Mediterranean Europe and the Common Market:

Studies of Economic Growth and Integration

EDITED BY

ERIC N. BAKLANOFF

Published for the
Office for International Studies and Programs
by
The University of Alabama Press
UNIVERSITY, ALABAMA

FOR MY MOTHER

Library of Congress Cataloging in Publication Data
Main entry under title:

Mediterranean Europe and the Common Market.

(Mediterranean Europe series)

Includes bibliographical references and index.
European Economic Community.
1. Mediterranean region—Economic conditions—Addresses, essays, lectures. 2. European Economic Community—Mediterranean region—Addresses, essays, lectures. I. Baklanoff, Eric N. II. Series.
HC244.5.M4 1976   330.9′4   75–19056
ISBN 0–8173–4605–8

Contents

Foreword

Mediterranean Europe has been undergoing significant social and economic changes during the post-World War II decades. No visitor to the region, whether vacationer or student, can avoid noticing the manifold evidences of development: intensive urbanization—and urban sprawl; industrialization, if unevenly; mass tourism with hundreds of kilometers of shoreside, multistory battlements to house it. These are not the whole story of development, of course, but we may be assured that the process is total. Less visibly, the more thoughtful observer may find also in 1975 that the term "Mediterranean Europe" reflects an internal shift of emphasis from preceding times.

The operative concept now seems to be increasingly *Mediterranean* in focus, rather than European. The econocentric view of nineteenth-century Western Europe, bemused then by its own industrialization, has been modified in these decolonializing decades of the twentieth century. Trans-Mediterranean concerns are major European preoccupations of these days, with the result that the national experiences described in this book may also be seen as being concerned with "bridging." Much of what happens in these countries may provide models for the whole region. The studies in this volume, therefore, carefully selected by Professor Baklanoff, have an unusually timely pertinence, as well as a general analytical value.

If the Mediterranean region is the first principal character in this book, the second is the European Economic Community. For all its political hesitations and internal problems of adjustment, the community is a major mechanism for development in the Mediterranean. Of the nineteen countries that line the littoral or dot the center of the middle sea, four are members of the community itself, and fourteen other states have agreements with the Common Market of varying scope. Moreover, these relationships can be more significant than their specifically economic content suggests.

For a ministate such as Malta, a fully developed relationship with Europe may mean not only economic survival but also the maintenance of a cultural tradition. Once the sentinels posted in the Sicilian channel that divides the eastern and western Mediterranean, the island's sales or rental value to the West as a naval and air base now has less tactical military importance, but its economic dependency on a larger market is reinforced by the cultural momentum of centuries of integration with western Christendom.

Similarly, the republic of Cyprus was afflicted at birth by intercommunal tensions: a Turkish minority confronts a Greek majority. The local conflict, frequently exacerbated by unrelated national rivalries (or by internal problems) of Greece and Turkey, flared to grave proportions in the summer of 1974, when zealots for the island's union with Greece set off a chain of grave events that ultimately led to the occupation of nearly half of Cyprus by Turkish forces. Cyprus has thus not completed its decolonializing process, but a second attempt at independence based on a principle of federation of the two communities may hold more promise of success than the now failed unitary state.

However, at least a minority of Cypriot leadership believe that by the full membership in the EEC of Greece, Turkey, and Cyprus, the island's communal problem might be subsumed in a reinforced independence. This does not seem to be an imminent possibility, but the association of political and economic objectives here suggests that the concept of Mediterranean Europe can be more complex than it might otherwise be considered to be. A "family" of neighbors may mean more than support; it can mean cultural identity as well as pluralistic peace.

Israel's case may be even more complicated, if more obvious. Its natural interest in European markets for its citrus fruit, textiles, and industrial specialties cannot be easily separated from its need for friends in its beleaguered situation. Here also, the cultural self-image of the state is European despite (perhaps because of) the overwhelming influx of non-European Jewry since independence in 1948. The ideological roots of Israel remain in the mainstream of European history, and so does its commitment to a modern economy of high technology and a democratic polity.

These are elements of a Mediterranean Europe where speeded economic and social development is the common denominator and where the *civiltà* of Europe provides the style. Braudel, the eminent French historian, describes the Mediterranean as "the sum of its routes," in which the essence of the region is the product of intellectual and commercial intercourse.* The sea is a means of concourse of more than 1.4 million square miles; with the reopening of the Suez Canal, it may regain an even greater prominence in world commerce. It is surrounded by nearly 300 million plainsmen and mountain persons, two-thirds of whom are a part of Mediterranean Europe. More than 8 million of this population work elsewhere as migrant labor, chiefly in Western Europe. As the new petroleum prosperity of the Islamic Mediterranean is expressed in development (and perhaps sooner as the European economy

*Fernand Braudel, *The Mediterranean and the Mediterranean World in the Age of Philip II*, vol. 1 (London, 1972).

adjusts to the massive shift of financial resources involved), these migrant workers will return to their native economies, bringing techniques and modified life styles with them. Investment may then flow all the more to where the labor is in the Mediterranean, rather than bringing people to Europe, where industry traditionally has been concentrated.

Mediterranean development is what this important group of studies is about. As an intellectual partner of the University of Alabama in exploring and exposing the problems of the Mediterranean region, the Center for Mediterranean Studies of the American Universities Field Staff welcomes this contribution to the literature of the region. We hope that this signifies the beginning of a continuing series of studies by Alabama scholars examining the interrelated phenomena of the area. The word *mediterranean* can be translated as the "middle of the earth," and the Mediterranean region may be as central to history now as it has been in past millennia.

Rome, Italy
September, 1975

E. A. Bayne, *Director*
AUFS CENTER FOR
MEDITERRANEAN STUDIES

Preface

Mediterranean Europe, extending from Portugal and Spain in the west through southern Italy and Malta to Yugoslavia, Greece, Cyprus, and Turkey in the east, offers the social scientist and student of business a rich, relatively unexplored research frontier. Significantly, such international agencies as the World Bank, the Organization for Economic Cooperation and Development (OECD), and the United Nations Economic Commission for Europe have identified Mediterranean or southern Europe as a distinct developing region. Also, because our western civilization was born and nurtured in these lands, Mediterranean Europe offers, particularly to undergraduates, the opportunity to vitalize the experience of their common heritage.

The American president's diplomatic journey in the autumn of 1970 to both Spain and Yugoslavia emphasized the growing strategic importance of the Mediterranean basin to the United States. The protracted Arab-Israeli conflict, the build-up of Soviet naval power in the Mediterranean Sea, the changing balance of power in the Persian Gulf (the location of over one-half the world's proven oil reserves), and the 1973/74 Arab oil embargo—all these factors are receiving increasing attention from United States and NATO policymakers.

Mediterranean Europe has become a region of major interest for the University of Alabama. A number of institutional links have been established, giving this university a firm footing for its research and study activities there. These ties include the association with the American Universities Field Staff (AUFS) Center for Mediterranean Studies in Rome, the supporting membership in the American Academy in Rome, the Summer Academic Program in Spain (in cooperation with the University of Madrid), and the seminar in Comparative Law of Mediterranean Societies. The AUFS Mediterranean Studies Institute, offered each spring for advanced undergraduate and graduate students, focuses on the social, economic, and political problems of the nations bordering the Mediterranean Sea. Both the institute and the Seminar in Comparative Law of Mediterranean Societies offer students the opportunity to study and carry on research in the region.

This study is the outcome of a joint venture that drew much of its inspiration and expertise from the AUFS relationship. Thus Dennison Rusinow and Jon McLin, both AUFS Associates, lecture at the Center for Mediterranean Studies; Seymour Goodman (Tulane), Douglas Lamont (Wisconsin), and Eric Baklanoff (Alabama) are associated with the AUFS member universities, and Dale Doreen received his Ph.D. from the University of Alabama. Each contributor is familiar with his country of special interest and has recently been engaged in research there.

This book is intended not only for professional economists, but also for social scientists generally, and for men of affairs who share a concern for the Mediterranean world and its evolving relationship with the European Community. The introductory chapter compares the economic performance of Mediterranean Europe with the other developing regions. It also brings out similarities and differences among the nations comprising the region under consideration. Chapters two through seven review and evaluate the postwar economic experiences of Turkey, Greece, Yugoslavia, Malta, Southern Italy, and Spain. They undertake to answer a number of important questions. How have geographical and historical-institutional factors conditioned the character of development? How has the economy responded to "indicative" planning and what kinds of policies contributed to either goal achievement or under achievement? How have international economic relationships evolved, and how are the growing links with the European Economic Community (EEC) viewed from the national perspective?

The final chapter analyzes the rapidly developing network of special relationships of the Common Market with countries of the Mediterranean basin. What are the implications for Southern Europe of the EEC relationship? From the perspective of European Community headquarters in Brussels, can one discern a "Global Mediterranean Policy"?

I am grateful to the University of Alabama's Office for International Studies and Programs, and particularly to Dr. Edward Moseley, its coordinator, for sponsoring this volume as the second in its Mediterranean Europe Studies.

The origins of my own chapter on Spain date back to the summer of 1968 when I began research in that country with the assistance of a research fellowship from the Louisiana State University Foundation. I owe a special debt to William D. Ross, dean of the College of Business Administration at LSU, who encouraged me in this project. I have also benefitted as a participant in the week-long Scholar-Diplomat Seminar for European Affairs, during the autumn of 1973. Special thanks are due Marie Bland, program director of the seminars, Jack Smith, deputy director of the Office of Iberian Affairs, and Henry Y. McCowan, who served as my host officer in that office.

A U. S. State Department travel grant through the Alabama Consortium for the Development of Higher Education enabled me to complete my field research in Madrid during the summer of 1974, and a summer stipend from the University of Alabama Research Grants Committee made it possible for me to put the manuscript into its present form.

Finally, I wish to acknowledge a debt to my colleague Enrique Ruiz-Fornells, Professor of Romance Languages at Alabama and Secretary of the University of Madrid's Summer School, from whom I have gained over the past years a greater appreciation of the *cultura hispanica.*

University, Alabama   ERIC N. BAKLANOFF
September, 1975

Contributors

1. ERIC N. BAKLANOFF, Board of Visitors Research Professor of Economics at The University of Alabama, was Dean for International Studies and Programs at the same institution from February, 1969, to January 1974. Before joining the University, he directed the Latin American Studies Institute (1965–69) at Louisiana State University and Vanderbilt University's Graduate Center for Latin American Studies (1962–65). In 1950–54 he was associated with the International Division of Chase Manhattan Bank, including three years with its Puerto Rican branches. Dr. Baklanoff received his Ph.D. from The Ohio State University, was the recipient of a Fulbright Fellowship to Chile, and in 1964/65 was a Fellow at the Center for Advanced Study in the Behavioral Sciences in Palo Alto, California. He is the author of *Expropriation of U. S. Investments in Cuba, Mexico and Chile* (1975) and edited *New Perspectives of Brazil* (1966) and *The Shaping of Modern Brazil* (1969).

2. MICHAEL BARTOLO is Program Management Officer in the Office of Technical Cooperation, United Nations. He received his B. A. from The Royal University of Malta, his M. A. in economics from the University of New Hampshire, and is currently a doctoral candidate at the New School for Social Research in New York. Since June, 1973, Mr. Bartolo has been responsible for all United Nations economic-development and public-finance projects in Asia and the Middle East.

3. DALE D. DOREEN is an Associate Professor of Quantitative Methods at the Sir George Williams Campus of Concordia University in Montreal, Canada. He received his Ph.D. in Business Administration from The University of Alabama in 1972 and subsequently pursued post-doctoral studies at the Wharton School of the University of Pennsylvania while working as a research associate on projects in corporate planning, management systems design, and marketing at the Wharton School's Busch Center. For two summers, Dr. Doreen was associated with the research department of the Central Bank of Malta. He has also worked in a research capacity for private and public institutions in Denmark, Switzerland and Czechoslovakia, including Swissair and the Economic Institute of the Czechoslovak Academy of Sciences.

4. SEYMOUR S. GOODMAN, Professor of Economics in the Graduate School of Business Administration, Tulane University, received his Ph.D. from The Johns Hopkins University. Dr. Goodman was the recipient of a Ford Foundation Dissertation Fellowship and served as Visiting Associate Professor of Economics in the Institute of Economic Develop-

ment, Istanbul University, Turkey, under the auspices of UNESCO. He is the author of *Turkey's Trade Prospects in the Common Market: An Exploratory Study* (1969) and *Essays on Trade and Finance* (1968).

5. ALEXANDER J. KONDONASSIS is David Ross Boyd Professor of Ecomics at the University of Oklahoma. Dr. Kondonassis is particularly interested in economic development and integration with emphasis on the Mediterranean region and the EEC. He received his Ph.D. from Indiana University, and has served as a Fullbright Professor at the Athens School of Economics and Business (1965-66). He is the author of several monographs and many articles. Among his administrative assignments have been positions as Chairman of the Department of Economics (1961–71) and as Director of the Advanced Program in Economics (1971–), both at the University of Oklahoma.

6. DOUGLAS F. LAMONT is Senior Academic Planner for the University of Wisconsin System. He has been a consultant to FORRAD of Milan, Italy, and a Fulbright Professor in Ecuador and Peru. Dr. Lamont was formerly Professor of Marketing and Coordinator for the MBA Program in international business in the Graduate School of Business, University of Alabama. He received his B.S. from the Wharton School, University of Pennsylvania, his MBA from Tulane University, and his Ph.D. from The University of Alabama. He is the author of *Managing Foreign Investment in Southern Italy: U. S. Business in Developing Areas of the EEC* and of articles in academic and professional journals.

7. JON B. McLIN is an Associate with the American Universities Field Staff. His current research and lecturing interests are focused on EEC and UN affairs. A Rhodes Scholar, Dr. McLin studied for his B.A. and M.A. at Wadham College, University of Oxford, and received his Ph.D. from The Johns Hopkins School of Advanced International Studies. Before joining the AUFS, he served as Assistant Professor of Political Science and Assistant Dean for International Programs at The University of Alabama. He is the author of *Canada's Changing Defense Policy, 1957–1963* (1967) and of articles and AUFS reports.

8. DENNISON L. RUSINOW, Associate Director of the American Universities Field Staff, has been interested in Adriatic Europe since 1952, when he traveled to Vienna, Trieste, and Yugoslavia while specializing in the problems of Hapsburg successor states as a Rhodes Scholar at the University of Oxford. Dr. Rusinow was a Fellow at the Institute of Current World Affairs and hold a B.A. from Duke University and an M.A. and D.Phil. from Oxford, where he also held an appointment as temporary lecturer in politics and modern European history. The author of *Italy's Austrian Heritage 1919–1946* and of a forthcoming interdisciplinary history of Yugoslavia, Dr. Rusinow has reported for the AUFS from Belgrade and Vienna since 1963.

List of Organizations and Abbreviations

AID	Agency for International Development (U.S.)
AUFS	American Universities Field Staff
CAP	Common Agricultural Policy (EEC)
COMECON	Council for Mutual Economic Assistance (Communist bloc)
EC	European Community (Common Market)
ECA	European Cooperation Administration
EDF	European Development Fund (EEC)
EEC	European Economic Community (Common Market)
EFTA	European Free Trade Association
EIB	European Investment Bank (EEC)
ENI	National Petroleum Company (Italy)
FAO	Food and Agricultural Organization
GATT	General Agreement on Tariffs and Trade
GDP	Gross Domestic Product
GNP	Gross National Product
IBRD	International Bank for Reconstruction and Development (World Bank)
ICOR	Incremental Capital Output Ratio
IMF	International Monetary Fund
IRI	Institute for Industrial Reconstruction (Italy)
MFN	Most-Favored-Nation (Tariff Treatment)
NATO	North Atlantic Treaty Organization
OECD	Organization for Economic Cooperation and Development
OPEC	Organization of Petroleum Exporting Countries

1

Mediterranean Europe:
Perspective on a
Developing Region

ERIC N. BAKLANOFF

IN THE 1950s the countries comprising Mediterranean Europe manifested numerous common features: a relatively low per-capita income
associated with technological backwardness; landholding systems
polarized between excessive fragmentation and very large estates; a
predominance of unskilled workers, and a large fraction of the
active labor force in agriculture and other primary activities and a
highly stratified society in which kinship and ascription rather than
achievement continued to exercise an important influence in the assignment of economic roles. With some notable exceptions, industry was
fragmented into small, inefficient family-owned enterprises using obsolete equipment. These lands shared a roughly similar topography and
climate and were among the least developed in Europe. They were, as
Gustav Schachter wrote, "much more akin to each other than to the
countries of northern Europe."[1]

The pace of change in Mediterranean Europe accelerated during the
decade of the 1960s, and early in the 1970s Spain, Greece and Southern
Italy crossed the arbitrary dividing line between the "less-developed"
and "developed" countries. The region experienced sharply rising per-
capita income associated with rapid growth and diversification of both
industry and exports, and a sharp rise in tourism has opened new opportunities for work in the services sector and in construction.

Medium term "indicative" planning was introduced as an instrument
of government policy to guide the pace and direction of economic growth
in Portugal, Spain, Southern Italy, Malta, Cyprus, Yugoslavia, Greece,
and Turkey. Basic infrastructure—railways, ports, roads, and communications and electric power systems—has been expanded and modernized.
The nations of Mediterranean Europe have become more closely integrated with the European Economic Community (EEC) through association or preferential trade agreements. And in the words of Jon

McLin: "One of the strongest economic and human bonds tying the Mediterranean region to trans-Alpine Europe is the immense two-way flow of persons: Mediterranean workers and their families going north and European tourists heading south for the sun."

COMPARISON WITH OTHER WORLD REGIONS

When compared with the achievements of both the industrialized countries and the other less-developed regions in the sixties, Mediterranean Europe's performance was impressive. As Table 1 shows, Mediterranean Europe, in the period from 1960 to 1967, achieved an annual gross domestic product (GDP) per-capita growth of 5.6 percent compared with 3.6 percent for the industrialized nations and only 2.5

TABLE 1

ECONOMIC INDICATORS FOR LESS-DEVELOPED AND
INDUSTRIALIZED COUNTRIES: REGIONAL SUMMARY

Average Annual Rates of Growth (%), 1960–67

Region	Population	Total GPD	Per-Capita GDPa	Agricultural Production	Manufacturing Production	Exports b	Imports	Total Gross Investment
Less-Developed Countries	2.5	5.0	2.5	2.1	7.3	6.1	5.7	6.2
Africa	2.4	4.0	1.6	1.4	6.0	5.4	2.3	4.7
South Asia	2.4	4.1	1.7	0.6	6.9	1.5	3.0	5.5
East Asia	2.7	5.6	2.8	3.2	7.5	5.4	7.3	11.4
W. Hemisphere	2.9	4.5	1.6	2.9	5.5	4.8	4.6	2.5
Middle East	2.9	7.2	4.2	4.1	10.8	8.7	7.2	6.4
Mediterranean Europe	1.4	7.1	5.6	3.7	10.1	13.7	14.0	14.2
Industrialized Countries	1.2	4.8	3.6	1.8	5.6	8.8	8.8	5.9
Western Europe	1.1	4.2	3.1	1.6	4.5	8.6	8.8	4.6

Percentages of Average GNP, 1960–67

Region	Gross Investment	Savings	Current-Account Deficit
Less-Developed Countries	17.8	15.0	2.8
Africa	16.7	13.1	3.6
South Asia	13.9	11.3	2.6
East Asia	15.6	11.0	4.6
W. Hemisphere	17.7	16.3	1.4
Middle East	19.8	14.8	5.0
Mediterranean Europe	24.9	21.5	3.4
Industrialized Countries	21.2	21.7	–0.5
Western Europe	23.1	23.7	–0.6

aAt constant prices
bGoods and services at constant United States dollars

Source: *World Bank Annual Report 1969*, p. 47, table 2

percent average for the less-developed regions. As a group, the Mediterranean European countries surpassed each of the other less-developed regions—Africa, South Asia, East Asia, the Western Hemisphere and the Middle East—in the growth of per-capita output, exports, imports, and the annual expansion of gross investment. Only the Middle East matched or slightly surpassed Mediterranean Europe in the growth of GDP (including both agricultural and industrial production).

For the subsequent period, from 1968 to 1971, the Mediterranean Europe group was surpassed by the Middle East among the less developed regions in growth performance (5.1 percent and 6.4 percent in average annual rates of GDP growth, respectively). However, Mediterranean Europe's GDP per-capita growth rate exceeded the average for all less developed regions (4 percent annually) and with the exception noted above, the growth rates of Africa, East Asia, South Asia, and the Western Hemisphere.[2] Using the same criterion of growth, Mediterranean Europe outperformed the industrialized countries during the 1968–71 period (5.1 percent versus 3.2 percent, respectively).

Even more striking was the economic performance of some Mediterranean nations within the Organization for Economic Development and Cooperation (OECD). Among the twenty-three OECD nations, Greece, Turkey, Spain, and Portugal ranked second, third, fourth, and fifth, respectively, in annual gross national product (GNP) growth during the 1962–1972 decade.[3] Only Japan, with its phenomenal annual growth rate of 10.4 percent, surpassed the four Mediterranean countries.

Upon close examination, the statistics given in Table 1 suggest the existence of a rough positive correlation between the levels of gross investment (the accumulation of real capital), export-import performance, and the growth of per-capita production. Mediterranean Europe's high savings and investment levels (22 percent and 25 percent of GNP, respectively) were supported by a vigorous expansion of the region's capacity to import. By directing a growing share of production to exports of goods and services, and by attracting foreign capital (represented by the current account deficit), the region was able to transform savings into real investment through imports of machinery and equipment from the industrialized countries.

The recent economic achievements of Mediterranean Europe follow in large measure from national policies that have been growth-enhancing rather than growth-inhibiting. Nevertheless, it must also be recognized that this region has certain advantages over the other low-income regions of the world.

First, Mediterranean Europe lies close to its major market and major supply source. This locational advantage, translated into lower transportation costs, benefits its commodity trade with industrialized Europe and improves its attraction for tourists from across the Alps. Of added imporance to the development of the lands of the northern Mediterranean littoral have been the labor policies of industrial Europe, which have permitted the export of "surplus" workers from the south to the north. Emigrant-worker remittances constitute a major balancing factor in the international economic relations of Portugal, Spain, Greece, Turkey, and Yugoslavia.

Second, in sharp contrast with the other low-income regions, Mediterranean Europe has experienced a remarkable demographic transition: birth rates have been brought into closs balance with low and declining death rates. With the notable exception of Turkey, these lands are characterized by low rates of population growth (see Table 2). Spain, Yugoslavia, and Cyprus have demographic growth rates of a little over 1 percent annually, while the populations of Greece and Southern Italy are rising at only about one half that rate. Portugal's population has actually declined somewhat since 1960, a reflection of large-scale emigration. Turkey's population is growing at a rate (2.5 percent annually) that is over twice as great as that of the other countries in the region. That nation's crude birth rate, estimated to be in excess of 40 per 1,000, is far more typical of Asia and Latin America than of Europe (see Table 1).

TABLE 2

MEDITERRANEAN EUROPE: LANDS AND PEOPLES

	Area (Sq. MI.) (000)	Agricultural[a] Land (% of Total)	Acres Per Capita	Population[b] (000)	Population Growth Rate (Average Annual) % 1960-70	Urban[c] Population (%)	Literacy (%)	Share of Labor Force In Primary Sector (%)
Turkey	301.0	68	3.7	36,160	2.50	35	55	72
Spain	195.0	68	2.7	34,003	1.05	61	90	29
Yugoslavia	99.0	57	1.8	20,540	1.10	37	80	50
Greece	51.0	67	2.4	8,769	0.45	49	82	37
Southern Italy	40.8			18,052	0.60			34
Portugal	36.0	54	1.3	8,870	−0.05	37	65	31
Cyprus	4.0	57	2.0	625	1.10	44	82	38
Malta	0.1	50	0.1	330	0.00	68	82	7

[a]1969 or 1970
[b]1971
[c]1970 or 1971

Sources: The OECD Observer, no. 63 (April, 1973), pp. 20–21, and World Data Handbook, U.S. Department of State (August, 1972), p. 6.

COMMONALITIES AND DIFFERENCES

"It is a matter of some importance to the historian," writes Fernand Braudel of the Mediterranean region, "to find almost everywhere within his field of study the same climate, the same seasonal rhythm, the same vegation, the same colours and, when the geological architecture recurs, the same landscapes, identical to the point of obsession; in short, the same way of life."⁴ With the exception of Portugal and the island republics of Malta and Cyprus, all the countries of Mediterranean Europe are peninsulas that jut into the same water basin. Until the appearance of a new middle class in recent years, the Mediterranean plains were characterized by a considerable distance separating rich from poor; the rich were very rich, the poor very poor.⁵

Southern or Mediterranean Europe was the heart of the ancient Greek and Roman empires, the very center of world civilization, some two thousand years ago. Most of it also bears the imprint of its Muslim conquerors. Protracted Arab occupation of the Iberian Peninsula, Malta, and Southern Italy has influenced the customs and languages of these lands. In the Eastern Mediterranean Ottoman rule over what today includes modern Turkey, Greece, Cyprus, and much of Yugoslavia proved inimical to modernization and economic development. The societies dominated by the Ottoman Empire failed to participate in the technological advances of the agricultural and industrial revolutions that swept Northwestern Europe. The Ottoman elites—the civil, military, and ecclesiastical aristocracies—as Seymour Goodman observes, "regarded commerce and industry contemptuously as inferior pursuits, leaving them to the management of alien minorities—Western Europeans, Greeks, Armenians, Jews and Levantines."

While Spain and Portugal rank among Europe's oldest sovereign nations, Cyprus and Malta—both former British crown colonies—did not achieve nationhood until the 1960s. Greece gained independence from Ottoman rule in 1821, the provinces of the *Mezzogiorno* (southern Italy) were joined to the northern states to form modern Italy in 1861, and Turkey, the successor to the Ottoman Empire, was declared a republic after World War I.

Regardless of the nominal form of their government, the de facto political regimes of Mediterranean Europe incline toward authoritarian rather than stable democratic constitutional rule. Whether these modernizing authoritarian regimes are led by civilian heads or by military officers, they significantly restrict participation of the masses in the political processes, while at the same time allowing considerable freedom to business and consumer interests.

Portugal, Turkey, and the *Mezzogiorno* (as part of Italy) are members of NATO; Malta, Cyprus, and Spain have signed defense agreements with one or more NATO members, and Yugoslavia describes itself as a nonaligned nation. All the countries of the region, except perhaps Yugoslavia, are potential candidates for ultimate EEC membership. Greece, Turkey, Malta, and Cyprus are associate members in EEC; Spain and Portugal have signed preferential trade agreements with the Common Market. In March, 1970, Yugoslavia entered into a nonpreferential trade agreement with the European Community that provides for a Yugoslav ambassador to Common Market headquarters and the establishment of a mixed commission to investigate other possibilities.

For all the similarities in their recent economic policies and development patterns, these lands exhibit a rich diversity in their ethnic composition, their languages and religions, their territorial size, and their populations. Roman Catholicism is the established church in Portugal, Spain, Southern Italy, and Malta; the Orthodox church commands the allegiance of the Greeks and the majority of Cypriots; the Turks and a minority of Cypriots are Muslims; and Yugoslavia, a multinational state, include adherents of all three historical faiths.

Turkey, next to the USSR, the largest among the countries that are classified as European, contrasts greatly (see Table 2) with the small areas of the Maltese Islands (121 square miles) and Cyprus (about 4,000 square miles). The populations of Turkey and Spain, each exceeding 30 million, should be compared with those of Malta (330,000) and Cyprus (625,000) and the medium-sized lands of Greece and Portugal, with populations of less than 9 million each. Man/land ratios, in consequence, vary enormously, e.g., between 3.7 acres of agricultural land

TABLE 3

MEDITERRANEAN EUROPE:
GNP, PER-CAPITA GNP, AND GROWTH RATE

	GNP, 1973 (In Millions of Dollars)	GNP Per Capita 1973 (In Dollars)	GNP Per Capita Growth Rate 1960-1973 (%)
Spain	59,360	1,710	5.8
Southern Italy[a]	22,700	1,100	— —
Turkey	22,600	600	3.9
Yugoslavia	21,160	1,010	4.3
Greece	16,720	1,870	7.3
Portugal	12,690	1,410	7.4
Cyprus	930	1,460	6.1
Malta	340	1,060	5.9

[a]For 1970

Source: World Bank Atlas, International Bank for Reconstruction and Development 1975.

TABLE 4

MEDITERRANEAN EUROPE:
INDICATORS OF ECONOMIC AND SOCIAL DEVELOPMENT
(Countries Ranked by Declining Level of Development)

Country	Per-Capita GNP	Urbanization	Literacy	Physicians Per 10,000 Inhabitants	Telephones Per 1,000 Inhabitants	TV Sets Per 1,000 Inhabitants
Spain	2	2	1	3	1	1
Cyprus	3	4	3	6	5	4
Malta	5	1	2	2	2	2
Greece	1	3	4	1	3	6
Yugoslavia	6	6	4	4	6	3
Portugal	4	5	6	5	4	5
Turkey	7	7	7	7	7	7

Sources: Derived from *OECD Observer*, No. 63 (April, 1972), pp. 20–21. World Data Handbook, U. S. Department of State (August, 1972), p. 6. *World Bank Atlas,* International Bank for Reconstruction and Development, 1975. U.N. *Statistical Yearbook 1971* (New York, 1972).

per capita in Turkey and 0.1 of an acre per capita in densely populated Malta.

Greece and Spain reached per-capita GNP levels of over $1,700 in 1974 (see Table 3), and Cyprus and Portugal attained comparable levels of more than $1,400. Yugoslavia ranked fifth among the nations of Mediterranean Europe with a per-capita GNP of about $1,000, followed by Turkey, with a per-capita GNP of only $600. A ranking of these nations on the basis of other socio-economic indicators (see Table 4) further reveals the comparative backwardness of Turkey. Of the seven nations, Turkey ranks last in the degree of urbanization and literacy, in the number of physicians per 10,000 population, and in the numbers of telephones and TV sets per 1,000 inhabitants. Spain and Malta at the other extreme demonstrate the highest rankings for urbanization, literacy, and the ownership of telephones and TV sets.

OBSTACLES TO DEVELOPMENT

In mobilizing for a more effective effort to overcome economic backwardness, each nation has encountered major obstacles arising out of its special circumstances. Thus, hyperinflation in Greece was associated with World War II, German occupation, and postwar Communist insurgency. Monetary stability was finally achieved, together with political stability, after the 1949–1952 reconstruction period.

Malta, after a century and a half of economic dependence on the British military presence on the island, was faced with the necessity of rapidly diversifying its economy. When Malta's invisible exports consisted largely of services rendered to the British military base, the island enjoyed a position akin to that of monopoly; now it must increasingly sell its goods and services in a competitive market of an enlarged EEC. With the decline of British military expenditures in Malta, the island must develop manufacturing in lines of high export potential and further promote its tourist industry.

The prosperity of Cyprus has been based, as with Malta, on a high level of British military-base expenditures and to a lesser degree on a protected commonwealth market in the United Kingdom for its agricultural exports. With the signing of an association agreement with the EEC, effective in June, 1973, Cyprus reduced its ties with the United Kingdom, and the Mediterranean island economy is now faced with a challenging period during which its principal export products—citrus fruits, potatoes, sherry, and copper—will meet increasing competition within the European Economic Community.

Communal strife in Cyrus, leading to intermittant armed conflict between Greek Cypriots (about 80 percent of the population) and Turkish Cypriots, has continued to threaten economic stability and progress. Despite these political difficulties, the economy grew at an accelerating rate during the sixties. The renewal of communal fighting between the two factions in the summer of 1974, leading to Turkish military occupation of more than 40 percent of the island, poses a serious question regarding the integrity of Cyprus as a viable nation and economy.

The outbreak of guerrilla warfare in Angola in 1961, Portuguese Guinea in 1963, and Mozambique in 1964 forced the late Premier Antonio de Oliveira Salazar to modify his nation's introverted economic posture associated with the *Estado Novo* (his version of the "corporate state"). Salazar reasoned that to preserve Portugal's "multiracial pluricontinental" state it was necessary to accelerate economic development both on the mainland and in the overseas provinces. And a more rapid pace of development required a greater degree of reliance on foreign capital and technical know-how. The new externally oriented policies succeeded in increasing Portugal's GNP and industrial-growth rates; however, the military expenditures associated with the defense of the overseas provinces in Africa absorbed almost half of the national budget during the sixties.

The liberalization of the Portuguese economy was given new impetus under Prime Minister Marcello Caetano (1968–1974). His government promulgated the long-awaited Industrial Development Law that, among its several provisions, removed the cumbersome licensing requirements for new enterprises in many fields.

Large-scale industrial projects were on the horizon on the eve of the military coup that ousted the Caetano government in April, 1974.[7] The most ambitious project was the $1.2-billion Sines Peninsula industrial port complex. Other long-term government projects included a $400-million Lisbon airport, a major renovation and expansion of railroads, superhighway construction between Lisbon and Oporto, new hospitals, nuclear energy and conventional thermal power plants, and a municipally financed expansion of the Lisbon subway system. Large private projects included the building of a new shipyard in Setubal, the expansion of steel and petroleum refinery capacity, and the construction of a cement plant, a fertilizer and synthetic fibers plant, two new breweries, and a plywood factory.

Southern Italy, known as the *Mezzogiorno*, faced the special problem of a backward region within an industrialized nation. As Douglas Lamont has shown, there has been no progress over the past two decades in closing the gap between the two Italian regions. The considerable investments carried forward by the *Cassa per il Mezzogiorno* (Fund for the South), Italian public- and private-sector firms, Italian and United States-based multinational corporations did not succeed in helping the south catch up with the more prosperous industrialized north. Nevertheless, the economy of southern Italy did undergo substantial change from the early fifties to the latter sixties with real per-capita income growth accelerating during this period. Lamont suggests that the imposition of free trade upon the backward south after establishment of the EEC in 1957 was inimical to the region's development: "The *Mezzogiorno*, unlike its counterpart Mediterranean countries, was unable to negotiate a transition period during which its industry could be protected from the full winds of economic integration."

Turkey, the largest and poorest country of Mediterranean Europe, confronts two continuing problems that it shares with other "least-developed" societies: a high demographic growth rate and a large traditionally oriented peasantry.

In the 1950s both Yugoslavia and Spain embarked upon systemic reorganization of their economic systems in order to overcome the rigidities and inefficiencies imposed by centralized state control. Around 1952 Yugoslavia abandoned the Stalinist economic model for a highly innovative socialist market economy. Spain, at the other end of the Mediterranean basin, modified the autarchic "corporate state" in the direction of an increasingly open European-style capitalist market economy. A disregard for the productivity of capital characterized both the Stalinist and corporate-state economic models. In both nations centralization of economic decision making gave way to a decentralized market orientation. Holders of monopoly of effective economic power in Yugoslavia (the members of the Communist party) and Spain (members of the Falange) were forced to relinquish much of that power. Significantly, increased scope for economic freedom has existed under the authoritarian regimes of Marshall Tito in Yugoslavia and General Franco in Spain. Medium-term plans, indicative in character, became the principal expression of government economic policy. In both nations integration with the world economy became a primary goal: tourism was promoted, the emigration of workers was permitted, joint ventures with multinational corporations were encouraged, and foreign trade was stimulated.

The momentum of growth during the balance of this decade will probably decline as Mediterranean Europe adjusts to the impositions of the OPEC oil cartel. The huge increase in the price of internationally traded crude oil will directly affect balances of payments and rates of industrial growth in the region. Since the autumn of 1973 there has occurred a dramatic shift in the terms of trade between Southern Europe and the trans-Mediterranean countries that supply the region with oil—a shift that has affected most particularly such energy-deficient countries as Spain.

The growing dependency of Spain, Greece, Portugal, and the other nations of the region on the international economy—what was until recently a major source of growth—may now have become a source of vulnerability. As industrialized Europe, and especially the EEC, adjusts to the higher price of energy, its diminished growth rate will adversily affect Mediterranean Europe through slackened tourist expenditures, commodity trade, and emigrant-worker remittances.

NOTES

1. Gustav Schachter, *The Italian South: Economic Development in Mediterranean Europe* (New York: Random House, 1965), p. 198.
2. *World Bank/IDA Annual Report* (1972) pp. 76–77.
3. Department of State, *Economic Growth of OECD Countries, 1962–1972*, News Release (August, 1973), p. 8.
4. Fernand Braudel, *The Mediterranean and the Mediterranean World in the Age of Philip II*, vol. 1, trans. by Sian Reynolds (London: William Collins Son & Co., 1972), p. 235.
5. Ibid., p. 76.
6. Gustav Schachter, *The Italian South*, p. 197.
7. *Foreign Economic Trends*, U.S. Department of Commerce (June 29, 1972), (ET 72-074), p. 10.

2

Turkey

SEYMOUR S. GOODMAN

TURKEY—successor to the Ottoman Empire, the "Sick Man of Europe" during the nineteenth and early twentieth centuries, and heir to that empire's homeland, religion, traditions, and backwardness—has endured a lingering malaise. The republic, the nearly single-handed creation of the reformist genius and inspirational, if authoritarian, leadership of one of the century's truly outstanding statesmen, Mustafa Kemal (Atatürk), has now achieved its semicentennial. Yet it still finds itself engaged in conflict with its traditional Aegean rival, Greece; it is still in some danger of forfeiting its paltry yet painfully purchased social and economic progress; it is still not the modern secular state of Atatürk's dream; it is still lacking in sustained goverance by democratic processes; and it is financially beholden to its allies.

The as-yet-unrealized objectives of national development cannot easily be rationalized as owing to a failure of will. In the early days of the republic, Atatürk's crusading zeal produced extensive changes in the political and judicial system. The purpose of these changes was to provide a foundation for the kinds of continuity and orderly sequence of political processes as were to be found in the West. Instability and its correlate, military control, while averted in the interval between the world wars, has emerged since. Twice in less than a decade military intervention has terminated freely elected national administrations, leading in the first instance to a change of constitution and execution of the topmost political leaders of the deposed regime, and later to a situation of limited martial law that almost subverted even the semblance of civilian rule.

In the social realm, Atatürk's attempted secularization of human affairs through the institutions that govern them has succeeded in affecting the life style of the urban population alone. The customs and traditions of Islam still maintain their hold on the peasantry, while religious influences in the national arena have been periodically reasserted at politically propitious times, exacerbating the political tensions between the cities and the villages as the cultural gap between them has widened.

Economic planning, institutionalized in the Atatürk era along with the policy of state capitalism *(étatism)* for key sectors of the economy, has been revitalized and modernized during the past decade after a period of disuse. Alliances with the West have cemented economic as well as political ties. But neither the rationalization and guidance of economic growth within the framework of a national plan nor the considerable material advantages the country has reaped from its strategic importance to the West have as yet succeeded in lifting it from its state of marked economic underdevelopment.[1]

However uncertain her progress to this point and her immediate prospects, Turkey's drive for status in the Western community of nations will continue undiminished in intensity. This seems assured by the deep pride and love of independence of a remarkably homogeneous people, ethnically and religiously,[2] whose conquering spirit fashioned one of the world's most durable, magnificent empires and, when its remnant finally lay in shambles following the *coup de grâce* of defeat in World War I, rescued its sovereignty with a triumph over Greek invaders. But a candid survey of the present scene cannot generate optimism regarding the near-term achievement of viable nationhood without some considerable gains in the economy. In a nation whose per-capita income is barely a twentieth of that of the United States and hardly more than a quarter of that of Greece, and whose problems are compounded by a population growth rate far in excess of the Western mean, compounded further by a vast, primitive agricultural sector whose output is a hostage of the weather, and compounded still further by a chronic inability to balance international accounts without adding to an already burdensome foreign indebtedness—in such a nation, the economy is unquestionably crucial to the shape of the future.[3]

This obvious truth has of course not been overlooked by Turkish governments since the founding of the republic. It is clear from the record that concern over the economy has been and remains a constant prod to administrative decision making and policy. The burden of this paper, therefore, is a review of the economic record of the past two decades—the significant developments that have given direction to the economy and the important structural changes that have become visible —with a view to assessing the implications of this record, and with special emphasis on the unfolding economic impact of the deliberate political decision, taken more than a decade ago, to associate Turkey with the European Economic Community (EEC.)

DESCRIPTIVE BACKGROUND

The territory of modern Turkey straddles the continents of Europe and Asia, covering the land bridge of Anatolia (Asia Minor) in westernmost Asia and a portion of Thrace across the Bosporus in southeastern Europe. The latter includes the principal and historic city of Istanbul, the site of Byzantium, later Constantinople of pre-Ottoman days. European Turkey takes up only 3 percent of a land area approximately twice the size of California and the largest among countries classified as "European" other than the USSR. The Anatolian peninsula is ringed by the Black Sea on the north, with a coastline steep and rocky, and by the Aegian on the west and the Mediterranean to the south, where fertile plains and river valleys abound. But the most prominent features topographically are the sprawling, rainfall-scarce central Anatolian plateau, on which the capital city, Ankara, is situated, and the mountainous eastern highlands, which border on Soviet Armenia, Iraq, and Syria and include the biblical Mt. Ararat.[4]

Most present-day Turks are descended from certain central Asian tribes that began migrating to Anatolia in about the eleventh century. Over 90 percent of the population still speaks Turkish, a member of a language family originating in Soviet Asia, as their primary native tongue. The people are overwhelmingly Muslim, their conversion to Islam having predated the Anatolian invasion.[5] Earning renown as fierce and courageous fighters, the Turks became the "sword of Islam" under the Ottoman sultans and were the unchallenged spiritual leaders of the Muslim world as well as its military spearhead. The material glories and territorial conquests of the empire were equally esteemed as victories of Islam over the infidels.[6] This centuries-long lack of any real distinction between the state and the religion it served perhaps lies at the root of the persistent reluctance of the peasantry to accept secularization of such traditionally religious responsibilities as education. Perhaps more to the point is the fundamental inconsistency between a progressive state that stresses the possibilities of self-improvement and the submissive Muslim fatalism (insallah) that permeates the Weltanschauung of the typical Anatolian peasant.

Turkey's population in 1970 numbered 35.7 million people. The overall population density is low by European standards—about that of the Irish Republic—but the people, both rural and urban, tend to be concentrated along the coastal areas. The growth rate is currently slightly over 2.5 percent, which is far more typical of Asia and Latin America than of Europe. The high rate of population growth is due to a crude birth rate that is estimated to be in excess of 40 per 1,000 population, which is reflected in more than 40 percent of the population under age fifteen, compared to 25–30 percent for advanced countries. Though the overall death rate is not high, the infant mortality rate is estimated to be in excess of 150 per 1,000 live births, more than seven times the rate for the United States and even five times larger than that of Greece.[7]

The population is predominantly rural, between 70 and 75 percent, reflecting an overall illiteracy rate of 45 per cent of those aged eleven and over. The hub of rural life is the village—a cohesive self-governing unit of closely grouped houses, a marketplace, a school, a mosque and a cemetery—which serves as a symbol of identity to its inhabitants, who range in number from 100 to 2,000 people. There are more than 35,000 such villages. There are only about a dozen cities of 100,000 and over, but these are the true centers of economic and political power in the country. Since the midfifties, urban population growth has exceeded that of the rural because of heavy emigration from the countryside to the cities, and the failure of the cities to absorb them fully has created sprawling shantytowns (gecekondu) along their outer perimeters.[8]

Harshness of climate and topography contribute measurably to rural poverty and the low level of development. Large areas of the country are relatively unsuited for agriculture because of rugged terrain, poor rainfall, and inferior soils. Only the coastal areas average more than thirty inches of rain per annum—along the Black Sea coast the figure is much higher—and have soils suitable for the cultivation of grapes and citrus fruits. Here also substantial stands of timber can still be found, covering 13 percent of the total land area. But in the interior plateau, the nation's breadbasket, the rainfall is only between ten and seventeen inches annually, temperature extremes are common, and the soils lack natural fertilizer.[9]

Thus, though agriculture presently engages 72 percent of the work force, it produces only 32 percent of the value of national output.[10] This indicates a rural per-capita income of less than half the depressingly low countrywide average, or under $100 annually,[11] a fact that readily accounts for the steady stream of migrants to the cities. Wheat is the dietary staple of the population, both urban and rural, and sharp annual fluctuations in agricultural yields and the total food supply are strongly associated with the effect of rainfall on cereals output. Agriculture also accounts for the great bulk of foreign earnings, especially in the form of cotton, tobacco, and fruits and nuts, and is similarly responsible for fluctuations in the total of such receipts. In the absence of secularly improving yields, the need to feed and clothe a growing population and still produce an exportable surplus has resulted in marked encroachments on meadow and pasture lands for crop-raising purposes, thus introducing a particularly vicious circle.

Manufacturing, however, is one bright spot, benefiting markedly from a belief shared by all Turkish leaders (beginning with Atatürk) that modernity cannot be achieved in its absence and cannot therefore be wholly trusted to private enterprise. Though often inefficient and wasteful of public funds, and though a contributor to both inflation and recession, state-owned-and-operated industry has assumed the principal role in more than doubling Turkey's manufacturing output, over the 1960s, through its prominence in a number of heavy industries—cement, iron and steel, fertilizer, paper, chemicals, sugar refining, to name only the more dynamic elements of the manufacturing sector.[12] A parallel expansion has also occurred in the extractive industries, especially iron ore. Turkey has a large diversity of mineral deposits but no outstandingly large deposits of any one. Chrome and copper are among the other commercially exploited ores. Coal production, including lignites, represents the main source of fuel; crude petroleum output is growing rapidly but is as yet insufficient to cover even domestic needs.[13]

Yet, in its essential aspect, the dualistic nature of the Turkish economy remains unchanged from Ottoman days, when it was characterized by a large subsistence sector and relatively small commercial and industrial enclaves in the cities along the western and southern coasts and occasionally inland. The empire never participated in the technological advances of the agricultural and industrial revolutions that swept western Europe, and it is hardly coincidental that its long military decline can be dated back to the seventeen century. Even commerce was ignored; the Ottoman elites were civil, military, and ecclesiastical aristocracies that regarded commerce and industry contemptuously as inferior pursuits and left them to the management of alien minorities—West Europeans, Greeks, Armenians, Jews, and Levantines. Economic control by outsiders became more firmly entrenched through the "capitulations," a series of agreements concluded by the Ottoman sultans with several European powers, beginning in the sixteenth century, which granted rights of extraterritoriality or immunity as well as commercial and financial privileges.[14] Irritation with foreigners so placed above the law must have later given way to bitterness when the declining empire, saddled with foreign debt from the financing of unsuccessful military ventures and other extravagances, suffered the humiliation of ceding to foreign interests liens on a number of sources of public revenues. The merely moderate encouragement that Turkey has traditionally given to foreign investors is surely an Ottoman legacy. Even more so has been the absence, until very recently, of an urban, entrepreneurially motivated, ethnically Turkish middle class of any significance. With respect to the economy, Turkey's heritage of the past is an object lesson for her future.

THE POSTWAR ERA[15]

Profiting from her non involvement in World War II, Turkey entered the postwar period favorably endowed with adequate reserve holdings of gold and foreign exchange in relation to imports, a larger industrial productive capacity than before the war, a substantial level of business savings (plus a greater acceptance of "business" as a respectable activity[16]), and, with it all, Marshall Plan aid in addition to the military assistance provided under the Truman Doctrine. In the late forties, the one-party system that had been in force since the republic's founding ended and political voice was given to elements who had been alienated by Atatürk's reforms, who had been excluded from participation in the important public decisions, or who were dissatisfied with the limited gains the regime was able to produce in the standard of living. Most notably, these included the religious councils *(ulema)*, the small urban entrepreneurial class, and the peasantry. These groups, allied with a few intellectuals and labor leaders, provided the basis of support for the Democrat Party, which was formed from a split within the Republican Peoples Party (the party of Atatürk and, after his death in 1938, led by his collaborator, Inönü), which hitherto had ruled without formal opposition. In the elections of 1950 the Democrats won a clear parliamentary majority and advanced an ambitious program for accelerating the economic development of the country.

The new program represented, as announced, a rejection of previous policy in two key respects. It included, first, greater encouragement of the private sector as a development agent and a commensurate de-emphasis of the role of state capitalism *(étatism)*, this to be implemented in part by the transfer to private control of certain State Economic Enterprises (SEE's) active in the industrial and infrastructure sectors; and, second, a greater concern with improving the lot of the peasant and with increasing agricultural output.

Over the fifties, the period during which the Democrats retained power, no significant change occurred in the relative importance of the private industrial sector. Denationalization was never more than token and was stopped after 1953. The number of *industrial* establishments (i.e., those employing ten or more workers or equipment of ten or more horsepower) approximately doubled between 1950 and 1960 in both the private and public sectors; the proportion of value added by the state establishments remained substantially unchanged while their share of employment declined slightly.[17] And though steps were also taken to encourage private foreign investment, this was never permitted to be more than a negligible fraction of domestic investment.[18]

As for agriculture, the results of the new program were mixed at best. It is clear that there were certain improvements in rural life, e.g., additional roads, more adequate drinking water supplies, continuance of a modest distribution of state land to the landless. And despite frequently unfavorable weather, real agricultural income managed to grow by 4 percent per annum over the decade, while the rural population grew only by 1.9 percent annually.[19] But the increase in agricultural output reflected largely the extension of the cultivated margin;[20] progress in irrigation and the use of chemical fertilizers was extremely slow.[21] Per-capita food output for the total population, however, did increase at a 5 percent annual rate between 1952/53 and 1960/61, but dietary improvement was limited by the absence of change in the net annual supply of meat per person.[22]

Midway through the decade the overall economic program ran into grave difficulties. The Democrats demonstrated a lack of both competence and will in dealing with some ill-considered consequences of their expressly expansionist policies—inflation, balance-of-payments deficits, and increased foreign debts—and by choosing to deal with a rising chorus of criticisms by increasingly repressive measures. The regime virtually invited the military takeover that took place a few years later and cost Premier Menderes and his closest associates their lives.

By any standard, the nation's bout with inflation was severe and sustained. Wholesale prices rose by 250 percent over the decade, all but 10 percent occurring after 1953,[23] and the cost-of-living indexes of Istanbul and Ankara rose at approximately the same rate. Though demand in the private sector was encouraged by the liberal extension of credit, the nearly sixfold increase in the money supply over the decade can be traced to an unbroken string of budget deficits, financed by the highly inflationary medium of Central Bank advances to the treasury. These developments mirrored an extraordinary emphasis on public investment or "developmental" projects, particularly in transportation, communications, and other public works, which underwent heavy criticism as ill-coordinated and economically unfeasible. Because their long-term nature precluded a rapid increase in the output they could be expected to help produce, they also contributed to the rise in prices.

Deficits in commodity trade, unrelieved throughout the fifties, was the predominant disequilibrating factor in the balance of payments. Export behavior turned sluggish following the end of the Korean Conflict, when Turkey faced increased competition in world markets for grains and was subsequently forced to subsidize these exports in order to keep foreign exchange receipts from plunging. The export problem was also aggravated by relatively poor harvests during most of the middle and late fifties, since the condition of domestic excess demand probably led to some diversion of output to the home market. Under the pull of demand, especially for capital goods needed to maintain the rate of investment, imports rose at a faster rate than exports. This forced restrictions on imports, especially of consumer goods, from relatively early in the decade, adding more fuel to inflation. The trade gap tended to be covered with short-term trade credits, which as the decade wore on became available only under steadily worsening terms. Hence, the Turkish lira became overvalued at its fixed exchange rate and black-market trading in the currency developed, showing it at a substantial discount on its official value. Before the decade ended, the country's external debt was nearly six times its 1950 level.[24]

By 1958 Turkey's allies recognized that they could no longer afford to overlook the country's difficulties. The United States joined with the International Monetary Fund (IMF) and the (now) Organization for Economic Cooperation and Development (OECD) to lend Turkey $359 million over the following two years. This arrangement was the quid pro quo for a wide-ranging stabilization program by which the government promised to combat domestic disequilibrium by sharply reducing public investment, increasing taxes, and financing agricultural subsidies out of budget revenues rather than by recourse to the Central Bank. Perhaps the most important part of the package of reforms was a de facto devaluation of the lira (later formalized) by means of premiums added to the official rate, which took it from 2.8 per dollar to effectively 9 per dollar for most transactions, including exports and imports.

Unfortunately, the government could not or would not implement restraints on its policy of economic expansion. Before the decade had ended, the stabilization program had become a complete failure. Capital expenditures never stopped rising, output fell, prices rose an additional 20 percent, and the trade deficit widened. Bribery and corruption emerged, particularly as a result of the allocations of foreign exchange for imports. Under extreme political pressure, the administration attempted to muzzle the press, gerrymander electoral districts, repress student demonstrations, and coerce the opposition Republican Peoples Party. In May, 1960, the army finally moved to end a situation it regarded as chaotic.

During the fifties Turkey developed a dependence on inflationary financing of development and began a serious cultivation of foreign aid. Yet the domestic savings rate did rise to a level more compatible with sustained growth (even if partly "forced" through inflation) and the infrastructure was expanded and improved, most notably in the case of road transport. The country did become somewhat more industrialized, though her industrial goods could not yet compete on the world market. The annual average growth rate of real per-capita gross domestic product was 2.8 percent for the decade, in excess of the 2.2 percent rate for all developing market economies for the period, despite one of the higher growth rates of population in the world.[25]

Yet the decade and more that followed has produced change having an even greater potential impact on Turkey's economic development, though in terms of structure there have been few signs of dynamism and certain problems and their consequences have recurred in an almost astonishingly similar sequence. Three major institutional changes affecting the economy can be distinguished in the sixties, all occurring early in the decade: first, the reintroduction of normal government planning as the principal expression of economic policy; second, association with the European Common Market (European Economic Community) through a series of stages leading ultimately to full membership; and finally, receipt of external aid on a systematic, continuing basis through a consortium of western European nations and the United States under the aegis of the OECD. These developments merit some amplification.

Disdainful toward the relatively uncoordinated investment policies of the Democrats, seeking a return to the more traditional, *étatist* ideal of a degree of authoritarian control over the economy, and encouraged by similar tendencies in other developing countries, the governing military authorities in 1960 reinstituted the prewar system of five-year economic and social plans. Less than six months after the coup, the State Planning Organization (SPO) was legislatively established within the prime ministry—thus giving it status at least equal to the other ministries—and charged with the responsibility of formulating detailed plans for the public sector and guidelines for the private that would chart the future progress of the economy. The planning principle was even embodied in the new Constitution of 1961, which created the Second Republic. By 1962, the framework of a long-term, fifteen-year development program had been sketched and approved, to be implemented by appropriate central government policies and reforms (especially fiscal) that would aim at the achievement of targets specified in a series of three medium-term five-year plans. Control over the planning process and a degree of flexibility in setting the magnitudes of the targets was provided through annual progress reports and "programs," which permitted significant corrections in midterm for each five-year plan.

Since the early 1960s, the planning machinery has been left largely intact, improving in efficiency with experience. Despite political tensions, the Third Five-Year Plan, to cover the final phase of the general development program, was ready for implementation in 1973. But the political role of the SPO and its consequent responsibility for prescribing the broad form and rate of economic change has been curtailed since the midsixties, its activities now being confined to the more technical areas of plan formulation.

After an extended period of negotiations, Turkey signed Articles of Association with the European Economic Community (EEC) in 1963. Considering its enormous potential impact on the economy, no single factor can adequately rationalize this truly momentous decision to seek eventual full membership. A general desire to hedge an uncertain future by obtaining firmer trade agreements with her single largest market must be counted as one reason. Moreover, remaining nonassociated meant not only having no voice in the fixing of Common Market duties and other restrictions on access to this market of the agricultural commodities that dominate Turkey's exports, but there was a felt risk of discrimination against at her goods by virtue of Greece's association with the Common Market, Greece being a country with a similar range of exports. Another reason may have been the feeling that the external financial aid deemed vital to the achievement of planning goals might thus be secured more easily and on more convenient terms. Indeed, the arrangements for the Aid Consortium had been concluded while the negotiations with the EEC were in progress. But this commitment to economic integration with Western Europe also may have been another in a series of more or less conscious expressions of an on-going Turkish "passage . . . to the West"[26] that began a millenium ago when the Turkic tribes of Central Asia turned from China, became Islamic converts, and invaded Anatolia.

Arrayed against these reasons is the unadorned fact that, though considerable time is expected to elapse before Turkey can meet the requirements of full membership, the state of development of the economy is far too inferior to her Western partners to warrant belief that the industrial sector could hold its own in competition with the Six (now the Nine, with the United Kingdom, Denmark, and Eire) at any time before, say, the end of this century at the earliest. The argument that is frequently advanced officially, that Turkish industry would benefit by increased competition, is clearly specious What is in question is the *survival* of industry, other than by efficiency-draining massive subsidization, which is already true for the "productive" (i.e., nonfinancial) State Economic Enterprises even in the absence of foreign competition.

Turkey's transition from associate to full membership is conceived to occur gradually through a sequence of "preparatory," "transitional," and "final" phases, pending mutual agreement that one phase had ended and the country was ready for the next. Agreement was reached in November, 1970, on arrangements for the "transitional" period, ending the initial phase somewhat after the minimum period considered necessary for its completion. Turkey gained a few concessions from the EEC during the "preparatory" interval and was not required to grant any. Over the "transitional" phase, however, which can last until 1982, she is required to cut duties on imports from member nations and to liberalize quantitative restrictions according to a fixed schedule, while imposing no addtional ones. Turkey is also "encouraged" to improve the treatment of private capital from EEC countries. On its part, the EEC undertakes to abolish all duties and quotas on Turkish imports, except for a handful of textile products and fruits. Additionally, financial arrangements similar to those agreed on for the "preparatory" phase allow Turkey to obtain further development loans on preferential terms from the European Investment Bank, a development arm of the EEC. The agreement also looks beyond this period to complete integration of Turkey into the Common Market no later than twenty-five years following ratification.

An agreement establishing an aid-to-Turkey consortium was reached in July, 1962, and by 1965 included fourteen creditor countries (the United States among them) plus the World Bank, the IMF, and the European Monetary Authority, all coordinated by the OECD. The groundwork for this combined multilateral and institutional lending program had already been prepared in connection with the stabilization program of 1958 and involved many of the same principals. In exchange for a promise to carry out certain reforms in foreign trade and fiscal and monetary policy, Turkey is to receive generally low-interest loans on an annual basis to meet the needs of her development programs as such, to cover the foreign-exchange costs of specific projects, and to enable her to meet payments on her external debt. Between 1963 and 1967, for example, over three-quarters of consortium loans were at rates lower than 3 percent, of twenty years duration, and with a seven-year grace period.[27]

Consortium aid, since its formal inception, has been the largest single source of capital imports for Turkey. Though the aid has doubtless been extremely helpful in meeting the foreign-exchange requirements of Turkey's planning efforts, there is some indication that a few disagreements have emerged between Turkey and the consortium regarding the administration of the program, thought they have been denied in one official quarter.[28] Nevertheless, on at least one occasion the consortium has eased Turkey's growing debt-service problem by extending repayment terms. And, though the republic expects to be able to reduce somewhat the proportion of program assistance in its total foreign borrowing in the near future, it appears improbable that such borrowing will be voluntarily curtailed at any time soon.

The course of the Turkish economy during the sixties and up to the midseventies is also worth summarizing, as are other developments having possible significance for the future, such as the terrorist activities that preceded and followed the ouster of the Demirel government in 1971 and the ouster of Makarios on Cyprus and the subsequent Turkish invasion of the island in the summer of 1974.

Early in the decade the economy was stagnating. Private investment was inhibited by heavy indebtedness accumulated earlier. Military rule had charged the atmosphere with uncertainty, U.S. economic aid dropped off sharply in 1960, recovering only partly in 1961, and public lending from other sources also declined on balance. Agricultural output (including food) and industrial production showed little or no growth between 1960 and 1962, while the value of industrial investment declined by a third. Public investment did not grow at its accustomed rate of the past and, for a change, the budget was not far out of balance. Though exports rose, imports rose still faster, but without any marked deterioration in the terms of trade. Real gross national product per capita was slightly lower in 1962 than in 1960.[29]

Recovery from stagnation began in 1963, aided considerably by a record cereals harvest, two years following the restoration of civilian rule under a coalition government. Only by 1966, however, had a fair measure of prosperity returned as adverse weather periodically hampered the growth of output. Not uncoincidentally, the increase in national product was again powered by a dramatic rise in fixed investment, this time equally divided between the public and private sectors. And again this effort could not be completely sustained by purely internal resources despite an improved fiscal effort exemplified by the removal of the tax exemption on agricultural income. A law passed in 1965 formally authorized short-term borrowing by the treasury from the Central Bank in an amount pegged to the size of the budget, and this device was fully exploited. Thus, funds from abroad (loans, grants, private investment, workers' remittances) amounting to 15.8 percent of total gross investment were required to close the savings gap in 1969, compared to only 5.5 percent in 1965.[30]

Though the money supply doubled between 1965 and 1969, the rate of inflation for the balance of the decade was still modest by the standards of the 1950s. It was more severe on the retail than on the wholesale level, especially in respect to food prices. Trade deficits were substantial and continuous throughout the decade, with exports remaining sluggish and imports tending to climb despite restraints. In the second half of the decade the balance of payments was helped immeasurably, however, by a swelling tide of foreign-exchange remittances from Turkish workers in West Germany and elsewhere in Europe. By the end of 1970 these remittances were adequate to cover nearly 30 percent of total commodity imports, but they also contributed to the growth of the money supply as a consequence of conversion of these receipts into domestic currency.

In summary, the 1960–69 period showed a growth rate of real gross national product per annum of 5.6 percent, compared to 5.8 percent for 1950–60. A somewhat lower rate of population growth during the sixties allowed the growth rate per capita to climb to 3.1 percent from 2.8 percent for the preceding decade.[31]

In August, 1970, a year after the Justice Party (the principal political heirs of the disbanded Democrats) captured Parliament, a sweeping new stabilization program was announced that included a new two-thirds devaluation of the lira. Precisely what provoked this step is not entirely clear at this writing. Several factors may have been involved, including the electoral evidence of increased dissatisfaction with recent economic accomplishments, which had fallen somewhat short of planned targets; fear of another military coup if fresh initiatives were not taken, especially since the military had recently made known its annoyance with the regime in a very pointed manner;[32] the pressure of rising food prices, bringing the embarrassment of renewed wheat shipments from the United States in 1969 and 1970, after a two-year absence; and possible pressure on the government by the OECD consortium to curb its increasingly heavier use of inflationary finance. It was also clear that a low level of international reserves was producing a growing backlog of import applications and that the sizeable discrepancy between the black-market and the official price of the lira was retarding the remittance of foreign-exchange earnings from workers abroad.

The program included a greater flexibility of interest rates to encourage more savings, a limitation of Central Bank credit for imports, additional indirect taxes, and management reorganization and consolidation of many of the debtridden SEEs. But the main response to these measures, seemingly, was a rise in prices not even experienced in the 1950s—23 percent from December, 1970, to December, 1971, in the wholesale and both the Ankara and Istanbul cost-of-living indexes[33]—as devaluation, the extra taxes, and an extraordinarily large pay rise for government employees conspired to take the roof off prices. Nor did exports increase as expected with the cheapened lira, so the increased cost of heavy, previously deferred imports pushed the trade deficit to record levels in 1970 and 1971. An offset was the flood of formerly withheld workers' remittances once the official exchange rate was put in line with market conditions—clearly a one-time phenomenon. Industrial growth was estimated by one source to have fallen to the extremely low annual rate of 2.5 percent in the first half of 1971 amid complaints by business of a profits squeeze, but this blow was softened by an apparently very good harvest.[34]

Economic instability was further complicated by the growing violence of left-wing terrorists—the so-called Turkish Peoples Liberation Army—seeking to mobilize the population against the government. Following a series of bombings, bank robberies, and kidnappings, culminating in the murder of the Israeli consul, the military, in March, 1971, demanded and obtained the dismissal of Premier Demirel and his cabinet, and replaced them with a government of academics and technocrats, with a sprinkling of professional politicians. This government lasted little more than a year before being replaced by a caretaker civilian group chosen by the military. With the general elections of 1973 and the coalition government that emerged, military influence receded, but it reasserted itself during the Cypriot crisis of 1974.

Greater insight into the pattern of development of the Turkish economy since 1950 may be obtained by a detailed examination of commodity production, specifically in agriculture and manufacturing, and external economic relationships.

COMMODITY PRODUCTION

The broadest picture of structural change in the agricultural sector since the fifties is shown below in Table 1. The rapidly declining contribution of agriculture to national income, from about a half to less than a third, has resulted from a lagging growth rate of agricultural output, which became particularly acute in the sixties, when it was less than 40 percent of the national growth rate. Diminishing productivity per worker in agriculture, relative to the national norm, is also evidenced by the only modest decline of the share of the labor force in this sector, a decline that may even be overstated.[35]

TABLE 1

PERCENTAGE SHARES OF AGRICULTURE[a] IN NATIONAL
INCOME AND THE LABOR FORCE, SELECTED YEARS

	1950	1955	1960	1965	1969
National Income	48.9	44.5	42.9	36.0	31.1
Labor Force	84.0	77.0	74.6	74.2	68.1

[a]Including forestry and fishing

Sources: Organization for Economic Cooperation and Development (OECD), *Agricultural Development in Southern Europe—Turkey* (Paris: 1969), Table 3, p. 291; United States Agency for International Development (USAID), *Economic and Social Indicators—Turkey*, 1969, Table 4D, p. 17; 1971, Table 3-C, p. 9, Table 4-D, p. 16; OECD, *Economic Surveys—Turkey*, January, 1972, inside front cover.

Food crops, wheat in particular, are the largest component of agricultural output and, as revealed in Table 2, show an increase of barely 50 percent over twenty years. These figures do not disclose periods of crop failure, and at such times (1957, 1962, 1970), sales of surplus wheat for local currency by the United States helped maintain consumption at accustomed levels.[36] This poor performance in food-crop production, when coupled with equally slow growth in poultry production and in livestock herds, is clearly reflected in the statistics of the Food and Agricultural Organization, which show per-capita food production in Turkey to have increased only slightly since the midfifties, growing at 4 percent annually between 1955–59 and 1960–64 but only 1 percent from then to 1965–69.[37] Industrial crops and fruits and nuts have shown more satisfactory rates of expansion. Lagging growth among the industrial crops in recent years is partly accounted for by the decline in the production of tobacco, a major export item.

TABLE 2

INDEX NUMBERS OF AGRICULTURAL OUTPUT
BY MAJOR CATEGORIES,
AVERAGES OF SELECTED YEARS
(1950–55 = 100)

	1950–55	1956–62	1963–67	1968–70
Food Crops[a]	100	136.6	155.5	149.7
Industrial Crops[b]	100	188.2	268.5	288.4
Fruits and Nuts	100	167.2	188.5	230.6
Poultry	100	121.0	132.8	148.9
Livestock[c]	100	117.9	119.4	123.8

[a]Cereals, pulses, and potatoes
[b]Sugar beets, tobacco, cotton, and oilseeds
[c]Sheep, goats, cattle, and buffalo

Sources: USAID, Economic and Social Indicators—Turkey, 1969, Table 6-C, p. 24, Table 6-E, p. 26; 1971, Table 6-C, p. 22, Table 6-E, p. 24.

Lack of structural change in agriculture is perhaps nowhere more apparent than in exports. Agriculture, as shown in Table 3, has completely dominated Turkey's exports and has shown no net tendency to decrease in relative importance. Moreover, the degree of commodity concentration has remained high and about constant since the midfifties, with cotton, tobacco, and fruits and nuts together accounting for about 65 percent of the value of all exports. Within this group, the only important change has been the substitution of cotton for tobacco as the leading export commodity.

What expansion has occurred in crop production has been very largely the outcome of extension of the area under cultivation, mainly at the expense of meadow and pasture land. Much of this occurred at the very beginning of the 1950s, when the Korean Conflict boom encouraged greater production for overseas markets. Between 1950 and 1955, the percentage of land area under cultivation (including vineyards and orchards) rose from 20.5 percent to 29.2 percent while meadows and pastures shrank from 48.4 to 39.8 percent. The expansion of crop land proceeded more moderately thereafter while meadow and pasture land continued to de-

TABLE 3

PERCENTAGE SHARES OF THE VALUE OF AGRICULTURAL
EXPORTS IN THE VALUE OF TOTAL EXPORTS,[a]
AVERAGES OF SELECTED YEARS

	1957–60	1961–65	1966–70
All Agricultural Exports	81.8[b]	86.3[c]	84.6
Fruits and Nuts, Tobacco, and Cotton[d]	64.8	63.9	68.9
Fruits and Nuts	21.6	22.3	24.6
Cotton	13.2	19.8	26.0
Tobacco	30.0	21.8	18.2

[a]Original value figures expressed in United States dollars
[b]Only average of years 1956 and 1960
[c]Only 1962–65
[d]Components may not sum to total because of rounding

Sources: USAID, *Economic and Social Indicators—Turkey*, 1969, Table 9-D, p. 36; 1971, Table 9-D, p. 34.

cline to 24.3 percent by 1969, some of this coming as a result of reforestation projects in the past few years. It is not surprising, therefore, that yields have shown no marked secular improvement except in a few cases (e.g., cotton, grapes, sugar beets) and in the years just past. What is surprising, in view of a consistently generous policy of price supports for grains over both decades, is that cereals have just maintained their share of cultivated area since 1950 (about 50 percent) and have recorded the slowest growth in yields.[38]

Turkish agriculture is handicapped by a combination of poor soil conditions in much of its arable area and an unchanging system of agricultural technique. Grain is grown mainly by dry-farming methods that produce only one crop in a year. Soil quality requires that much of the land be left fallow the next year, and sometimes for the next two or three years (this becomes necessary even more frequently with the tilling of meadow and pasture land). Since 1950 the percentage of cultivated area lying fallow has remained nearly constant at 30 percent.[39] Irrigation, however, could break this cycle, and OECD has estimated that a fifth of the cultivated area could be irrigated.[40] This compares to 6 percent actually under irrigation in 1967, at the conclusion of the First Five-Year Plan, up slightly from 4.5 percent at its beginning, with the use of inefficient traditional methods most common.[41] Commercial fertilizer could also be of considerable value in improving yields, but since a significant portion of what is presently used must still be imported,[42] the warranted extension of its use may not be realized for some time.

Mechanization, on the other hand, is a less than optimal type of investment for Turkish agriculture. What are needed are means that would profitably raise output per unit of land, not per man, and be labor absorbing, as is true of irrigation projects. Though mechanization might reduce the excessive fragmentation of peasant agricultural holdings in Turkey, there is no evidence that the large relative increase that has occurred in the number of tractors in the country—there were five times as many in 1968 as in 1950—has accomplished this.[43] Nor have tractors appeared to substitute for draft animals,[44] which suggests that tractors have been used mainly for plowing up pasture and meadow land. Hence, mechanization may even have contributed to the slow growth of the livestock population and to the lack of significant improvement in crop yields.

A sustained rise in agricultural productivity over an indefinite future must be considered indispensible to the development of the economy for two key reasons: first, the continuing high rate of population growth and, second, the heavy agricultural bias in the composition of exports. The statistics make it clear that agriculture has been a badly lagging sector through almost all of the postwar period and that there is a need for "industrializing" agriculture—for seeking ways and means of doing it most effectively under the particular natural and institutional conditions that govern agrarian life in Turkey. Accordingly, agriculture requires a very high priority in planned development schemes. Yet such perception appears badly lacking when one considers that under both the First and Second Five-Year plans the planning authorities allocated an investment share to agriculture of roughly only a half of its contribution to national income, permitted actual investment in the sector to fall short of the target during the First Five-Year Plan, and increased the emphasis on machinery and equipment investments in agriculture for the Second Five-Year Plan.[45] Under these circumstances, agriculture can hardly remain more than a "fair-weather" friend to the economy.

Table 4, below, points to the steady progress in the growth of the contribution of manufacturing to national income. The rise from 14 percent to nearly 17 percent between 1962 and 1967, the interval spanned by the First Five-Year Plan, was accomplished by a real growth rate in excess of 10 percent annually. Expansion of employment in manufacturing, shown for census years only, has proceeded at a slower rate (about 2.75 percent annually between 1955 and 1965) but about twice as rapidly in industrial (factory) establishments,[46] which comprise only 45 percent of all manufacturing plants.[47] Total manufacturing output grew an average of 13 percent annually during the First Five-Year Plan, slowing down slightly thereafter to achieve an annual average growth of 11 percent for the longer 1962–70 period.[48] It is clear, therefore, that during the sixties there occurred a very marked rise in output per worker in manufacturing. Nevertheless, employment in manufacturing barely kept pace with the growth of the population and thus has not alleviated the country's increasingly severe unemployment problem.[49]

TABLE 4
PERCENTAGE SHARES OF MANUFACTURING IN NATIONAL INCOME AND THE LABOR FORCE[a], SELECTED YEARS

	1955	1960	1962	1965	1967
National Income	na[b]	13.8	14.1	15.5	16.8
Labor Force	5.9	6.8	na	7.3	na

[a]Employed only
[b]na=not available

Source: USAID, *Economic and Social Indicators—Turkey,* 1969, Table 4 D, p. 17; 1971, Table 4-D, p. 16; OECD, *Economic Surveys—Turkey,* July, 1961, inside front cover; OECD, *Labour Force Statistics, 1958–1969* (Paris: 1971), p. 187.

In Table 5, below, the growth of physical output by selected manufacturing industries is shown. The list of industries is fairly representative of the range from two decades of experience. In nearly every case, the general industrial slowdown at the beginning of the sixties is apparent. In the heavy industries (e.g., cement and pig iron) growth in the sixties was greater than in the fifties and greater than for manufacturing as a whole in the sixties. Just the opposite appears to be true of industries more closely linked to consumer goods (e.g., cotton yarn and textiles, sugar refining and paper). This pattern should not be interpreted too literally, however, for data on a few other truly industrial items—sulphuric acid,, coke, alcohol—show either output declines or an average annual growth rate below 3.5 percent since 1962.[50] It is also clear that relative output growth by decade was heavily influenced by performances between 1962 and 1967, the period of the First Five-Year Plan.

TABLE 5
INDEX NUMBERS OF PHYSICAL PRODUCTION OF SELECTED MANUFACTURING INDUSTRIES, SELECTED YEARS
(1950 = 100)

	1950	1955	1960	1962	1965	1967	1969
pig iron	100	181.1	223.4	136.0	450.5	763.1	854.1
ingots and steel for casting	100	206.6	292.3	265.9	638.5	1091.2	1285.7
cement	100	206.3	515.2	587.9	818.2	1070.2	1463.4
cotton yarn	100	152.9	164.7	164.7	188.2	200.0	217.6
cotton textiles	100	144.6	151.5	153.5	179.2	187.1	199.0
sugar	100	186.1	414.6	290.5	438.0	483.9	429.2
paper	100	261.1	311.1	455.6	544.4	605.6	644.4
fertilizer[a]	100	766.7	400.0	1066.7	2400.0	2300.0	3333.3

[a]Nitrogen and phosphate content

Sources: USAID, *Social and Economic Indicators—Turkey,* 1969, Table 7-A, p. 28; 1971, Table 7-A, p. 26.

Some "unbalanced growth" in manufacturing can be expected under institutional conditions governing in Turkey, given that the state owns and operates about 30 percent of all industrial installations, mostly of relatively large size, and in manufacturing accounts for about 35–40 percent of total output and nearly 40 percent of employment.[51] Also, there is now a "mixed" sector involving joint participation by the state and private interests, though private enterprise has thus far contributed only a small portion of the capital of these establishments.[52] Since the avowed aim of all modern Turkish governments has been to enlarge the economy's industrial base, which requires substantial and continuing imports of capital equipment, it would be hard to believe that the public sector has not been favored in the allocation of scarce foreign exchange, as well as in the provision of domestic credit.

Table 6 provides some data on the relative importance of manufactures in Turkish exports since the midfifties. As is typical of developing countries, the share is very low, and concentration is evident in the disproportionately large portion accounted for by three categories of products. It is to be expected that processed food products would be important among exports of manufactures, and the abnormally high share of manufactured goods exports in 1960, apparently the result of the formal lira devaluation of that year (given the greater price elasticities of manufactures than raw agricultural produce), is largely accounted for by such products. This explanation, however, cannot apply to the high share in

TABLE 6

PERCENTAGE SHARES OF MANUFACTURED GOODS AND
SELECTED MANUFACTURING CATEGORIES IN THE VALUE
OF ALL EXPORTS AND EXPORTS OF MANUFACTURED GOODS,
SELECTED YEARS

	1956	1960	1962	1965	1967	1970
A. Shares in All Exports						
All manufactured goods	2.3	8.6	5.4	5.9	4.0	10.5
Food products, clothing and textiles, metals, and metal manufactures	1.0	7.7	3.2	3.9	3.2	8.2
B. Shares in Exports of Manufactured Goods						
Food products	34.3	70.0	47.3	41.1	50.7	20.7
Clothing and textiles	7.1	11.9	10.6	16.4	14.4	42.9
Metals and metal manufacturers	4.3	6.9	nil	8.0	9.6	14.9

Sources: See Table 3.

1970. Not only did the 1970 lira devaluation occur too late to be fully re-flected in the figures for that year, but textile and clothing exports had been accelerating since 1967, increasing by nearly eight times, to achieve a dominant position by 1970.

Hence, the increase in sales abroad of textiles and clothing has been occurring in spite of a considerable overvaluation of the Turkish lira. Moreover, in contrast to other manufactured commodities, the EEC has not agreed to an immediate and complete abolition of its duties on textile products (specifically, cotton yarn and fabrics and woolen carpets) in the agreement covering the "transitional" phase of Turkey's association with it. It is worth noting that the textile industry is not only largely in private hands but in 1963 accounted for more than a quarter of all manufacturing establishments with more than fifty employees.[53] Yet, the Second Five-Year Plan's anticipated investment increase in the textile and clothing in-dustry is substantially below the average for all manufacturing industries. Thus, if Turkey is developing a comparative advantage in some elements of textiles and apparel, its complete exploitation seems to be resisted at home as well as hindered by partners abroad.

The Second Five-Year Plan is not emphasizing export possibilities in the manufacturing sector. So far as language is concerned, the second plan explicitly mentions the goal of greater output of *import substitutes*.[54] Further, even in food products and metals and metal manufacturing the planned investment increase is less than the average for all manufacturing industries. Unless a stimulus comes in other ways, such as a further cheapening of the lira, it would appear that prospects are poor for much shift away from traditional agricultural exports in the near future.

FOREIGN TRADE, AID, AND INVESTMENT

In this era of rising expectations among the world's less-developed coun-tries and of impatience with the rate of material progress that has been characteristic of the past, the choice that governments face, between de-velopment by internal, self-sufficient measures or by means of a consider-able contribution from foreign sources (e.g., loans, foreign investments, "aid" of all descriptions), amounts to a choice between repression or frustration of these expectations indefinitely and making an observable at-tempt to meet them now. Whether because of simple political expediency or genuinely humanitarian impulses (or both), the governments of most less-developed countries have opted for development via external aid. Turkey is only one of many to do so.

The need for sacrifice and discipline, however, is not obviated by this choice. Care must be taken to conserve the nation's stock of the means of international payment, and this ordinarily cannot be accomplished by sustaining consumer demand for *foreign* articles or by *not* diverting more of existing traditional production to markets abroad. Preventing the trade gap from exhausting international reserves and impairing foreign-credit facilities as imports of the means of development rise is nothing but elementary economy—however difficult it may be to follow in practice. As Turkey's experience bears witness, violation of this discipline can only serve to produce difficulties that accentuate instability, political as well as economic.

Table 7, below, provides the factual basis for an analysis of Turkey's trade difficulties during the past two decades. Over this entire period, the growth of exports, just under 2.5 percent at an average annual rate, has lagged behind the growth of imports and that of the entire economy. The little growth that did occur seems to have been crowded into the latter years of the decade just past, but it was not sufficient to keep the trade deficit from virtually doubling in size over the last five years. This represents a very serious deterioration of the trade situation even in the context of the chronic deficits of the post-war period and the tendency in Turkey to regard trade deficits as "inevitable and natural."[55] The seriousness of the problem is underscored by the fact that during almost all of the postwar period imports have been subject to strict quantitative controls and have had a very small consumer-goods component.[56] Slightly

TABLE 7

EXPORTS, IMPORTS AND THE TERMS OF TRADE,
AVERAGES FOR SELECTED YEARS

(In Millions of United States Dollars)

	1950–53	1954–56	1958–61	1964–66	1968–70
(1) Exports (fob)	334	318	317	455	541
(2) Imports (cif)	445	461	441	609	838
(3) Trade Balance (1) – (2)	–111	–143	–124	–154	–297
		1963=100			
(4) Terms of Trade	92[a]	93	85[b]	75	77[c]

[a] 1950–52
[b] 1959–61
[c] 1968 only

Sources: USAID, *Economic and Social Indicators—Turkey,* 1971, Table 9-D, p. 34, Table 9-E, p. 35; OECD, *Economic Surveys—Turkey,* February, 1966, Table 8, p. 22; Goodman, S.S., *Turkey's Trade Prospects in the Common Market: An Exploratory Study,* Institute of Economic Development, Faculty of Economics, Istanbul University, Istanbul: 1969, Table 1, p. 9; International Monetary Fund (IMF), *International Financial Statistics,* Supplement to 1966–67 Issues, p. 259; 1971 Supplement, p. 267; July, 1972, p. 352.

more than half the record deficit for 1968–70 was incurred by trade with the present EEC (including the United Kingdom).[57]

With controls on imports, progress with the trade deficit is limited almost entirely to improvement of the export picture. Perhaps even more than most developing countries, Turkey is especially handicapped in this regard. First, the relative economic importance of exports is extraordinarily low for a developing country. Commodity exports represented less than 6 percent of the gross national product in 1969, and even that is an improvement from 3.2 percent back in 1955–59.[58] With products of low-demand elasticities dominating exports, there can be little hope of exports being increased substantially by greater production efforts along traditional (i.e., agricultural) lines. Repeated criticism of the lack of attention being given to quality, standardization, and marketing of traditional exports would indicate that even in this sector not everything is being done that could be done.[59]

Second, the nature of agricultural exports is such that any response of marketed quantities to a price improvement in the international market can only occur with a lag, at which time the stimulus may no longer be present, as occurred for Turkish cereals at the cessation of the Korean Conflict in 1953. Third, the long-range outlook for growth in world demand for several of these commodities—for example, tobacco and even cotton (and now, opium)—is not encouraging and they are among the most competitive sold on world markets. They must be sold despite high costs resulting from domestic inflation, agricultural price supports, and, until very recently, the overvaluation of the lira at its official price. Finally, the widening deficit cannot be blamed on a loss of markets; OECD figures show that Turkey slightly increased its share of total OECD exports to a large number of different world areas over the decade of the sixties.[60]

Difficulties on the export side have been compounded by an element not subject to control on the import side—prices. The last row of Table 7 gives values for the terms of trade, the ratio of an index of export prices to an index of import prices, which thus measures the import purchasing power of a unit of exports. As can be seen, the terms of trade have sharply worsened during the sixties, in effect transferring real income from Turkey to her trading partners, and have complicated the problem of maintaining a reasonable balance of trade. The principal cause has been a strong rise in import prices, mainly from the late fifties on, which far outstripped the gain in export prices.

A roughly appropriate measure of the imbalance in the international payments of Turkey would consist of the entire current-account balance (that is, the trade balance) the balance of invisibles, and net sales of goods and services to foreign military installations ("infrastructure and offshore"), plus the balance on direct private investment and debt repayments.[61] A reliable estimate of the balance-of-payments imbalance, as defined above, cannot be constructed from the published detail of the data available for years prior to the sixties. For the sixties, however, Table 8 reveals a rising trend in the overall payments deficit, a result mainly attributable, of course, to the growth of the trade deficit, which accounted for more than 80 percent of the decade's cumulative payments deficit.

A few additional components of the overall balance are also of interest. The swing from deficit to surplus in the invisibles balance over the decade is the result of the emergence of remittances from temporarily migrant workers in West Europe. Indeed, the average proceeds from this "export of services" in 1968–70, which has moderated domestic unemployment as well as the imbalance in foreign payments,[62] exceed those from any other single export commodity. Outpayments of property income, reflecting mainly interest payments on the external debt, also appear as a rising trend while private foreign investment remains very stable. And the effect of the United States balance-of-payments problem can be seen in the drastic decline in infrastructure and offshore receipts.

TABLE 8

PAYMENTS BALANCE AND COMPONENTS,
AVERAGES OF SELECTED YEARS

(In Millions of United States Dollars)

	1961–63	1964–66	1968–70
Payments Balance	−188	−219	−284
Trade Balance	−124	−154	−297
Invisibles	−42	6	85
Interest and profits	−31	−42	−72
Workers' remittances	−2	65	174
Tourism and travel	−9	−13	−3
Infrastrructure and Offshore	46	33	9
Direct Investment	30	26	32
Debt Repayment	−98	−130	−113
Trade Balance as Percent of Payments Balance	66	70	105

Sources: USAID, Economic and Social Indicators—Turkey, 1969, Table 9-A, p. 33; 1971, Table 9-A, p. 31.

The balance-of-payments pressures to which Turkey has been subjected for most of the postwar period could not have been met without external funding on a massive scale. The fact that such funding was forthcoming might be considered by some as a fortunate coincidence. But a less naïve view must recognize that Turkey's strategic position between East and West and her NATO membership were factors that could be exploited in aid of a development strategy based to a significant extent on foreign credits and grants. Put otherwise, the country could not have incurred the payments deficits shown were she not relatively secure about meeting her foreign-exchange needs.

External funding has been made available to Turkey in a variety of forms. As noted earlier, in the early and middle fifties the deficit tended to be financed by costly short-term commercial credits ("supplier credits").[63] Starting with the stabilization program of 1958, Turkey has relied much more on long-term credits extended under convenient terms.[64] Most important in this category of aid has been what the OECD calls "program assistance," or, loosely speaking, general development funding, as opposed to "project credits," which tend to be tied to the foreign-exchange cost of specific projects that are approved by the lender and that sometimes require purchase of needed imports in the lender's country ("tied loans"). Consortium credits have been also made available for debt relief. Turkey has enjoyed additional benefits from grant aid from the United States, covering both the receipt of surplus agricultural commodities and other goods and technical assistance. On the other hand, private foreign investment has never been a significant source of foreign savings. Some orders of magnitude of the different forms of external funding Turkey has received in recent years are shown in Table 9.

Foreign lending, therefore, has pushed Turkey's debt payable in foreign currency to a level two and a half times larger in 1970 than it had been as recently as 1962. The present authorized debt of $2.5 billion, three-quarters of which has already been incurred, can be compared with a 1970 GNP that cannot realistically be put above $9 billion.[65] A more appropriate idea of the burden this debt represents is given by the fact that the *average* annual payment of principal plus interest scheduled for the years 1971 to 1980 inclusive is just under $170 million,[66] which is close to 30 percent of the dollar value of Turkish exports in 1970.

Aside from public lending, "aid" (that is, grants) has been an important form of external assistance. According to figures supplied by the Agency for International Development (AID) of the United States government, sales of surplus agricultural commodities to Turkey under Public Law 480, which began in 1955, averaged just over $40 million annually for the balance of the 1950s and just about the same for the 1960–70 period. This was in addition to other grant aid supplied by AID and predecessor agencies in the form of technical assistance and general commodity imports. From 1950 to 1959, such aid averaged about $57 million annually, 3 percent of it in the form of technical assistance. From 1960 to 1970, with a switch away from grants to loans after 1963, grant aid still averaged about $35 million annually, of which about 12 percent was in the form of technical assistance by 1970.[67] Hence, loans aside, United States economic aid to Turkey appears to have averaged close to $100 million a year during the 1950s and approximately $75 million a year since then.

TABLE 9

SELECTED SOURCES OF EXTERNAL CAPITAL
INFLOW AND FOREIGN EXCHANGE DEBT,
SELECTED YEARS

(In Millions of United States Dollars)

	1962	1965	1967	1970
Consortium Credits	152	169	162	217
Direct Investment	36	22	17	58
Project Credits	26	57	83	179
TL Grain Imports[a]	71	29	nil	83
Foreign Exchange Debt	979	1383	1776	2522
Fully Incurred	na[b]	1081	1344	1929

[a]Purchases for domestic currency only
[b]na=not available

Sources: USAID, Economic and Social Indicators—Turkey, 1969, Table 9-A, p. 33; 1971, Table 9-A, p. 31, Table 11-G, p. 50; OECD, Economic Surveys—Turkey, May, 1963, Table 8, p. 62.

Compared to these other forms of external funding, private foreign investment has been insignificant. An extended time series in dollar values seems not to be available except for investment in petroleum exploration and refining. Conversion of Turkish lira figures into dollars by official exchange rates prevailing in different years over the past two decades suggests that, roughly, just over $400 million was invested between 1951 and 1970, 70 percent of it in petroleum.[68] This averages out to approximately $20 million annually, a figure that is supported elsewhere.[69]

The lack of greater foreign investment in Turkey is something of a puzzle in view of the considerable Western financial stake in the country and a set of foreign-investment laws that cannot be considered illiberal by standards of developing countries today. The legal framework under which foreign investment operates in the country was established in the early fifties and has since been amended several times with a view to encouraging additional investment. Repatriation of capital and profits has been assured, but it is not clear that the country's foreign-exchange regulations have always permitted full freedom on that score. The employment of specialized foreign personnel is permitted, and the country is covered under the investment-guarantee program (insurance against confiscation and expropriation) of the United States government.[70] By its association with the Common Market, the country could have advantages as a distributing and/or manufacturing center for sales to that trading bloc. But all foreign investments do require authorization (approval) by the Turkish government, and after the military-controlled Erim govern-ment took over in March, 1971, it was announced that majority interests by Turkish nationals were required for all new investments and that such investments had to satisfy criteria with respect to magnitude, technologi-cal transfers, and export potential. In fact, the recently concluded proto-col outlining the conditions of Turkey's "transitional" phase of its associa-tion with the EEC contains an implication that the government has not fully encouraged private investment from Common Market nations.[71] More recent news, however, suggests that these new investment rules are being interpreted somewhat flexibly.[72]

For reasons that are not obvious to this writer, realized investments have amounted to only 37 percent of the cumulative authorized foreign investments, excluding petroleum, since 1951, with extremely marked an-nual fluctuations in this percentage.[73] In nonpetroleum activities, foreign investment has been prominent in the chemical, tire, pharmaceutical, motor-vehicle, electrical equipment, and metal-manufacturing industries. British and United States interests appear to have dominated the foreign sector of the petroleum field, while in other industries, West Germany, Italy and the United States, in that order, have been most active in recent investments, accounting for well over half of foreign nonpetroleum in-vestment since 1966.[74]

Owing in large part to the absence of real change in the composition of exports and the continuing domination of imports by capital goods and industrial raw materials, there have been few permanent shifts in the di-rection of Turkish trade over the past two decades. Table 10 presents the picture for both exports and imports in this regard.

As in 1950, Turkey's present EEC partners currently represent the largest single market for her goods, taking between a third and 40 per-cent of exports, but there is no real evidence of a change in the relative importance of this market, either from 1950 or after 1962, following rati-fication of Turkey's associate membership. The EEC accounts for roughly the same share of imports with a similar lack of change over time, and for both exports and imports West Germany is the most important part-ner within the bloc, generally maintaining a reasonably balanced trade with Turkey. The major export to the EEC is cotton, with dried fruit and nuts and some mineral ores also of importance, while machinery, in-cluding automative equipment and parts, and chemicals, are heavily im-ported from this trading group.[75]

The notable shifts in the direction of trade that have occurred have been the relative decline in trade with the United States, especially in exports, and the generally increased trade with the Eastern bloc. Tobacco is by far the major commodity sold to the United States,[76] and declining United States demand for this single commodity has been instrumental

TABLE 10

DESTINATION OF EXPORTS AND ORIGIN OF IMPORTS, PERCENTAGE DISTRIBUTION BY WORLD REGION OR COUNTRY, SELECTED YEARS

Exports (%)

Region or Country	1950	1956	1960	1962	1965	1967	1970
EEC[a]	34.7	34.0	33.5	40.4	33.9	33.7	39.5
W. Germany	21.1	16.6	14.8	17.7	15.6	16.1	19.9
U. S.	16.9	19.6	18.3	19.6	17.7	17.8	9.6
EFTA[b]	24.5	15.1	17.4	19.3	18.0	16.9	17.7
U. K.	14.0	7.6	9.7	9.4	8.9	6.6	5.7
East Bloc[c]	6.9	19.6	12.2	7.0	14.7	16.7	13.8
Rest of World	17.0	11.7	18.6	13.7	15.7	14.9	19.4

Imports (%)

	1950	1956	1960	1962	1965	1967	1970
EEC[a]	32.8	37.0	35.6	30.2	28.5	34.7	34.2
W. Germany	17.6	23.6	21.0	17.1	14.7	19.5	18.6
U. S.	24.5	21.1	25.8	29.1	28.1	17.9	20.4
EFTA[b]	17.4	12.9	17.0	16.4	16.6	19.8	17.3
U. K.	10.4	8.2	11.3	11.3	9.7	12.9	9.6
East Bloc[c]	7.9	14.6	9.1	6.0	10.0	13.2	10.7
Rest of World	17.4	14.4	12.5	18.3	16.8	14.4	17.4

[a]For the years shown and until January 1, 1973, the European Economic Community included Western Germany, Belgium, Luxembourg, the Netherlands, France, and Italy.

[b]Until January 1, 1973, the European Free Trade Association included the United Kingdom, Austria, Denmark, Sweden, Switzerland, Norway, and Portugal.

[c]The East Bloc includes Eastern Germany, Bulgaria, Czechoslovakia, Hungary, Poland, Romania, and the USSR.

Sources: USAID, Social and Economic Indicators—Turkey, 1969, Table 9-B, p. 34, Table 9-C, .p 35; 1971, Table 9-B, p. 32, Table 9-C, p. 33.

in the reduction in the export share. Imports have also been relatively less important than in the immediate past because of the reduced need for cereals during most of the sixties.[77] Though there have been substantial yearly fluctuations in the importance of Eastern-bloc trade, which is conducted on a bilateral, essentially barter basis,[78] the increase from 1950 can be attributed more to Turkey's foreign-exchange problem than to any rapprochement with her Communist neighbors. This group has become an important customer for Turkey's dried fruits and tobacco.

Since the early fifties, Turkish trade with the erstwhile European Free Trade Association (EFTA), both exports and imports, has been remarkably stable. The United Kingdom traditionally accounted for more than half of imports from this group, showing no clear trend as a supplier. In exports, the United Kingdom has markedly declined as a trading partner since 1950. EFTA has imported proportionally more oil cakes and cotton and less dried fruit than the EEC, while exports from the

EFTA countries have also been heavily concentrated in the machinery and equipment category.[79]

Along with Denmark and (from outside of EFTA) the Irish republic, the United Kingdom formally entered the EEC on January 1, 1973. Though trade with the first two countries combined appears negligible, the United Kingdom has traditionally been an important market for Turkish dried fruits and nuts and olive oil.[80] If Turkey has had to compete against Commonwealth preferences in regard to these commodities, it is conceivable that the decreasing importance of this market may be arrested with English entry into the Common Market. On the other hand, if sterling continues to depreciate relative to other Common Market currencies as Turkey loosens restrictions on goods from the EEC, there can be a corresponding or greater increase in imports from England. The immediate outlook, therefore, seems promising for greater trade with the United Kingdom, but it may not ease Turkey's overall trade deficit unless English goods are substituted for other EEC imports.

One last development in Turkey's foreign economic relations should be noted. This is the formation of a regional bloc with the Muslim countries of Iran and Pakistan in 1964 (Regional Cooperation for Development), which by 1967 produced a multilateral payments arrangement as well as a freeing, or rather promoting, of trade with them.[81]

It is not apparent that much can be accomplished on the trade level, though cooperation is expected to be developed in other spheres. The economies of these countries are not complementary; they are alike especially in their dependence on agriculture, and at present, Turkish trade with Iran and Pakistan amounts to 1.5 percent or less of total trade.[82]

EVALUATING TURKISH ECONOMIC PROGRESS

Economic change is too multidimensional a phenomenon to lend itself to facile qualitative evaluation as to whether it has or has not represented "progress." The task of evaluation, of course, is still more complicated when values can come into conflict over the choice of criteria and when a long record of historical experience must be summarized. But these are really insufficient grounds for avoidance of formal judgment. Events are never merely recorded as they occur; rather, they are selected by and filtered through the observer's perceptions of what "ought" or "ought not" to be, leaving evaluation, however indistinct, always present. Fairness thus demands that one's accounting of the pluses and minuses be made explicit, even if the attempt should seem to be overindulgence of ego.

An eclectic approach to judging economic change in postwar Turkey is more likely to do justice to the problem than the use of a single perspective. Accordingly, Turkish economic accomplishments are judged below:

(a) in terms of the goals or targets the planners have set themselves,

(b) by success or failure in overcoming special obstacles to growth imposed by institutional or other conditions, and,

(c) by whether certain preconditions for accelerated future growth have been achieved, as well as this can be determined.

The essentials of the first approach mentioned is contained in Table 11, which is simply a checklist of important planning targets. Available at this writing is information on various aspects of the outcome of the First Five-Year Plan, 1963-67, and for two to three years into the period of the Second Five-Year Plan, 1968–72. Table 11 attempts to summarize this information by specifying the first-plan targets that were achieved and those that were not, and by indicating whether progress toward attainment of objectives outlined in the Second Five-Year Plan is or is not satisfactory in terms of the schedules set down. Targets are judged achieved or on schedule if they come to being met at least by 90 percent, producing a small bias in favor of optimistic results.

Table 11 presents a mixed bag. There is no unvarying pattern either in the results of the First Five-Year Plan or the accomplishments thus far under the second plan. The growth rate of GNP, which can be judged the key target variable, fell just short of being met over the period of the First Five-Year Plan, achieving an average of 6.7 percent annually in real terms instead of 7 percent. For the second plan, the same 7 percent growth rate is projected, but after lagging significantly behind the plan from 1968 to 1970, the growth rate is rather hesitatingly here considered on schedule only because of an estimated bumper crop for 1971, which pushed the estimated growth rate for that year well above the planned rate.

Investment and domestic savings goals were, relatively speaking, comfortably achieved over the First Five-Year Plan, but difficulties in the economy in the late sixties are showing up in a less-than-planned growth of private investment and domestic savings that could seriously interfere with the GNP growth target toward the close of the Second Five-Year Plan period. During the first-plan period, only the services sector realized the planned sectoral-output growth[83] and similar overestimation of growth may be true at the conclusion of the second-plan period. The lack of realization of projected investment in agriculture over the first plan was commented on earlier.[84] But the productivity of total investment, as indicated by the marginal capital-output ratio, which just barely satisfied the first-plan target, and which has been pegged as less favorable over the Second Five-Year Plan,[85] has been surprisingly high halfway into the second plan.

Targets in the trade sector seem to have been more easily met during the First Five-Year Plan than might have been expected, but the picture is definitely cloudier for the Second Five-year Plan. In some ways, however, the listing of "achievements" and "failures" as just that may be misleading. For example, it would appear that the trade-balance target for the first plan was attained only because the planners had allowed for a very large deficit in the anticipation of a substantial amount of borrowing that would permit it to be financed. But less than 65 percent of the amount of public lending expected under the first plan was obtained, and

TABLE 11

FIRST PLAN TARGETS ACHIEVED AND UNACHIEVED AND SECOND PLAN TARGETS ON OR AHEAD OR BEHIND TARGET SCHEDULE, SELECTED TARGETS

Target Variable	First Plan Achieved	Unachieved	Second Plan On or Ahead	Behind
Gross National Product, growth rate	x		x	
Private Consumption, growth rate		x	x	
Private Gross Fixed Investment, growth rate	x			x
Public Gross Fixed Investment, growth rate	x		x	
Total Gross Domestic Savings, percent of GNP	x			x
Private Gross Domestic Savings, percent of GNP	ns[a]		x	
Agricultural Output, growth rate		x		x
Industrial Output, growth rate		x		x
Investment in Agriculture, percent of total		x	na[b]	
Investment in Manufacturing, percent of total	x		na[b]	
Marginal Capital-Output Ratio, total economy	x		x	
Total Exports, growth rate of dollar value	x			x
Total Imports, growth rate of dollar value	x		x	
Agricultural Exports, growth rate of dollar value	x			x
Exports of Industrial Products, growth rate of dollar value		x	x	
Trade Balance, cumulative dollar value	x		x	
Interest Payments Abroad, cumulative dollar value		x	x	
Tourism and Travel, net cumulative dollar value		x		x
Workers' Remittances, cumulative dollar value	ns[a]		x	
Other Invisibles, cumulative dollar value	x			x

Target	First Plan		Second Plan	
Variable	Achieved	Unachieved	On or Ahead	Behind
Debt Repayments,[c]				
cumulative dollar value		x	x	
Private Direct Investment,				
cumulative dollar value	x			x
Official Loans,				
cumulative dollar value		x	x	
U. S. Agriculture Surpluses[d]				
cumulative dollar value	x			x

[a]ns=not specified
[b]na=not available
[c]Gross of debt relief
[d]Public Law 480 shipments

Sources: OECD, *Economic Surveys—Turkey*, July, 1968, Tables 7-8, p. 21, Table 9, p. 22, Table 10, p. 23, Table 11, p. 24, Table 12, p. 25; December, 1970, Table 5, p. 17; January, 1972, Table 1, p. 7, Table 5, p. 18, Table I, p. 39, Table II, p. 40; USAID, *Social and Economic Indicators—Turkey*, 1971, Table 4-B, p. 14, Table 4-D, p. 16; Republic of Turkey, State Planning Organization, *First Five Year Development Plan, 1963-1967* (Ankara: 1963), Table 49, p. 108; OECD, *Capital and Finance in Agriculture*, Volume II: *Country Studies—Turkey* (Paris: 1971), Table 3, p. 7.

this undoubtedly forced the trade gap to a narrower position than was planned for.[86] Also, no surplus agricultural commodity shipments from the United States were anticipated in the period 1968–72. Thus, the fact that some shipments were required in 1969 and 1970 means that this variable is permanently off-target for the second plan. Nevertheless, it does appear that in tourism and travel, in other invisibles, and in private investment there has been a substantial overestimation of foreign receipts over the second-plan period, so that a favorable final outcome of the balance of payments by 1972 is heavily dependent on a marked improvement in exports.

As a summary judgment, it would appear that the major targets of the First Five-Year Plan were essentially met, albeit with some deficiencies, and that these targets were probably not unrealistic, considering the productive capacity of the economy and the rate at which it had to grow to prevent the continuing high rate of population growth from unduly interfering with planned development. In the evidence relating to progress under the Second Five-Year Plan, however, there is a strong indication that the goals may fall far short of accomplishment; if they do, this will leave the relative position of the economy about where it was in the early sixties, which is to say, before the implementation of the first plan.

It is probably true that the historical record of any developing country can be successfully combed for instances of unfavorable developments or special situations that can be used to rationalize inadequate economic performance. This, however, does not invalidate the search for or the accuracy of conclusions based upon that record. One must consider that Turkey's economic growth rate over two decades compares quite favorably with the achievement of many developed countries, despite her share of problems more or less in common with other developing countries. These include a probably greater-than-desired defense budget as a result of the continuing tension over the Cyprus issue. Other real restraints on development, mentioned or alluded to earlier, include political instability and the resulting uncertainty about possible military take-over or control; the inability to keep budgetary deficits from upsetting the money and credit mechanism and producing chronic inflation, which would tend to divert private funds from long-term productive investments; the considerable and persistent financial drain caused by the inefficient and politically harrassed industrial State Economic Enterprises, still a firmly entrenched institution; and the lack of receptivity to modern methods of agriculture and animal husbandry by a very traditionally oriented peasantry.

When economic gains can be made even in the face of such obstacles, the country that makes them cannot be greatly faulted. Yet the assessment should not be limited to the narrowly economic record. Efforts that can be genuinely labeled "developmental" must also be addressed to those institutional areas in which reform can be equally or more productive than some additional enterprises or capital formation—population control, fiscal integrity, and land use, for instance. And in these respects, much remains to be done in Turkey.

Economic science is not yet sufficiently advanced to lend itself to rigorous determination of whether any country is currently prepared for accelerated development, or "takeoff." Perhaps a special sort of insight, derived from an intimate knowledge of social conditions in the country and a general competence in the recognition and analysis of economic forces and trends will always be necessary for an enlightened judgment along these lines. But if this paper lends itself to at least a tentative conclusion on this score, it must be that such a development stage is not yet imminent for Turkey. Turkey's real per-capita income is, realistically, hardly more than an eighth of the average for Western Europe.[87] Assuming, for example, that "takeoff" would be a genuine possibility for a country if per-capita income was only a third of the current Western European average (about $2,400), it would take Turkey a third of a century to achieve that higher income level with an annual growth in per-capita income of 3 percent, the maximum realized thus far. And this would also assume that whatever additional growth Turkey's Western European partners achieved over this period did not represent a hindrance to her "takeoff."

Leaving this statistical finding aside, it seems appropriate to conclude that the conditions of "takeoff" for Turkey will include much more than the development of her infrastructure and industrial base, which conceivably has reached (or is about to reach) a stage of adequacy for a more rapid future growth of industrial production. The possibility of sustained growth appears to rest much more on the development of a more advanced and stable agricultural sector, on a larger and more diversified export base (which includes the products of the most rapidly expanding industrial sectors), on better control of monetary aggregates, and on a substantially diminished rate of population growth. These are the variables that hold the key to Turkey's economic future.

NOTES

1. Two recent English-language economic histories of Turkey which make this point, with somewhat differing emphasis, are Hershlag, Z. Y., *Turkey: The Challenge of Growth* (Leiden: Brill, 1968), and Cohn, E. J., *Turkish Economic, Social and Political Change: The Development of a More Prosperous and Open Society* (New York: Praeger, 1970).

2. Although, as will become increasingly evident in the pages that follow, this homogeneity has not proved to be an unmitigated blessing.

3. Some recent comparative economic statistics on Turkey and neighboring European countries can be scanned in Organization for Economic Cooperation and Development, *Economic Surveys: Turkey*, January, 1972 (Paris: 1972), folded page at rear (hereafter referred to as OECD *Survey* and date). The 1970 Turkish GNP is listed here as $350 per head, but this figure is most questionable, and seems to have been obtained by conversion of the Turkish lira (TL) to the United States dollar on the basis of the official exchange rates existing both before and after the devaluation of the lira in August, 1970. Since the lira was considerably overvalued for several years at the predevaluation rate, exclusive use of the postdevaluation rate for all of 1970 income would have been far more appropriate. This would have reduced the OECD per-capita income estimate by about $100.

4. Roberts, T. D., Reese, H. C., Comeau, P., Jones, M. C., Reck, G. and Siffing, P., *Area Handbook for the Republic of Turkey* (Washington, D.C.: Superintendent of Documents, United States Government Printing Office, 1970), pp. 11–22. Hereafter referred to as *Handbook*.

5. *Handbook*, pp. 80–81, 33.

6. Gallagher, C. F., "Contemporary Islam: The Straits of Secularism—Power, Politics and Piety in Republican Turkey," *American Universities Field Staff Reports Service*, Southwest Asia Series, Vol. 15, No. 3 (New York: 1966), pp. 16–17.

7. *Handbook*, pp. viii, 55, 60; United States Department of Commerce, Bureau of the Census, *Statistical Abstract of the United States, 1971* (Washington, D.C.: Superintendent of Documents, U. S. Government Printing Office, 1971), Table 1269, p. 797 (hereafter referred to as *U. S. Statistical Abstract* and date); and United Nations Conference on Trade and Development, *Trade and Development*, Vol. VI: *Trade Expansion and Regional Groupings*, Part 1 (New York:

United Nations, 1964), Table 2–2, p. 83 (hereafter referred to as *UNCTAD Conference*).

8. OECD *Survey* (January 1972), inside front cover; *Handbook,* pp. 23, 25; and Republic of Turkey, State Planning Organization, *First Five Year Development Plan, 1963–1967* (Ankara: 1963), p. 24 (hereafter referred to as *First Plan*).

9. Ibid., p. 13.

10. OECD *Survey* (January, 1972), inside front cover.

11. *The Economist* (January 2, 1971), pp. 47–48, reports annual rural per-capita income at about $50. The relatively large share of services in total output, 42 percent, is probably also indicative of the large extent of urban poverty. In Turkey, as in other equally poor countries, substantial numbers of city dwellers are effectively unemployed but manage to scratch out a bare subsistence income by rendering petty, menial personal services to businesses and households.

12. See Table 6.

13. *Handbook,* p. 15.

14. Cohn, op. cit., p. 4.

15. The materials in this section are drawn from a wide number of contemporary sources, which include: OECD *Surveys,* for selected years from 1958 to 1972; *Newsweek,* selected issues of 1971 and 1972; *The Economist,* selected issues of 1971 and 1972; *Handbook;* Hershlag, op. cit.; Cohn, op. cit.; Gallagher, op. cit.; *First Plan;* Republic of Turkey, State Planning Organization, *Second Five Year Development Plan, 1968–1972* (Ankara: 1969; hereafter referred to as *Second Plan*) and *Partners in Development-Turkey* (Report of the Commission on International Development, Lester B. Pearson, Chairman), (New York: Praeger, 1969), hereafter referred to as *Pearson Report.*

16. Cohn, op. cit., p. 17.

17. Hershlag, op. cit., pp. 139–140.

18. Ibid., Table 25, p. 345.

19. United States Agency for International Development, *Economic and Social Indicators-Turkey,* 1969, Table 1–A, p. 1 (hereafter referred to as *Indicators* and date).

20. Ibid., Table 6–A, p. 22.

21. Organization for Economic Cooperation and Development, *Agricultural Development in Southern Europe-Turkey* (Paris: 1969), Table 6, p. 296 (hereafter referred to as OECD, *Agricultural Development*).

22. Hershlag, op. cit., Table 39, p. 356.

23. *Indicators,* 1969, Table 5–B, p. 20. Price stability earlier was maintained by record harvests.

24. Hershlag, op. cit., Table 13, p. 338.

25. *UNCTAD Conference,* Tables 2–2 and 2–3, p. 83, Table 2–5, p. 85 and *Indicators,* 1969, Table 1–A, p. 1.

26. Gallagher, op. cit., p. 16.

27. OECD *Survey* (July 1968), p. 26.

28. Hershlag, op. cit., p. 262 and *Pearson Report,* p. 323.

29. Hershlag, op. cit., Table 47, p. 361, Table 33, p. 352, Tables 24 and 25, p. 345, Table 58, p. 369, Table 12, p. 337; *Indicators,* 1971, Table 4–A, p. 12; and Cohn, op. cit., Appendix Table 5, p. 171.

30. *Indicators,* 1971, Table 11–F, p. 49 and Table 4–B, p. 14.

31. Ibid., Table 4–A, p. 12.

32. The military hauled tanks into view of the Parliament building in May, 1969, to register opposition to a bill seeking to restore political rights of former leaders of the Democrats. See Cohn, op. cit., p. 40.

33. OECD *Survey* (January, 1972), Table 2, p. 12.

34. *The Economist* (Jan. 2, 1971, Oct. 23, 1971), pp. 47–48 and p. 94, respectively.

35. The OECD has revised downward its estimate of the total and agricultural labor force for 1967 and thereafter, which may or may not be validated by the results of the 1970 Census when it is published. *Cf.* OECD *Survey* (July, 1968, and August, 1969), inside front cover.

36. *Indicators*, 1971, Table 12–D, p. 61.

37. Food and Agricultural Organization, *Production Yearbook: 1970* (Rome: 1971), Table 11, p. 31.

38. *Indicators*, 1969, Tables 6–A, 6–B, pp. 22–23; 1971, Tables 6–A, 6–B, pp. 20–21.

39. Republic of Turkey, State Institute of Statistics, *The Summary of Agricultural Statistics, 1944–1965* (Ankara: 1966), p. 5 and *The Summary of Agricultural Statistics, 1970* (Ankara: 1971), Table 1, p. 7.

40. OECD, *Agricultural Development*, p. 294.

41. Hershlag, op. cit., p. 222.

42. OECD, *Agricultural Development*, Table 6, p. 296.

43. Organization for Economic Cooperation and Development, *Capital and Finance in Agriculture*, Volume II: *Country Studies—Turkey* (Paris: 1970), Table 5, p. 9 (hereafter referred to as OECD, *Capital and Finance*) and OECD, *Agricultural Development*, Table 12, p. 303. In 1950 there was an average of seven different plots per farm, with no indication of subsequent improvement except in some newly irrigated lands.

44. OECD, *Agricultural Development*, Table 5, p. 295.

45. OECD, *Capital and Finance*, p. 8.

46. I.e., establishments employing ten or more workers or equipment using ten or more horsepower.

47. Cohn, op. cit., Table 16, p. 120 and *Second Plan*, Table 195, p. 400.

48. OECD *Survey* (August, 1969, January, 1972), Table IV, p. 56, and Table IV, p. 42, respectively.

49. Unemployment has been estimated to have nearly doubled to two million between 1965 and 1971. *Economic News Digest* (of Turkey) (July 1, 1971), p. 5.

50. Cohn, op. cit., p. 114; *Handbook*, pp. 285, 292; and Türkiye Is Bankasi, A. S., Economic Research Department, *Economic Indicators of Turkey, 1966–1970* (Ankara: n. d.), p. 4 (hereafter referred to as *Economic Indicators*).

51. Cohn, op. cit., p. 125.

52. Ibid., p. 124 and *Economic Indicators*, p. 4.

53. *Second Plan*, Table 195, p. 400.

54. Ibid., p. 327.

55. Union of Chambers of Commerce, Chambers of Industry and Commodity Exchanges of Turkey, *Economic Report*, 1967 (Ankara: 1968), p. 265 (hereafter referred to as *Economic Report* and date).

56. *Handbook,* p. 329. From 1965 to 1970, the value of consumer-goods imports have averaged less than 10 percent of total imports. See OECD *Survey* (January, 1972), Table IV, p. 44.

57. *Indicators* (1971), Table 9–B, p. 32 and Table 9–C, p. 33.

58. OECD *Survey* (January, 1972), folded page at rear, and Ibid. (July, 1961), inside front cover. Export levels of the last half of the fifties were depressed relative to the first half, making for a higher rate of growth in exports than for the general economy from the late fifties as well as a higher rate than for exports since the early fifties. See Table 7, above.

59. *The Economist* (Jan. 2, 1971), pp. 47–48.

60. OECD *Survey* (January, 1972), folded page at rear.

61. Long-term public foreign credits, including foreign aid in cash or kind, can legitimately be considered as bolstering foreign-exchange reserves required by other international transactions rather than directly contributing to the magnitude of Turkey's balance-of-payments deficit. Similarly, all short-term capital movements are traditionally treated as financing in nature.

62. The number of workers unofficially estimated to be employed abroad, in-

63. See above, pp. 18–19.

cluding legal and illegal emigrants, has been put between 480,000 and 500,000. The official estimate is about 150,000. *Economic News Digest* (of Turkey) (July 1, 1971), p. 5, and *Economic Indicators,* p. 8.

64. *Pearson Report,* p. 323.

65. This estimate assumes that the devaluation of August, 1970, can be applied to the entire year's income in lira because of the preceding overvaluation of the lira by about the percentage of the devaluation. See above, note 3.

66. *Indicators* (1971), Table 11–H, p. 51.

67. Ibid., Table 12–A, p. 57.

68. Ibid., Table 10–B, p. 40, Table 10–C, p. 41.

69. *Pearson Report,* p. 323.

70. *Handbook,* p. 344.

71. See above, p. 21.

72. *Indicators* (1971), Table 10–B, p. 40; OECD *Survey* (January, 1972), p. 29; and *The Economist* (Oct. 23, 1971), p. 94.

73. *Indicators,* 1971, Table 10–A, p. 39.

74. *Handbook,* p. 286, and *Indicators* (1971), Table 10–A, p. 39.

75. *Economic Report* (1967), Table 158, p. 215, Table 193, p. 257, and *Handbook,* p. 333.

76. *Economic Report* (1967), Table 196, p. 260.

77. *Indicators* (1971), Table 9–C, p. 33.

78. *Handbook,* p. 332.

79. *Indicators* (1971), Table 9–B, p. 32, Table 9–C, p. 33, and *Economic Report* (1967), Table 163, p. 221, Table 195, p. 259.

80. *Indicators* (1971), Table 9–B, p. 32. Table 9–C, p. 33, and *Handbook,* p. 333.

81. Ahmad, Y. "Iran, Pakistan and Turkey: 160 Million Customers," *Ceres* (November/December 1968), pp. 43–44.

82. *Indicators* (1971), Table 9–B, p. 32, Table 9–C, p. 33.

83. OECD *Survey* (July, 1968), Table 9, p. 22.

84. See above, p. 26–27.
85. OECD, *Capital and Finance*, Table 3, p. 7.
86. OECD *Survey* (July 1968), Table 12, p. 25.
87. See footnote 3, above.

3

Greece

ALEXANDER J. KONDONASSIS

W HEN Constantinople was conquered by the Turks, A.D. 1453, most of the Greek mainland had also come under Turkish rule, and so far as Greece was concerned, this rule continued intermitently until 1821. As a consequence, many Greeks left their country and settled elsewhere in the Mediterranean region, in Southern Russia, and in some areas where they thought they might be free to pursue their interests. To achieve some measure of personal security, many of those who did not leave the country began clustering around the local church, becoming so dependent upon it that eventually the church came to perform not only religious but many educational and political functions for them. A number of other Greeks who stayed in the country rose to high positions in the Turkish administrative hierarchy. By and large, then, it can be argued that Greece experienced a serious setback as a result of Turkish occupation, for during almost four centuries of Ottoman rule she was cut off from the significant social, political, and technological changes that were taking place in Western Europe during the Renaissance and the early industrial revolutionary periods. Thus, when a large part of Greece's mainland became independent from Turkish rule, Greece was a poor, agricultural nation with an even smaller land area than before the Turkish rule, and a fragmented internal market.

The Greek people won freedom from Ottoman rule in the War of Independence of 1821–30. A monarchy was established in 1832 under the tutelage of England, France, and Russia.[1] Greece more than doubled its territory during its first century of independence and emerged from World War I with approximately its present frontiers.[2]

A continuing struggle for power between the palace and antimonarchist elements occurred during the interwar period. Greece was proclaimed a republic in 1924, but King George II was recalled to the throne in 1935. The monarchy was reconfirmed by a plebiscite in 1946.

GENERAL CHARACTERISTICS OF THE ECONOMY, 1940

By 1940[3] Greece had achieved its present boundaries. Its total area is about 130 thousand square kilometers, with a population, in 1940, of 7.3 million people. Approximately three-fourths of this land is rocky and mountainous.[4] Before World War II, Greece was basically a primary-product-producing country that derived about a third of her national income from agricultural production.[5] According to the Greek ministry of agriculture the average size of land plots was less than a hectare and the average dispersion of farm plots was about 2.5 kilometers. The prevalent methods of cultivation were quite inefficient and included no concerted effort toward soil conservation or irrigation; the use of chemical fertilizers was limited and soil exhaustion and low productivity were common phenomena. The main crops were wheat, grapes, olives, and tobacco.

Greece possessed mineral deposits (e.g., nickel and bauxite) that, in the absence of technical skills and appropriate local industries, were mostly exported as raw materials. Moreover, owing to the lack of adequate sources of power, handicrafts were comparatively strong.[6] The typical Greek business firm was rather small in size. In most Greek cities, small shops were the rule, not large enterprises.[7] The 1930 census shows that 93.2 percent of Greece's manufacturing establishments employed five persons or less, 5.7 percent employed from six to twenty-five persons, and only 1.1 percent employed twenty-six persons or more.[8] The great majority of firms were family-owned-and-managed enterprises whose small size limited the possibility of introducing modern technology. Most of these firms, protected as they were from foreign competition by government tariffs, were operated inefficiently, utilized anarchronistic methods of production, incurred high production costs, and were low in productivity.[9]

Other characteristics of the Greek society included strong family ties, social inertias and labor immobilities, and a pronounced cultural and economic stratification of the Greek people into two groups, one of the villages and one of the cities, a social dualism contributed to and perpetrated by a rather inadequate transportation system and a highly centralized and bureaucratic governmental structure.

Before World War II, per-capita income in Greece was quite low and so was the volume of savings. Though prewar national-income data are not too reliable, various estimates suggest that, in 1938, per-capita income was only about $100 (U.S.) and total savings with the banks plus undistributed corporation profits amounted to only 6 percent of gross national product.[10] It is further estimated[11] that during the 1928–39 period real national income increased by 1.2 percent per year, while population increased by 1.3 percent. In addition the Greek tax system was built around indirect taxes. In 1938, for example, more than two-thirds of the government revenue was derived from such taxes.[12]

Another characteristic of the Greek economy was its relatively high foreign-trade orientation. Before the war, approximately 20 percent of the economy's total requirements were imported from abroad.[13] A large part of these were raw materials and foodstuffs. At that time Greek exports paid for about 70.5 percent of the value of imports. Tobacco, raisins, olives, olive oil, and wine constituted the most important Greek exports. A large part of the remaining balance-of-trade account was paid by invisible income (e.g., shipping and private remittances.)[14] However, because of the luxury character of Greek exports and the fluctuating behavior of "invisibles" the Greek balance of payments was often in trouble.

In the financial sector, a few privately owned and a number of state-owned banks were in operation in 1939. An important characteristic of the Greek commercial banks was that they did not create demand deposits as a general consequence of lending and investing operations. The majority of business and financial transactions have always been settled in cash. A major part of their prewar deposits were savings or time deposits, and even in those cases where larger business firms made payments by check, the checks were ordinarily cashed in exchange for currency.

The Bank of Greece, the country's central banking institution, was established in 1927 following an agreement between the Greek government and the Council of the League of Nations, which provided for a loan of 9 million pounds sterling to the Greek government.[15] The Bank of Greece was founded as a limited-liability company with an original share capital of 400 million drachmae.[16] The head office of the bank was established in Athens and branch offices were set up in various parts of the country.

Before World War II, the primary objective of the Bank of Greece was to control the money supply through its vested monopoly power of note issue.[17] The only limitation upon this power was the provision that the bank must maintain a 40 percent gold reserve against all bank notes in circulation.[18]

Before the war, the bank did not exercise active quantitative or qualitative credit controls as these are understood in the Western world today. It made a relatively small volume of direct loans to the economy for general welfare projects,[19] in which the other banks were not interested, and it attempted to influence the bank rates of interest by rediscounting commercial-bank portfolios.[20] However, this so-called British banking tradition proved to be not very effective[21] in Greece because there was no organized discount market and because the commercial banks, which held a rather sizable volume of private deposits of about 24 billion drachmae in 1938, did not choose to call on the Bank of Greece for an appreciable volume of assistance through rediscount of their portfolios. Moreover, in the absence of a liquid call-loans market and bills market, the Bank of Greece had no opportunity to carry on open-market operations for the purpose of implementing monetary and credit control.

On the basis of the brief review presented above it is not difficult to generalize that external and internal political conflicts and an unfavorable combination of resources and institutions go a long way toward explaining the underdeveloped condition of the pre-World War II Greek economy.

THE ALBANIAN WAR, OCTOBER, 1940–APRIL, 1941

Greek involvement in the Albanian War began with the Italian invasion of Greek territory in the north on October 28, 1940. The Greek government, confronted with the problem of financing the war, proceeded to borrow the necessary funds from the Bank of Greece, which in turn resorted to the privilege of issuing notes. Consequently, the volume of bank notes in circulation increased during this six-month period by about 72 percent.[22] Internal transportation and domestic production were adversely affected and imports of goods and services substantially declined as a result of the war, during which the cost-of-living index rose by 12 percent.[23] The rise would undoubtedly have been greater had it not been for certain offsetting factors, including: (1) relatively high public confidence in the drachma, (2) a decline in the velocity of circulation of money, and (3) stability in the foreign-exchange value of the drachma in terms of gold. In addition, the fact that the war lasted only about six months prevented the development of greater economic dislocations that would have led to more intense inflationary price pressures.

THE OCCUPATION PERIOD, APRIL, 1941–OCTOBER, 1944

Greece was occupied by the Axis forces from April, 1941, to October, 1944. During this period the foundations were laid for the continuing price-level inflation that would plague Greece after World War II.

The administrative, monetary, and productive machinery of the Greek economy were unable to function effectively during the occupation period. Fear, uncertainty, and political and economic chaos prevailed. The occupation forces appropriated the largest possible volume of Greek commodities for their own use and for export to their respective homelands. Allied aid was largely nonexistent, the internal transportation system deteriorated, and domestic production levels fell substantially below prewar levels. Commodity hoarding became common practice and black markets developed rapidly. Simultaneously, the Bank of Greece was compelled, by both the occupation forces and the puppet Greek government, to issue more and more bank notes to provide the occupation forces with the means with which to pay for their respective operations.

The interaction of these monetary and nonmonetary developments resulted in continuous deterioration of the purchasing power of the drachma and in deterioration of the drachma's foreign-exchange value in terms of gold, which in turn led to loss of confidence in the drachma and an increase in the velocity with which money circulated. As these trends assumed greater amplitude, an additional medium of exchange made its appearance: the gold sovereign.[24] It was first introduced by the occupation forces in order to facilitate their domestic purchases of goods and services, but as confidence in the drachma deteriorated, it largely replaced the paper drachma as a medium of exchange and as a store of value.[25] In effect, Gresham's law was reversed; that is, the good money (the gold sovereign) pushed the bad money (the paper drachma) out of circulation.

Table 1 illustrates developments with respect to the indices of banknote circulation, of the cost of living, and of the gold sovereign in Athens.

TABLE 1

INDICES OF BANK NOTE CIRCULATION, COST OF LIVING, AND GOLD SOVEREIGN

Date	Bank-Note Circulation Index	Cost-of-Living Index	Gold-Sovereign Index
April, 1941	1.	1.	1.
December, 1942	15.7	127.7	156.5
December, 1943	135.5	1,319.2	1,572.7
October, 1944	2,276,320.0	1,633,540,989.0	2,305,948,911.1

Source: Bank of Greece, *Annual Report for 1946* (Athens: 1947), p. 28.

The data show clearly the magnitude of the monetary expansion effected by the Bank of Greece and the tremendous deterioration of the drachma's purchasing power and gold value during the occupation period.

By the time of the liberation, in October, 1944, the Greek economy had been reduced to a condition of paralysis. Domestic production was at a very low level as compared to the prewar period, and there was an almost complete lack of confidence in the drachma. The bank-credit mechanism was defunct because bank deposits, the basic source of credits to the Greek economy prior to the war, had been wiped out by the hyperinflation of the occupation period. All prewar debt/asset relationships had been repudiated and the only acceptable means of payment was the gold sovereign.

THE PERIOD OF GENERAL UNREST, OCTOBER, 1944–1948

In October, 1944, it was quite obvious to everyone concerned with Greece's future that the monetary inflation and its consequences, which had plagued Greece throughout the occupation, could not be tolerated for long by the newly formed Greek government, and as early as November 11, 1944, a monetary reform was attempted. The basic provision of this reform was the creation of a new drachma related to the inflated occupation drachma at the ratio of one new drachma to fifty billion of the old. In addition, the new drachma was officially linked to the pound sterling at the ratio of one pound sterling to six hundred drachmae.[26] The reform failed, however, and a few months later, in June, 1945, another reform was undertaken by Kyriakos Varvaressos who, in his newly created capacity as deputy prime minister in charge of all ministries of economics, attempted to establish currency stability in Greece by instituting measures aimed both at correcting the Greek balance-of-payments disequilibrium and at balancing the government budget. The Varvaressos reform included the following proposals: (1) price controls and commodity rationing, (2) heavier taxes, (3) import restrictions, and (4) more foreign economic aid.

This reform, like its predecessor, failed to achieve its objective of liquidating the inflationary past and establishing conditions conducive to currency stability. Both reforms failed largely because of the same factors that characterized the occupation period.

A more detailed review of the monetary and nonmonetary forces that were at work during the 1944–48 period reveals the following developments.

The volume of private deposits in the Greek banking system was very low indeed. Though total bank deposits in billions of drachmae in current prices increased about forty-seven times between December 31, 1945, and December 31, 1948, the total volume of bank deposits in December 31, 1948, was about one-twelfth of that in December 31, 1938.[27] The inability of the banks to attract private deposits becomes more obvious if notice is taken of the fact that a large fraction of bank deposits in 1948 were obligatory public-corporation deposits.[28] In view of this and because of the high demand for loanable funds for economic reconstruction and government budgetary purposes the role of the Bank of Greece was expanded. Thus the volume of Bank of Greece credits to the economy and the government derived from note issue increased from 91.5 billion drachmae in 1945 to 2,533 billion drachmae in 1948.[29]

It will be remembered that during the hyperinflation of the occupation period the Greek public developed a strong preference for gold. During the 1945–48 period of guerrilla warfare confidence in the drachma continued to be low, and the gold sovereign continued to act both as an alternate medium of exchange to the drachma and as a more trustworthy store of value than the drachma. Because increases in the price of the gold sovereign were invariably followed by increases in general price levels, it was believed that if the Bank of Greece implemented a gold-sovereign sales policy at least those speculative pressures associated with the rise in the drachma-price of the sovereign would be alleviated. There was also another aspect to this policy of gold sovereign sales. Whenever monetary expansion was followed by a rising demand for gold sovereigns, the Bank of Greece, by stepping up its sales, could absorb corresponding amounts of drachmae and thus reduce the quantity of money in circulation. In furtherance of this policy, the Bank of Greece sold about 3.6 million gold sovereigns and absorbed an equivalent amount—about 562 billion—in drachmae.[30]

Table 2 summarizes the monetary situation in terms of the volume of notes in circulation, the drachma price of the gold sovereign and the cost-of-living index between December 31, 1945, and December 31, 1948. Table 2 shows that between December 31, 1945, and December 31, 1948, the volume of notes in circulation increased by about 1,056 percent, the price of gold sovereign rose by approximately 118 percent, and the cost-of-living index went up by 258 percent.

TABLE 2

NOTES IN CIRCULATION, PRICE OF GOLD SOVEREIGN
AND COST OF LIVING INDEX AT END OF YEAR
1945–48

Year as of December 31	Notes in Circulation (In Billions of Drachmae)	Price of Gold Sovereign (In Thousands of Drachmae)	Cost of Living Index in Athens 1938 = 1
1945	104	104	74.2
1946	537.5	136	145.5
1947	973.6	193	216.2
1948	1,202.2	226.5	265.6

Source: Bank of Greece, Confidential Report for April, 1951.

Review of the agricultural-production index compiled by the Greek ministry of agriculture, and of the industrial-production index, compiled by the Association of Greek Industrialists, shown in Table 3, indicates that both agricultural and industrial production, during the 1946–48 period,[31] were below the levels achieved in 1938.

Aggregate data of net national income,[32] shown in Table 4, confirm the observation that the Greek economy's performance was marked by improvement between 1946 and 1948 but had not yet in 1948 achieved the 1938 level.

TABLE 3

INDICES OF AGRICULTURAL AND INDUSTRIAL PRODUCTION
1938 and 1946–48

Agricultural Production		Industrial Production	
Year	Index 1938 = 100	Year	Index 1939 = 100
1938	100	1938	100
1945	na[a]	1945	na[a]
1946	77.9	1946	53
1947	90.4	1947	67
1948	83.5	1948	73

[a]na = not available

Source: Xenophon Zolotas, Currency Problem and the Greek Economy (published in Greek), (Athens: Papazessis, 1950); and National Statistical Service of Greece, Statistical Summary of Greece, 1954 (Athens: National Printing House, 1955).

TABLE 4

NET NATIONAL INCOME
1938 and 1945–48

Year as of December 31	In Millions of Drachmae in 1938 prices	Index 1938 = 100
1938	67,372	100
1945	na[a]	na[a]
1946	34,235	51
1947	45,800	68
1948	48,267	72

[a]na = not available

Source: Xenophon Zolotas, Currency Problem and the Greek Economy (published in Greek), (Athens: Papazessis, 1950).

Table 5 shows, moreover, that the dependence of the Greek economy on imports was substantial. Developments with respect to both the trade balance and the current-account balance of the Greek balance of payments was disappointing. In 1946, for example, contrary to the optimistic expectations that prevailed at the end of World War II, exports paid only about 17 percent of the value of the imports.[33] This trade-account adversity continued in 1947 and 1948, when exports paid approximately 24.8 percent and 22.8 percent of the value of imports, respectively,[34] as compared with the prewar period, when exports paid around 70.5 percent of the value of imports.[35] In addition, income from private remittances, which before the war was substantial, was relatively small between 1946 and 1948, and income from shipping, which was also sizable before the war, was nonexistent between 1946 and 1948. The general causes of this state of affairs were the adverse effects of war on domestic production, the deteriorating foreign-exchange value of the drachma, and the fact that many Greek shipowners chose to register their ships under foreign flags in order to take advantage of lower tax rates and greater political security than Greece then had to offer.

To cope with the precarious balance-of-payments situation, the Greek government decided to subsidize exports of goods and services beginning in the fall of 1947. To meet the cost of this subsidy program, the government imposed a special tax on foreign exchange for all purchases of nonessential goods and services. The apparent objectives of these measures were to restrict imports of nonessential goods and services and to encourage the increase of receipts from abroad (i.e., on account of exports), but their adoption did not lead to an improvement in the Greek balance of payments. Indeed, the trade deficit increased in 1948. The implementation of the system of subsidies proved to be cumbersome. The distinction between essential and nonessential, or luxury, imports was a difficult one to make and to administer. As a result, the authorization of imports of foodstuffs and other basic commodities was beset by delays and discon-

TABLE 5

TOTAL OF GOODS AND SERVICES AVAILABLE
TO THE GREEK ECONOMY AND THEIR USE
1946–48

(In Billions of Drachmae)

(in current prices)

	Item	1946	1947	1948
	Gross National Product	6,947	11,252	18,209
Plus:	Imports of goods and services	1,805	1,943	4,055
Minus:	Exports of goods and services	301	663	1,308
	Total of goods and services at the disposal of the economy	8,471	12,532	20,956
	Total Consumption	7,785	10,770	19,049
	a. Private	6,708	9,030	16,448
	b. Government	1,077	1,740	2,601
	Total Fixed Asset Formation	686	1,762	1,907
	a. Private	253	817	1,227
	b. Government	193	374	973
	c. Change of Stocks	240	571	−293
	Total Gross National Expenditures	8,471	12,532	20,956

Source: Ministry of Financial Coordination, National Accounts of Greece, 1946–1953 (Athens: National Printing House, 1955), p. 35.

tinuities[36] that adversely affected the supply of goods and services available to the economy, contributed to the worsening of the prevailing mood of economic uncertainty, made speculation and artificial scarcities profitable, and hence promoted higher prices. Thus, the status of the Greek balance of payments can be considered to have been both a cause and an effect of the prevailing currency instability.

A high rate of capital formation did not occur during the 1946–48 period.

Table 5 shows that during the 1946–48 period[37] the volume of expenditures for fixed-asset formation was relatively small as compared to consumption expenditures. This conclusion becomes stronger if the item "change of stocks" is not counted as part of fixed-asset formation since changes (+) in stocks represent accumulations of goods by firms and not fixed or permanent capital formation.[38] After this adjustment, fixed asset formation amounted to 446 billion, 1,191 billion, and 2,200 billion drachmae for 1946, 1947, and 1948, respectively, or, expressed in percentage terms, to 4.26, 9.5, and 10.5 percent of total gross national expenditure.

The major basic conclusion that emerges from the preceding description and analysis of the economic phenomena that characterized the World War II and the postwar periods is that currency instability was a permanent characteristic of the Greek economy from 1940 through 1948. The intensity of currency instability varied during these years, with the most pronounced upward trend in general prices (i.e., hyperinflation) occurring during the occupation period. All three periods were characterized by the same general causes and effects of currency instability. The causative factors can be identified as real and as psychological. The real factors included the monetary expansion effected by the Bank of Greece and the paralyzing effects of the Albanian War, occupation, and guerrilla-warfare periods on domestic production. The psychological factors, which closely interacted with the real ones, reflected the adverse psychological influences of the war, the occupation, and the guerrilla warfare on the public's expectations. The psychological factors accounted for the general lack of confidence on the part of the Greek people. This lack of confidence took two forms: political and monetary. As a consequence, bank deposits were low, savings were diverted to gold hoarding, and the velocity of money circulation was high. The result of the interaction of the real and psychological factors was the continued deterioration of the internal and foreign-exchange value of the drachma and the perpetuation and worsening of inflation. The inflationary environment magnified the problem of economic reconstruction and development confronting the Greek economy. Such was the economic situation in Greece at the end of 1948.

THE RECONSTRUCTION PERIOD, 1949–52

Two important developments initiated the reconstruction period and influenced the economic and political environment of Greece during the entire 1949–52 period. These developments were the end of the guerrilla war (associated with the Communist threat) in 1949 and the increase of American economic assistance to Greece under the Marshall Plan aid program. Both of these events were expected to have a favorable influence on Greece's efforts toward monetary stability and economic reconstruction and development.

Monetary Developments

During the 1949–52 period, monetary expansion continued to be substantial. There were four main factors affecting the volume of notes in circulation: (1) unbalanced government budgets, (2) Bank of Greece credits to the various sectors of the economy, (3) gold-sovereign sales by the Bank of Greece, and (4) disposition of the drachmae-counterpart account of the European Cooperation Administration (ECA).

During the period under review, the Bank of Greece continued to make advances to the Greek government for the purpose of covering current budget deficits. Current deficits were 1,557 billion drachmae, 1,467 billion drachmae, 1,007 billion drachmae, and 852 billion drachmae in 1949, 1950, 1951, and 1952, respectively. Total current budget government expenditures for these same years were 2,873 billion drachmae, 3,851 billion drachmae, 4,835 billion drachmae, and 5,435 billion drachmae.[39]

Public-corporation deposits–which, it will be remembered, were obligatory deposits of public institutions–continued to constitute a significant part of total deposits with the banks. These deposits were 54.7 percent, 57.6 percent, 52 percent and 47 percent of the total volume of bank deposits for 1949, 1950, 1951, and 1952, respectively.[40] This trend tends to dramatize the fact that the banks did not regain their position as major depositing institutions and also explains the continued reliance of the banks on Bank of Greece funds, derived from note issues, for credit extension to the economy. Total credits to the economy were 3,388 billion drachmae, 4,560 billion drachmae, 5,612 billion drachmae, and 5,428 billion drachmae in 1949, 1950, 1951, and 1952, respectively. About two-thirds of the total volume was derived from Bank of Greece funds.[41]

A problem of continuing importance was the strong preference of the public for gold. Thus, the Bank of Greece was under constant pressure to persist in its sale of gold sovereigns.

Available data show that the price of the gold sovereign did not vary widely during the period under review. The yearly average price in thousands of drachmae was 227.1 in 1948, 226.9 in 1949, 223 in 1950,

225.4 in 1951, and 208.5 in 1952.[42] The achievement of this relative stability can be better appreciated when one considers the substantial upward fluctuations experienced by the drachma-price of the gold sovereign from 1946 to 1948, when the policy of sales was also in force. However, success in halting the rise in the drachma-price of the gold sovereign did not mean overall monetary stability. Despite the offsets provided by gold-sovereign sales[43] the money supply expanded from 1,202.2 billion drachmae in December 31, 1948, to 2,475.9 billion drachmae in December 31, 1952.[44] More significantly, general prices increased considerably during the same period, when the drachma price of the gold sovereign was kept relatively stable. The cost of living index rose from 247.3 in December 31, 1948, to 359.8 in December 31, 1952. On an annual basis it increased 14.7 percent, 8.2 percent, 12.2 percent, and 4.4 percent in 1949, 1950, 1951, and 1952, respectively.[45]

Another factor that affected the Greek economy during this period was the United States aid-generated account of counterpart drachmae held with the Bank of Greece.

The counterpart-drachmae funds were drachmae deposits equal to the value of goods and services imported and made available to the Greek economy under the American economic-assistance program. Of these funds, 5 percent was allocated to cover the operating expenses of the American Mission to Greece, and the remaining 95 percent was to be held unused or to be spent as agreed to by the Greek government and the ECA administration in Greece. If counterpart-drachmae funds were spent, they were to serve the objectives of monetary stability and economic reconstruction and development. By being held unused, the counterpart-drachmae funds were to help check inflation, since accumulated but unspent drachmae represented withdrawals from circulation.

During fiscal years 1948–52 a total of 10,054 billion drachmae in counterpart funds accumulated. Reconstruction by the government and the private sector claimed 3,531.2 billion. Government deficits absorbed 1,300 billion and the operating expenses of the United States Mission in Greece took 604 billion. The unused portion stood at 4,621.8 billion drachmae in 1952.[46]

Production Levels and the Supply of Goods and
Services Available to the Economy

To appraise accomplishments in the area of domestic production during the 1949–52 period, we may review the evidence provided by agricultural- and industrial-production indices. These are shown in Tables 6 and 7. The data show that agricultural production increased by about 35 percent over these years.

The factors responsible for the general increases in agricultural production during the 1949–52 period include the following: (1) the defeat of the Communist movement in Greece in 1949, which permitted farmers to return to their countryside homes, (2) the "crash" rehabilitation and reconstruction program for agriculture, which was initiated by the American economic-aid program, and (3) the credit assistance that was given farmers by the Bank of Greece through the Agricultural Bank.

Behavior of the general index of industrial production shown in Table 6 indicates that the considerable increase in such production included manufacturing and electric-power output but excludes mining. Table 7 shows that both components of the general index of industrial production increased substantially during this period.

TABLE 6

GENERAL INDICES OF AGRICULTURAL AND
INDUSTRIAL PRODUCTION
1948–52

	General Index of Agricultural Production 1938 = 100		General Index of Industrial Production 1939 = 100	
Year	Index	Percentage of Change Over the Previous Year	Index	Percentage of Change Over the Previous Year
1948	83.5		73	
1949	116.0	+38.9	88	+20
1950	98.2	−15.4	110	+25
1951	119.7	+22.8	125	+13.6
1952	109.0	− 7.7	124	− 0.8

Source: National Statistical Service of Greece, Statistical Yearbook of Greece, 1954 (Athens: National Printing Office, 1955), p. 51; Bank of Greece, Confidential Report for February, 1952.

Increases in electric-power output were mainly the result of immediate postwar repairs and of improvements and modernization of electrical plant and equipment, primarily in the Athens-Piraeus area, which started as early as 1948.[47] This development was apparently induced by the anticipated high demand for electricity that was expected to result from the oncoming reconstruction effort. Increases in manufacturing activity were undoubtedly the result of many factors, among which the most important were the American economic aid for long-term financing of industrial-development projects and the credit assistance from the banking system for the short-term financing of industrial raw-material purchases.

TABLE 7

GENERAL INDEX OF INDUSTRIAL PRODUCTION
COMPONENTS, AND INDEX OF MINING
1948–52

	General Index of Industrial Production 1939 = 100			General Index of Mining 1939 = 100
Year	Total	Manufacturing	Electricity	Total
1948	73	65	148	20
1949	88	79	178	16
1950	110	100	210	24
1951	125	114	240	45
1952	124	111	256	64

Source: National Statistical Service of Greece, Statistical Yearbook of Greece, 1954 (Athens: National Printing Office, 1955), p. 51.

Though mining output, shown in Table 7, increased by 220 percent during the 1949–52 period, in 1952 it was still far below the prewar level. This lag can be attributed to the destruction of countryside mines during World War II and the subsequent abandonment of these mines during the guerrilla war, and to the slowness of mining repairs during the reconstruction period.[48] Apparently, these repairs were not forthcoming because of the prevailing low demand for the high-cost, high-priced Greek mineral ores in the foreign markets to which Greece had traditionally sold most of her mineral output.[49]

Table 8 presents aggregate data on goods and services available to the economy and their utilization during the 1949–52 period. It must be noted that the GNP changed at variable rates and so did gross fixed-asset formation. The adjusted (i.e., adjusted for "changes in stocks") value of gross fixed-asset formation increased by 10.8 percent in 1949 and by 43.5 percent in 1950, and decreased by 20.5 percent in 1951 and 8.2 percent in 1952. As a percentage of total gross national expenditure, the adjusted value of gross fixed-asset formation was 11.1 percent in 1949, 15.6 percent in 1950, 12 percent in 1951, and 11.5 percent in 1952.

Table 9 shows the composition of total gross fixed-asset formation. During this period of reconstruction and development the obvious emphasis of fixed-asset formation in housing, infrastructure development, (e.g., transportation, communication, power and manufacturing) is not at all difficult to understand. It should be pointed out, however, that the large role of investment in housing cannot be explained solely by the increased housing needs of an economy in the process of reconstruction; another factor was the public's propensity to hedge against inflation by investing in apartment buildings.[50]

TABLE 8

GOODS AND SERVICES AVAILABLE TO THE ECONOMY AND THEIR USE
1948–52

In Millions of New Drachmae (in 1951 market prices and in percentage of change over the previous year)

Goods and Services and Their Use	1948 Amount in Millions of Drachmae	1949 Amount in Millions of Drachmae	1949 Percentage Change	1950 Amount in Millions of Drachmae	1950 Percentage Change	1951 Amount in Millions of Drachmae	1951 Percentage Change	1952 Amount in Millions of Drachmae	1952 Percentage Change
Gross National Product	26,840	31,763	+ 18.7	31,794	+ .09	34,425	+ 8.3	34,071	− 1
Plus: Imports of Goods and Services	5,632	6,690	+ 19.6	7,715	+15.3	6,542	−15.2	5,696	−13
Minus: Exports of Goods and Services	1,576	1,753	+ 10.8	1,874	+ 6.9	2,213	+18.0	2,755	+24.5
Total of Goods and Services Available to the Economy	30,896	36,700	+ 18.8	37,635	+ 2.5	38,754	+ 3.0	37,011	− 4.5
Total Consumption	27,750	30,594	+ 10.0	30,777	+ .6	32,327	+ 5.0	32,237	− 3.0
a) Private	22,736	25,886	+ 14.0	26,375	+ 1.9	27,274	+ 3.4	27,428	+ 5.6
b) Public	5,014	4,708	+ 6.0	4,402	− 6.5	5,053	+14.8	4,809	− 4.8
Total Gross Asset Formation	3,146	6,106	+ 96.8	6,858	+12.3	6,472	− 6.3	4,774	−25.7
a) Private Fixed-Asset Formation	2,014	2,083	+ 3.4	3,207	+53.9	2,986	− 6.9	2,829	− 5.3
b) Public Fixed-Asset Formation	1,582	2,002	+ 27.2	2,654	+32.5	1,673	−36.9	1,446	−13.6
c) Change in Stocks	−450	2,021	+549.0	997	−50.7	1,768	+77.3	449	−71.1
Total Gross National Expenditure	30,896	36,700	+ 18.8	37,635	+ 2.5	38,754	+ 3.0	37,011	− 4.5

Source: Ministry of Financial Coordination, *National Income Accounts of Greece, 1953–1955* (Athens: National Printing House, 1956), pp. 91–94.

TABLE 9

COMPOSITION OF TOTAL GROSS FIXED ASSET FORMATION
1948–52

In Millions of New Drachmae (in 1951 prices and in percentage of total)

Type of Fixed-Asset Formation	1948 Amount in Millions of Drachmae	1949 Amount in Millions of Drachmae	1949 In Percentage of Total	1950 Amount in Millions of Drachmae	1950 In Percentage of Total	1951 Amount in Millions of Drachmae	1951 In Percentage of Total	1952 Amount in Millions of Drachmae	1952 In Percentage of Total
Agriculture	278	444	10.9	606	10.3	566	12.2	361	8.5
Mining	21	7	.1	71	1.2	187	4.0	121	2.7
Manufacturing	519	456	11.2	858	14.6	712	15.4	740	17.3
Power	54	109	2.7	161	2.8	538	11.6	402	9.5
Transportation and Communication	1,344	1,025	25.0	1,427	24.3	671	14.4	506	12.0
Housing	1,070	1,347	33.0	1,817	31.1	1,404	30.0	1,351	31.8
Government Administrative Services	103	265	6.5	381	6.5	44	.9	238	5.5
Other	107	432	10.6	540	9.2	537	11.5	556	13.0
TOTAL	3,596	4,085	100.0	5,861	100.0	4,659	100.0	4,275	100.0

Source: Ministry of Financial Coordination, *National Income Accounts of Greece, 1953–1955* (Athens: National Printing House, 1956), p. 94.

The Balance of Payments. It is estimated that the value of Greek exports covered less than 30 percent of the value of imports during the period under review.[51]

Prior to World War II most Greek exports were "luxury" agricultural products such as tobacco, currants, and olive oil. Of these, tobacco was the most important and was solidly established as an export to the United States and Germany. It is estimated that about half of the value of Greek exports before the war was derived from tobacco exports.[51] Following the end of World War II Greece experienced difficulties in exporting tobacco. While the political and economic turmoil that prevailed in Greece during the 1945–48 period adversely affected the domestic production of tobacco, a neighboring country, Turkey, increased its tobacco exports and quickly began to outsell Greece in the markets to which Greece had hitherto been the major exporter of "oriental" tobacco. In addition, the prevailing Greek inflation and the associated deterioration of the foreign-exchange value of the drachma tended to aggravate the situation by making the foreign-currency price of Greek tobacco continually less attractive even after production of tobacco in Greece had reached (in 1951) the prewar level. Similar difficulties beset the export of other agricultural products (e.g., currants and olive oil). Needless to say, the deteriorated foreign-exchange value of the drachma continued to have an adverse impact on income from such other sources as private remittances, shipping, and tourist travel.

To cope with the adverse balance-of-payments situation the Greek government, in addition to the corrective measures that were applied as early as the fall of 1947, devalued the drachma on September 21, 1949. Prior to this devaluation the exchange rate of the drachma in terms of the United States dollar was set at $1 = 10,000 drachmae. On September 21, 1949, the exchange rate of the drachma in terms of the United States dollar was changed to $1 = 15 drachmae.

Following the 1949 devaluation, invisible income from remittances, travel, and transportation and income from exports increased in 1950, 1951, and 1952. However, the value of imports of goods and services in these years increased more than the value of exports of goods and services. A partial explanation of this trend may be the liberalization of import-restriction agreements between Greece and Western Europe, which had an expansive effect on the volume of Greek imports and the rising trend of world prices, following the Korean Conflict, which tended to increase the value of Greek imports more than the value of the "luxury" Greek exports.

The problems that confronted Greek attempts to eliminate balance-of-payments deficits would have been considerably more difficult if substantial economic assistance had not been given Greece under the Marshall

Plan aid program. The substantial deficits on current account were largely offset by capital transfers from the rest of the world and primarily from the United States. However, the significant dependence of Greece on imports of foodstuffs and manufactured products induced the use of a relatively large portion of the foreign exchange, made available to Greece under the economic-aid program, for the financing of imports of consumption goods rather than for imports of capital goods.

Moreover, the relatively large import surplus that Greece experienced during the 1949–52 period tends to support the contention that internal monetary stability was susceptible to externally created destabilizing influences. For instance, following the outbreak of the Korean Conflict, rises in import prices were transmitted into the domestic level of prices.[52]

THE PERIOD OF MONETARY STABILITY AND ECONOMIC DEVELOPMENT, 1953–62

A number of rather unusual developments characterized this period. Perhaps the most important of them were the achievement of relative stability (mostly after 1956) and rapid economic growth throughout the decade. Both were the result of several interacting forces, among which the establishment of political stability and the substantial devaluation of the Greek drachma (in April, 1953) were the most prominent.

General Trends

Upward price changes continued to be rather pronounced until 1956, the consumer price index rising by an average annual rate of 6.75 percent during the 1953–56 period.[53] One of the main reasons for these price increases was a 50 percent devaluation in the Greek currency in 1953. However, following the initial price adjustments connected with the devaluation, domestic prices rose at a much slower rate, and the average annual rate of increase in the consumer price index was only 1.67 percent during the 1956–62 period.[54] That the inflation psychosis of the previous periods had begun to heal was indicated by substantial increases in the volume of private deposits in commercial banks and a concurrent decline in gold hoarding. Total private deposits with the banks increased about fifteen times in the course of the decade. Particularly noticeable were the increases in savings and time deposits. The increased importance of private savings and time deposits can also be seen in the changes that occurred in the ratios of savings and time deposits to total private deposits. These ratios were about 10 percent and 1 percent in 1953 and 62.8 percent and 14.4 percent in 1962.[55] However, increases in the volume of private deposits with the banks and decreases in gold hoarding must not be attributed solely to the establishment of relative price stability and restoration of confidence in the currency and in the banks. Additional factors that reinforced the public's propensity to deposit funds with the banks were the absence of a well-organized capital market, which deprived individuals of alternative investment opportunities, and the government's policy of exempting from taxation income earned on bank deposits.

It will be remembered that among the main forces tending to expand the money supply in previous periods were Bank of Greece advances to the government for the purpose of covering current budget deficits. During the 1953–62 period the Bank of Greece continued to extend credit to the economy from note issue. However, the relative participation of commercial banks and other financial institutions in financing the needs of the economy increased steadily and the Bank of Greece's relative participation decreased. Thus, in 1953 the Bank of Greece and the other banks contributed, respectively, about 54 percent and 43.7 percent, of the total credit extension to the economy; by 1962 the Bank of Greece participation had declined to about 30 percent and that of the other banks had increased to about 62 percent.[56]

Concerning the role of the Bank of Greece in assisting the government to cover its current budget needs, it also changed during the 1952–62 period. Beginning in fiscal year 1952/53, a concerted effort was made to reduce the government's current budget deficits. The size of these deficits experienced a drastic reduction to 161 million drachmae in 1952/53 and then rose to 459 million drachmae in 1955/56. To minimize the inflationary pressures associated with these deficits, the Greek government curtailed its public-investment expenditures during the 1953–56 period to a point that seemed consistent with the availability of United States-aid drachmae-counterpart funds, which were eventually used to offset the government's annual deficits. After 1956 the current budgets of the government incurred continuous surpluses, which averaged about 850 million drachmae per year for the 1957–62 period. They were used, along with private savings (which the government began to tap via the issuance and sale of bonds and treasury bills), temporary advances from the Bank of Greece, and money borrowed from abroad,[57] to finance a greatly expanded program of public investments. In this connection, it should be pointed out that the total amount of public investments increaed (in 1954 prices) from 2,251 million drachmae in 1953 to 7,204 million in 1962.[58] It is also interesting to note that total investments increased by an average annual rate of 8.9 percent and 13.4 percent for the 1952–57 and 1958–62 periods, respectively. Moreover, the average annual rate of increase in public investments was 3 percent for the 1953–57 period and 19 percent for the 1958–62 period. Of the total volume of investments, public investments accounted for 19.2 percent during the 1953–57 period and 33.4 per cent during the 1958–62 period. In absolute figures, total public investments amounted (in 1954 prices) to 12,842 million drachmae and 26,929 million drachmae for 1953–57 and 1958–62, respectively.[59] Total investments accounted for 12.7 percent and 19.7 percent of total gross expenditure in the economy for 1953 and 1962, respectively. Ministry of Coordination data show that energy, transportation, communications, and housing construction absorbed about 65 percent of public investments during the 1953–57 period.[60] During the 1958–62 period public investments in energy, transportation, and communications continued to be large, but public investments in housing construction experienced a sizable decline. These data also reveal a pronounced and continuing propensity of the private sector to invest in housing.[61] It will be remembered that interest in housing construction dated back to the preceding period and can be explained by the following: (1) the expanded housing needs of the economy following the end of the guerrilla war in 1949 and the establishment of peace in Greece, (2) the migration of relatively large numbers of people to urban centers such as Athens and Salonica, and (3) the public view that housing, especially apartment buildings, represented a safe investment for private savings.

It can be concluded that during the years under review the government's role in establishing monetary stability and economic development, especially after 1956 when political stability prevailed, was generally positive. It should be pointed out, however, that the facts that credit extension to the economy from Bank of Greece funds declined and the current budgets of the government experienced surpluses after 1956 did not mean that monetary policy was contractionary. The truth of the matter is that during the 1953–62 period the money supply increased at fluctuating but more rapid rates than did the gross national product. In 1958 constant prices, the GNP increased from 71,266 million drachmae in 1953 to 117,507 million drachmae in 1962, while the total money supply more than tripled during the same interval.[62] During the last six years of the decade the average annual rate of growth of the money supply was about 15.3 percent, and that of gross national product (in constant prices) was about 6.5 percent. Yet such a disproportionately large increase in the means of payments was accomplished without any serious effects on prices as we have mentioned above. Among the factors that made relative price stability possible were:

(1) The more rational import policy that was induced by the devaluation of 1953. Following the devaluation an increase in capital inflows and in income from invisibles improved the ability of Greece to finance an expanded volume of imports of foodstuffs and capital goods. These imports, in turn, had depressing effects on the level of domestic prices.

(2) The greatly improved confidence of the people in the drachma and the banking system that helped put an end to the inflation psychosis of the war and immediate postwar periods. This development, as we mentioned above, was marked by a diminished tendency to hoard gold and a rather spectacular increase in the volume of private deposits with the commercial banks.

(3) The establishment of political stability, beginning in 1953 and lasting through 1961, which not only had a favorable effect on the overall economic environment but also made possible the implementation of monetary, fiscal, and public-investments policies that contributed positively to monetary stability and economic growth.

It has been observed that the 1953–62 decade was characterized by rapid rates of economic development: in constant prices, the GNP increased by an average annual rate of growth of 6.5 percent, and GNP per capita increased by 5.3 percent.[63] Even so, the Greek economy continued to be confronted in 1962 with a number of structural problems of long standing. These included strong emphasis on primary production; small-size, domestic-market-oriented manufacturing; and pronounced balance-of-payments difficulties. We turn our attention now to a brief examination of these problem areas.

Agriculture

During the 1953–62 period agricultural production increased by an average annual rate of about 4 percent. Increases in agricultural production were attributed largely to the fact that more land came under cultivation as a result of land-reclamation and irrigation projects. An increased use of farm machinery and chemical fertilizers must also be acknowledged. Production increases were particularly noticeable in wheat, cotton, tobacco, fruits, vegetables, and live-stock products. For instance, the production of wheat increased from 1.4 million tons in 1953 to 1.722 million tons in 1962, and that of citrus fruits from .179 million tons in 1953 to .428 million tons in 1962.[64] But as was pointed out above, agriculture was handicapped in a number of ways—by the insufficient market orientation of the farmers, by the use of out-of-date methods of production, by the low yields per unit of land, and by the small size of farms.[65] Another problem that apparently began to confront Greek agriculture in the early 1960s was a scarcity of labor. Contrary to the assumed large disguised unemployment in Greece, the volume of surplus labor experienced a decline and Greek agriculture began to experience labor shortages during peak seasons.[66] Presumably, the sharp increase in emigration to Western Europe[67] was a major contributing factor.

TABLE 10

LAND FRAGMENTATION IN GREECE, 1959

Areas	Average Size of Farms (In Hectacres)	Average Number of Land Plots by Farm	Average Size of Land Plots	Average Disposition of Farm Plots (In Kilometers)
Macedonia	4.53	7.5	.61	2.5
Thessaly	6.81	10.0	.68	2.4
Central Greece	8.57	11.0	.78	2.8
Peloponnesus	5.68	7.9	.72	2.2
Islands	5.99	12.5	.48	2.2
For Total Area	5.99	9.2	.65	2.5

Source: Greek Ministry of Agriculture.

Industry

Industrial production, in constant 1954 prices, increased at an average annual rate of about 7.5 percent during the period 1953–62. Although this rate of increase was not insignificant, it was exceeded by the rate of increase of imports of industrial products, which was about 11.5 percent. About three-fourths of these imports were consumer and intermediate goods. The contribution of manufacturing to the gross national product continued to be relatively low. In 1962 it stood at about 16.5 percent of gross domestic product (in current prices).[68] Moreover, Greek manufacturing in that year included a high degree of domestic-market orientation that was compounded by the high tariff protection afforded firms by the government and the dominance of small family-owned-and-managed firms. Data in Table 11 show that in 1958 only about 2 percent of all manufacturing establishments employed more than twenty persons. Finally, an inadequate supply of modern entrepreneurial talent, an adverse climate of tax incentives, and cumbersome and bureaucratic systems of licensing new firms added to the difficulties of Greek manufacturing in 1962.

The Balance of Payments

According to all accounts, the Greek currency was overvalued, prior to 1953, relative to other main foreign currencies. It will be remembered that a rather cumbersome system of subsidies and import controls was used to conserve on foreign exchange. However, following the April, 1953, 50 percent devaluation of the drachma, more liberal policies of import and exchange control were introduced. The basic goal of the new policies was to keep imports within the limits consistent with the maintenance of balance-of-payments equilibrium and, at the same time, to encourage imports of capital goods for development purposes. It was also

TABLE 11

SIZE DISTRIBUTION OF MANUFACTURING
ESTABLISHMENTS, 1930 and 1958

Size of Group (In Numbers of Persons Employed)	Percentage of Total
Census 1930	
Up to 5	93.2
6 to 25	5.7
20 and over	1.1
Census 1958	
Up to 5	84.9
5 to 9	9.8
10 to 19	3.2
20 to 49	1.4
50 to 99	.4
100 and over	.3

Source: George Coutsoumaris, *The Morphology of Greek Industry*, 1963.

anticipated that, as a result of the devaluation, Greek exports would become more competitive, and that an improvement in the trade balance would ensue. Immediately following the devaluation, a decline in the balance-of-trade deficits occurred. This development was short lived, however, and from 1956 to 1962 a rapidly expanding trade deficit emerged. Thus, in 1962 the trade deficit was more than three times what it had been in 1953.[69]

To be sure, exports did expand during the period under review but not as rapidly as imports. Between 1953 and 1962 imports increased from $245.9 million to $608.5 million, and exports increased from $134.1 million to $242.6 million. As a percentage of gross national product, imports and exports were 17.9 percent and 6.4 percent in 1962.[70]

A review of the composition of imports reveals that of the total volume of imports in 1962, 14 percent were foodstuffs, 24.9 percent were raw materials, 7.9 percent were fuels and lubricants, 22.3 percent were capital goods, and 30.9 percent were manufactured consumer goods.[71] One of the basic reasons for this high consumption-oriented pattern of imports was the liberal import policies that were followed after the 1953 devaluation. These policies were partly motivated by the desire to avoid rapid increases in domestic prices subsequent to the devaluation. However, in order to prevent the wholesale importation of luxury products, the Greek government imposed qualitative and quantitative restraints on credit extensions for foreign trade in 1954 and 1955. After 1960 many of these regulations were removed.

The structure of exports for the period of three years prior to Greece's association with the EEC is shown in Table 12. The data clearly establish the dominance of agricultural exports. A gradual decline in the role of some traditional exports such as tobacco and currants and an increase in the importance of cotton and fruit exports is also obvious. Low income elasticity of demand for currants and continuing shifts in world preferences from the high-quality oriental type of Greek tobacco to the lower-quality tobacco made possible by filter cigarettes at least partly explain the relative decline in the exports of currants and tobacco.[72] It is important to keep in mind that of the total of Greek imports and exports in 1962, 43.4 percent and 35.7 percent were with EEC countries.[73]

Notwithstanding Greece's widening trade deficits, balance-of-payments equilibrium was attained during the period under review because of a substantial rise in receipts from "invisibles" (e.g., emigrant remittances, shipping and tourism) and increased capital inflows. Beginning in 1952, United States economic aid to Greece was substantially curtailed as a general consequence of the shift in the emphasis of United States foreign policy in favor of national security. Thus, this previously important

TABLE 12

STRUCTURE OF GREEK EXPORTS
1960–62

(In Percentages)

Category	1960	1961	1962
Agricultural Products	74.4	74.9	74.4
Tobacco	34.7	34.4	28.0
Cotton	9.2	11.7	16.1
Currants	13.1	12.5	11.7
Olives and Olive Oil	5.4	2.2	4.3
Fruit	5.1	6.7	7.8
Other	6.9	7.4	6.9
Ores	8.6	6.7	6.4
Industrial and Handicraft			
Products	3.7	3.4	4.5
NATO Commodities	2.3	3.3	2.4
Other	11.0	11.7	11.9
Turpentine, etc.	3.5	3.4	2.0
Leather	4.5	4.6	4.1
Printed Matter, Films, etc.	3.0	3.7	5.8

Source: The Bank of Greece.

source of financing the Greek trade deficits began to disappear. Undoubt-edly, financing an increasing portion of imports by exports represented a continuing challenge for Greece in 1962. This must have been an im-portant motivation leading to her association with the European Eco-nomic Community.

THE ASSOCIATION OF GREECE WITH THE EUROPEAN ECONOMIC COMMUNITY

The dominant economic event of the decade of the 1960s, so far as Greece was concerned, was her association with the EEC. Because of this, our emphasis in this section will center, first, on the association agreement (i.e., the Athens Agreement) and its implementation and, second, on the probable impact of the association on the Greek economy.

The Athens Agreement

The Athens Agreement is based on Article 238 of the Treaty of Rome, which provides for associate memberships in the EEC. Under the agree-ment, Greece began on November 1, 1962, a twelve-to-twenty-two-year period of transition, during which the immediate goal is establishment of a full customs union with the EEC. Some of the main provisions of the agreement, which is still in effect at this writing, are the following:[74]

(1) The agreement stipulated that Greek exports to the EEC would be granted immediately all the reductions in tariffs that had taken place among the EEC members since the Treaty of Rome became effective in January 1, 1958. It was further provided that all subsequent tariff reduc-tions among EEC members would also be applicable to Greek exports.

(2) The agreement gave special attention to certain key Greek exports such as tobacco, olive oil, olives, raisins, fresh fruits and wine. For in-stance, EEC tariffs on Greek leaf tobacco and raisins were scheduled to be eliminated by the end of 1967. Concerning fresh fruits, Greek exports to the EEC would be subject to the same duty provisions as were applic-able to the EEC countries. But to protect the interests of a number of EEC fresh-fruit exporting countries, certain quantitative export limits were imposed on Greece. Moreover, special provisions were agreed upon by the different EEC countries concerning Greek wine exports to the EEC.

(3) In regard to Greek imports from the EEC, the Athens Agreement classified products into three basic categories, or "annexes." Annex 1 lists most industrial products produced in Greece. Annex 2 includes agricul-tural products that are of no current export interest for Greece. Annex 3 lists exportable agricultural products of Greece. On the basis of these categories the agreement provided the following: (a) For all imports

from the EEC, except those listed in Annex 1, complete customs disarmament was scheduled to occur within a twelve-year period. This disarmament should take place in ten successive stages each stage involving a 10 percent tariff reduction. The duration of each stage ranged from one year to eighteen months. Article 18 of the agreement allows Greece to reimpose, increase, or introduce new tariffs on products not included in Annex 1, provided this action would help stimulate new activity and economic growth. This escape clause, however, was subject to considerable restrictions. (b) For imports listed in Annex 1 a complete tariff reduction was scheduled to occur more gradually, i.e., in twenty-two years and in fourteen successive stages.

(4) Article 33 of the Athens Agreement provided that Greece would harmonize its agricultural policies to the common agricultural policies of the EEC within twenty-two years from the effective date of the agreement.

(5) Greece agreed to adjust her tariffs to third parties so that they conformed to the common external tariff of the EEC. This adjustment would take place in three stages for products subject to the twelve-year transition, and in four stages for products subject to the twenty-two-year transition.

(6) The agreement established an Association Council, which would be responsible for supervising implementation of the agreement.

7) A provision for the free movement of labor, capital, and services between Greece and the EEC countries was also included in the agreement. Details concerning implementation of this provision were to be worked out by the Association Council.

(8) Greece was promised by the EEC $125 million in loans to be made available during the first five years of the association and to be used for development purposes (i.e., infrastructure and industrial projects).

(9) Finally, the agreement emphasized the commitment of the EEC and Greece to pursue coordinated economic policies aimed at balance-of-payments equilibrium, balanced economic growth, and price stability. The ultimate objective of the Athens Agreement, as stated in Article 2, is to help accelerate Greek economic development.

IMPLEMENTATION OF THE ATHENS AGREEMENT: ACCOMPLISHMENTS AND PROBLEMS BY THE END OF THE 1960s

Accomplishments. (1) Since July 1, 1968, Greek industrial products have entered the EEC without any quantitative restrictions, and since November 1, 1968, without any tariffs.

(2) Beginning in January 1, 1970, most Greek agricultural exports have

entered the EEC free of tariffs and quantitative restrictions. Tariffs on Greek tobacco and raisins exports were eliminated by the EEC on January 1, 1968, and on June 1, 1968, respectively.

(3) In accordance with the Athens Agreement, Greek duties have been brought closer to the common community tariff by 60 percent and 20 percent, depending on whether the products involved are subject to the twelve-year or the twenty-two-year transition period.

(4) Tariffs on industrial imports from the EEC have been reduced by 20 percent or 70 percent, depending on whether they are listed in Annex 1 or not.

(5) Greek exports of fresh fruit and wine to the EEC have "generally" received the treatment prescribed in the agreement. However, a number of violations by the EEC have been noted.

(6) In general, all provisions designed to move Greece toward the establishment of a customs union with the EEC have been adhered to rather routinely.

Problems. (1) No progress has been made in the much-heralded area of harmonizing the agricultural policy of Greece with that of the EEC countries. The EEC has claimed that political developments in Greece since April 21, 1967, have caused the freeze in the negotiations. It must be observed, however, that even before that date, no visible substantive progress on the question of harmonization had been made.

(2) The Athens Agreement provided that Greece would be granted, via the European Investment Bank, loans amounting to $125 million to be used for development projects. By 1970 only about $69 million in such loans had been approved. The EEC has suggested that the reason for this obvious delay has been the political situation in Greece. According to the agreement, however, the total amount of $125 was supposed to be committed by the Investment Bank during the first five years that the Athens Agreement was in force.

(3) The Asociation Council, the governing body of the association, has proven to be rather ineffectual in promoting Greek interests. Greece, to be sure, has been consulted by the EEC on several occasions when its decisions appeared to be affecting Greek interests (e.g., EEC trade agreements with Turkey, Morocco, Tunisia, Iran, Spain, and Israel), but these consultations have been largely for the purpose of informing Greece of decisions already made and have afforded the Greeks little opportunity for negotiation and dissent. Furthermore, provisions in the Athens Agreement that were not clearly spelled out (e.g., harmonization of agricultural policies, financial and technical assistance to Greece) and were left for the council to clarify and implement have been generally unsuccessful. In this connection, Greece's membership in the Association Council may be viewed as a poor substitute for membership in the powerful EEC Com-

mission. There seems to be little doubt that decisions of the commission have affected directly or indirectly, immediately, or with some time lag all associate members, including Greece. Nonparticipation of the associate members in the deliberations of the commission has placed them in a decidedly disadvantageous position so far as their future integration into the EEC is concerned.

The Impact of the EEC Association on the Greek Economy

It is not easy to disentangle the precise economic effects of the association of Greece and the EEC. Nevertheless, most observers of the Greek economy would agree that the association has had a generally favorable, stimulating effect. Under the impetus of the tariff disarmament provided in the Athens Agreement, Greece has been able to expand its exports to the EEC by substantial margins. Moreover, because of the gradual removal of tariffs on EEC exports to Greece, the Greek economy has been challenged to modernize in order to be able to raise its productivity and become more competitive with the EEC.

Following the association, an obvious improvement in the ability of the industrial sector to compete has occurred as demonstrated by the rather phenomenal increases of industrial exports to the EEC. As Table 14 shows, exports of manufactured products increased from $4.2 million in 1961 to $67.2 million in 1968, or by 1600 percent. Agricultural exports to the EEC did not exhibit the same type of strength. They increased from $54.7 in 1961 to $138.4 million in 1968 or by about 152 percent. Also, during the 1961–70 period, as Table 13 shows, exports to the EEC increased at a more rapid rate than did exports to the rest of the world. Imports from the EEC also increased at a faster rate than did those from the rest of the world. The total value of Greek exports to the EEC rose from 30.50 percent in 1961 to 45.90 percent in 1970. On the other hand the total value of imports from the EEC rose from 38.10 percent in 1961 to 40.50 percent in 1970.

It has been noted above that the response of Greek agriculture to the opportunities made available by the EEC Association was not as pronounced as that of industry. Table 14 shows that agricultural exports to the EEC as a percentage of total exports to the EEC fell from 80.3 percent in 1961 to 62.2 percent in 1968. The relative importance of the role of tobacco in the Greek trade balance continued to decline and generally for the same reasons mentioned earlier. In addition, the association of Turkey, a tobacco competitor of Greece, with the EEC militates against the likelihood of a relative expansion of Greek tobacco exports to the EEC.

However, as data in Table 14 show, exports of olive oil, olives, wine, and fresh fruits and vegetables (including canned fresh-fruit juices and citrus products) all experienced absolute and relative increases between 1961 and 1968. Exports of olive oil fluctuated from year to year largely because of variations in weather conditions affecting production. Increases in wine exports appear to have been due to a marked improvement in the quality and standardization of Greek wines. Moreover, better methods of refrigeration, shipping, and marketing and a high income elasticity of demand for fresh fruits and vegetables seem to account for the relatively large increases in the exports of these products to the EEC. It is quite likely that, in view of the rising incomes in the EEC countries, expansion in the exports of these products, including citrus fruits, would have been greater if it were not for the trade preference agreements that the EEC has signed with competitors of Greece such as certain North African and other Mediterranean countries. Notwithstanding these positive developments, Greek agriculture did not experience any major widely spread reorganization and modernization. Thus, by 1970 productivity in agriculture continued to be low, the average size of farms continued to be small, and the much-hoped-for commercialization of agriculture continued to be a goal for the future.

Greek industry, in contrast to agriculture, responded more innovatively to the association of Greece and the EEC. The rather remarkable inroads made by Greek industrial products in the EEC have been cited above.[75] This response has also taken the form of a gradual expansion in the size of firms and the introduction of modern technology made possible by new investments. In addition, the government's contribution in building the industrial infrastructure has been a significant factor. But perhaps what appears to be even more significant, though rather intangible, is the gradual transformation that has occurred in the attitudes of many Greek industrialists. These attitudinal changes include the broadening of their business horizon and an increasing willingness to move in the direction of making the changes necessary for their enterprises to become competitive in the EEC. Censuses of Greek industries taken in 1963 and in 1969 show that the number of enterprises employing more than fifty persons increased from 884 in 1963 to 935 in 1969—not a spectacular increase, but a good beginning. The trend toward larger enterprises was particularly noticeable in the paper, plastic, chemical, oil-refining, basic-metals (aluminum), and electrical industries. It is also interesting to note that the greatest industrial-export increases, in both absolute and relative terms, have been in basic metals, chemicals, and oil products.

Contrary to the expectations of advocates of the Athens Agreement, EEC capital inflows to Greece have been rather disappointing. Available data show, for instance, that total net capital inflows were $232.9 million, $160.9 million, $235.3 million, and $322.1 million in 1966, 1967, 1968, and 1969, respectively. Net capital inflows from the EEC in the same years were $54.6 million, $60.5 million, $64.2 million, and $170.4 million, respectively.[76] It will be remembered that about $56 million in promised development loans from the European Investment Bank have not been granted to Greece, nor has any concerted EEC effort been made to encourage capital to move to Greece, where the availability of "surplus" labor might be advantageous to European businesses. Actually, what appears to have happened is that EEC capital not only did not move to the periphery in anything like the amounts expected but "surplus" labor has moved to the center. It is estimated that the number of Greeks working in the EEC countries increased from about 62,500 persons in 1962 to 216,-000 persons in 1969.[77] In the absence of a strong regional EEC policy it is not likely that this lack of enthusiasm of capital to move from the established industrial centers of the EEC countries to her outlying regions will continue.

Nevertheless, the continued contribution of capital inflows to achieving general equilibrium in the Greek balance of payments cannot be minimized. Moreover, receipts from the remittances of emigrants who have been employed in EEC countries have constituted an important source of foreign exchange. It is estimated[78] that exports, receipts from invisibles, and capital inflows have contributed 36 percent, 39.6 percent, and 24.4 percent of the total financing of imports in 1970.[79]

Greece and the New Members of the EEC

The recent admission of England, Ireland, and Denmark into the Euro-

TABLE 13

EVOLUTION OF GREEK EXPORTS AND IMPORTS
1961–1970

	Exports (In Millions of United States Dollars)			Imports (In Millions of United States Dollars)		
Year	With the EEC	With the Rest of the World	Total	With the EEC	With the Rest of the World	Total
1961	68.1	155.2	223.3	272.2	441.8	714.0
1962	88.7	159.9	248.6	303.8	387.4	702.2
1963	95.0	195.1	290.1	320.2	484.0	804.2
1964	115.6	193.0	308.6	374.6	510.5	885.1
1965	121.6	205.9	327.8	469.1	646.6	1,133.7
1966	144.0	261.9	405.9	503.9	718.8	1,222.7
1967	199.9	295.3	495.2	527.3	658.9	1,186.2
1968	222.6	245.1	467.7	607.1	785.9	1,393.0
1969	249.8	303.8	553.6	668.8	925.3	1,594.2
1970	295.0	348.0	643.0	792.0	1,166.0	1,958.0

Source: Statistical Office of the European Communities, Basic Statistics of the Community, 1964, 1971.

TABLE 14

THE STRUCTURE OF GREEK EXPORTS
1961 and 1968

In Millions of United States Dollars and in Percent of Total Exports

Type of Export	1961						1968					
	With EEC		With the Rest of the World		Total		With EEC		With the Rest of the World		Total	
	In Millions of Dollars	In Percentages	In Millions of Dollars	In Percentages	In Millions of Dollars	In Percentages	In Millions of Dollars	In Percentages	In Millions of Dollars	In Percentages	In Millions of Dollars	In Percentages
1. Tobacco	26.3	38.6	56.6	36.5	82.9	37.1	46.0	20.7	53.9	22.0	99.9	21.4
2. Food & Beverages												
a. Fresh Fruits, Vegetables & Canned Products	15.2	22.3	33.2	21.4	48.4	21.7	41.4	18.6	48.0	19.6	89.4	19.1
b. Olives & Olive Oil	.5	0.7	4.0	2.6	4.5	2.0	24.3	10.9	5.9	2.4	30.2	6.5
c. Wines	1.0	1.5	1.4	.9	2.4	1.1	5.1	2.3	1.8	0.7	6.9	1.5
d. Other	.6	.9	1.9	1.2	2.5	1.1	10.4	4.7	11.9	4.9	22.3	4.8
3. Other Agricultural Products	11.1	16.3	29.3	18.9	40.4	18.1	11.2	5.0	43.2	17.6	54.4	11.6
Total Agricultural Products	54.7	80.3	126.4	81.4	181.1	81.1	138.4	62.2	164.7	67.2	303.1	64.8
4. Industrial Raw Materials	9.2	13.5	9.0	5.8	18.2	8.1	17.0	7.6	23.3	9.5	40.3	8.6
5. Manufactured Products	4.2	6.2	19.8	12.8	24.0	10.7	67.2	30.2	57.1	23.3	124.3	26.6
Total Industrial Products	13.4	19.7	28.8	18.6	42.2	18.9	84.2	37.8	80.4	32.8	164.6	35.2
TOTAL Exports	68.1	100.0	155.2	100.0	223.3	100.0	222.6	100.0	245.1	100.0	467.7	100.0

Source: European Community Press and Information, *European Community*, No. 9, 1970.

pean Economic Community could have a number of possible consequences for Greece:

(1) Expansion in the marketing opportunities for Greek products may materialize. The new members are obligated to accept all prior agreements of the EEC, including the Athens Agreement. To make for a smoother transition in the trade relations between the new members and the associates of the EEC, additional protocols are expected to be signed. The special protocol that Greece will sign with the three new EEC members (and especially with England) can have a significant immediate effect on the Greek balance of payments, if the provisions of the protocols remove, as expected, trade restrictions on Greek exports (and particularly on agricultural and textile exports) to England. For many years past Greece has incurred a substantial trade-account deficit with England.

(2) Admission of a less industrialized country such as Ireland may constitute an example to be imitated and thus may hasten Greece's full integration into the EEC.

(3) Enlargement of EEC membership may delay the formulation and implementation the so called "uniform" Mediterranean policy of the EEC, as proposed in the 1972 Rossi Report.

(4) Pragmatism may govern future relations of the EEC and Greece because of the leading role that England will probably play in EEC's external policies.

In the final analysis, however, because of the divergent interests and views that appear to influence deliberations in the EEC councils it is rather difficult to forecast the precise impact of the new admissions on the future development of the EEC and on its relations with the expanding network of associates such as Greece.

EXPERIENCES WITH ECONOMIC PLANNING, 1968–72

During the ten years following its association with the EEC the Greek economy made substantial progress in a number of areas. We have already noted a few of the apparent effects of the association on the Greek economy. In view of the fact that many of the goals and aspirations of the Greek society in the decade of the 1960s were incorporated in the 1968–72 economic development plan of Greece we will now briefly review this plan in the hope of revealing the accomplishments and problems of the economy as it moved closer to the date of possible complete integration with the EEC in 1984.

In summary form, the main goals of the plan included the following:[80] (1) to raise the level of per-capita income to that of the developed economies, (2) to improve income distribution among different groups and

regions of the country, (3) to provide full employment and equal economic opportunities for all people, (4) to improve the competitiveness
of the economy, (5) to change the structure of the balance of payments
and lessen the dependence of financing Greek economic development on
foreign sources, and (6) to upgrade the levels of education, health, welfare, and social security.

Admittedly, the complete attainment of these goals, even under the
best of circumstances, required a time horizon beyond that of the plan's
five years. Consequently, a number of targets that were viewed either as
attainable within five years or as necessary preconditions for the achievement of the main long-run goals of the plan were established. These
targets were seven in number: (1) to attain an average annual rate of
growth of between 7.5 to 8.5 percent, resulting in a per-capita gross national income of $1,020 in 1972 as compared with $710 in 1967, (2) to
maintain monetary stability and balance-of-payments equilibrium (in this
regard, monetary stability was defined as a maximum increase in the general consumer-price level of 2 percent), (3) to initiate desired changes
in the composition of production, employment, investments, and balance of payments so as to raise the productivity and competitiveness of
the economy, (4) to create 300,000 new jobs in order to increase employment and limit emigration, (5) to reduce inequalities in the distribution
of income among different groups and regions of the country, (6) to
extend and modernize the basic infrastructure of the economy (e.g.,
transportation, communications, energy), and (7) to introduce institutional reforms aimed at developing and modernizing the areas of education, public administration, capital and labor markets, and the tax system.

It must be apparent that both the goals and the targets of the 1968–72
plan were quite ambitious. It remains to be seen to what extent they were
attained. A study of the available government data suggests the following
conclusions: [81]

(1) An average annual rate of increase in gross national product (in
1967 constant prices) of 8.2 percent was attained during the five years of
the plan. This compares favorably to the average annual rate of increase
for the decade of 1960–70, which was 7.5 percent, and the target of the
plan, which was set between 7.5 to 8.5 percent. Also, estimates place per
capita gross national income, in 1967 constant prices, at $1,050 in 1972, as
compared to the target figure of $1,020. The accomplished rate of growth
was largely attributable to increases in the nonagricultural sectors of the
economy, which progressed more rapidly than the plan anticipated. For
instance, industrial production increased at the average annual rate of 13
percent, while agricultural production increased at the rate of 2 percent.
The targets of the plan for industrial production and for agricultural production were 11.4 percent and 5.2 percent per year, respectively. More-

over, the services sector was targeted to increase at the rate of 7.4 percent but its actual rate was 8 percent. Reference has been made to the reasons for the slow progress of agriculture and the dynamism of Greek industry following Greece's association with the EEC. It also appears that government tax and credit incentives offered to business contributed not only to the development of Greek entrepreneurship but also helped attract foreign entrepreneurial activity.

(2) An average annual rate of increase in the consumer price index of 2.6 percent, as compared to the target of 2 percent, was attained. This obvious accomplishment of monetary stability continued to encourage confidence in the currency and in the banking system and, as a general consequence of this development, private deposits with the banks increased by substantial margins. For instance, total private deposits doubled and time deposits increased two and a half times during the 1967–70 period.

The evolution of the Greek balance of payments was discussed earlier. The situation was basically no different in 1971 and in 1972, except perhaps that substantial inflows of foreign exchange in the form of deposits with the banks occurred in 1972 and that receipts from invisibles expanded more rapidly than anticipated.

(3) Concerning structural changes, some of the results were as follows: (a) The labor force increased from 3.35 million in 1967 to 3.43 million in 1972, or at an average annual rate of 0.45 percent as compared to the targeted 0.60 percent. Total employment increased from 3.220 million in 1967 to 3.350 million in 1972, or at an average annual rate of 0.80 percent as compared to the target of 1 percent. This increase in employment meant 280,000 new nonagricultural jobs, as compared to the 300,000 anticipated. Moreover, agricultural employment declined by 150,000 people, as compared to the target of 110,000 people. On the other hand, industrial employment increased from 730,000 people in 1967 to 850,000 in 1972, and employment in services increased from 990,000 people in 1967 to 1,150,000 people in 1972. Industrial employment was below the target by 29,000, and employment in the services exceeded the target by 9,000. Employment in agriculture fell to 40.3 percent of total employment in 1972. The average annual rate of productivity for the period of the plan was 7.5 percent as compared to the target of 7 percent.

(b) The targets for investments (gross fixed-asset formation) were met in manufacturing, tourism, transportation, and housing. They were not met in the areas of education, health, and welfare. In general, total private investments for the five year period of the plan exceeded the set target by about 12 percent, while public investments fell short of the target by 7 percent.

Particularly strong was the contribution of heavy industry to gross product of the industrial sector, which increased from 41 percent in 1967 to 46.6 percent in 1971. The target for 1972 was 46.4 percent. Also, the value of industrial exports for the 1968–72 period increased by about 340 percent as compared to the target of about 245 percent.

(4) Available data show that during the period of the plan gross domestic product by regions did not change in a way consistent with an improvement of income distribution among the different regions of the country. Instead, there has been a widening of the differences. The Athens and Salonica regions, which contributed 53.6 percent and 14.9 percent of gross domestic product in 1967, increased their share in 1972 to 53.9 percent and 17.2 percent, respectively. All the other regions experienced decreases in their relative contributions to gross domestic product. In general, it appears that the incentives provided by the regional-development policy did not prove to be enough to attract industrialists to the country's less-developed regions.

(5) Reforms in education (e.g., improvement in the student/teacher ratios, changes in curriculum, and construction of new school facilities) and improvements in social services and public health (e.g., extension of social security and better hospital care) were of rather limited nature during the period of the plan. Though some progress was made in the direction of decentralizing government activity, the results of reforming the overall system of government services were not impressive: at the end of the five-year plan, excessive bureaucracy continued to plague the public-administration system.

Other planned reforms—including the redistribution of land to economical plots, the reorganization and modernization of the capital market, and the introduction of major tax reforms—were not implemented to a significant degree.

A POSTSCRIPT ON THE ECONOMIC PLAN

Our brief review of the 1968–72 economic-development plan of Greece suggests that the Greek economy took some positive steps toward growth. On the other hand, several problems in areas such as regional development, education, public administration, money and capital markets, etc., remained to be tackled. It must also be pointed out that a substantial expansion in the money supply accompanied the growth-oriented policies of the period covered by the plan and helped increase the liquidity of the economy to a point that posed a threat to the maintenance of monetary stability. The inclination of the economy toward inflation began to be manifested in 1972, when a combination of prevailing high levels of demand and liquidity, along with declines in the levels of domestic agricultural output and increases in the costs of imports, generated intense inflationary pressures. Though a number of corrective monetary and fiscal measures were adopted in late 1972 and in 1973, the inflationary pressures continued unabated throughout 1973 and during most of 1974. Certainly, the increases in oil prices that followed the 1973 Arab-Israeli War were also instrumental in causing higher domestic prices generally and larger trade deficits for the Greek economy in 1973 and in 1974. In connection with the emergence of the above situation, it should be noted that the volume of currency in circulation increased by 17.6 percent in 1972 and by 28.5 percent in 1973. The value of imports increased by 24.9 percent in 1972 and by fully 67 percent in 1973. Finally, the consumer price index rose by 6.5 percent in 1972, by 30.6 percent in 1973, and by about 11 percent during the first seven months of 1974.

THE RETURN TO REPRESENTATIVE GOVERNMENT: A NEW ERA

Beginning toward the end of July, 1974, a new era began for Greece. It is an era marked by the return of representative government to its ancient birthplace after an absence of some seven years. But it is also destined to be an era of major problems and challenges. In the economic arena, one of these problems is the restoration of monetary stability. Another is the "unfreezing" of relations with the EEC and, possibly, the quickening of the pace by which Greece moves toward full membership. Other unresolved and largely structural problems have been mentioned above. Though it is not easy to predict how effectively these and other problems facing Greece will be resolved, it augurs well for Greece's future that the present leadership of the nation is, at this writing, in the hands of the seasoned statesman Constantine Caramanlis, to whom the Greek people gave an overwhelming vote of confidence in national elections held on November 17, 1974. The resulting politically stable climate may prove to be a decisive force in favor of resolving constructively many of the short- and long-run problems that have continued to confront the Greek economy, for as this study has shown, economic development cannot be explained solely in terms of economic factors. In the case of Greece, political stability has been, and seems likely to be, an important condition for rapid economic development.

NOTES

1. Department of State, *Kingdom of Greece*, Background Notes (May 1968), p. 1.
2. The population of Greece in 1821 was about one million people and its total area about 48,000 square kilometers; in 1920 the nation's population in-

creased to about five million people and the total area to 127,000 square kilometers.

3. The only addition to Greece's area after 1940 was that resulting from the annexation of the islands of Dhodhekanissos in 1947.

4. V. Damalas, *The Greek Economy*, published in Greek (Athens: Papazessis, 1957), p. 57.

5. National Statistical Service of Greece, *Statistical Summary of Greece*, 1954, (Athens: National Printing House, 1955).

6. V. Damalas, op. cit., p. 61.

7. G. Halkiopoulos, *Supply of Capital for Industrial Development: European Productivity Project No. 212* (Athens: European Productivity Agency, 1955), p. 4.

8. George Coutsoumaris, *The Morphology of Greek Industry* (Athens: Center of Economic Research, 1963).

9. K. Varvaressos, *Report on the Economic Problem of Greece* published in Greek, (Athens: Nafteboriki, 1952), p. 101; and Xenophon Zolotas, *Currency Problem and the Greek Economy*, published in Greek (Athens: Papazessis, 1950), p. 117.

10. X. Zolotas, op. cit., p. 83 and *Technica Chronika*.

11. K. Bantaloukas, *Review of Economic and Political Sciences*, VI, Athens, 1951, p. 20.

12. X. Zolotas, op. cit., p. 88.

13. D. Delivanis and W. C. Cleveland, *Greek Monetary Developments 1939–1948* (Bloomington: Indiana University Press, 1949), p. 130.

14. Bank of Greece, *Report for 1951* (Athens: 1952), p. 130.

15. Bank of Greece, *Statutes* (Athens: Printing House Pyrsos, 1952), p. 3.

16. Eighty thousand shares, at a nominal value of 5,000 drachmae each, were sold to the public at home.

17. The Bank of Greece provided the almost exclusive means of payments of Greece, i.e., Bank of Greece notes. Coins constituted a relatively insignificant part of the currency in circulation.

18. Bank of Greece, *Statutes* (Athens: Printing House Pyrsos, 1952), p. 27.

19. Kyriakos Varvaressos, *Report on the Economic Problem of Greece*, published in Greek (Athens: Nafteboriki, 1952), p. 31.

20. Ibid.

21. Ibid., and Xenophonon Zolotas, *Currency Problem and the Greek Economy*, published in Greek (Athens: Papazessis, 1950), p. 88.

22. D. Delivanis and W. C. Cleveland, *Greek Monetary Developments 1939–1948* (Bloomington: Indiana University Press, 1949), p. 58.

23. Ibid.

24. The gold sovereign was a British gold coin whose weight was approximately .23 of an ounce of pure gold.

25. The supply of gold coins was also increased from private sources, i.e., arbitrage and from Allied forces, which shipped gold to the partisans to assist them in their operations against the Axis forces.

26. Bank of Grece, *Report for 1946* (Athens: 1947), p. 42.

27. Xenophon Zolotas, *Currency Problem and the Greek Economy*, published in Greek (Athens: Papazessis, 1950), p. 85.

28. These public-corporation institutions fell into two categories: (1) public bodies whose revenues were derived exclusively from taxation and that performed governmental functions both national and local in character (e.g., defense, road building, seaport construction, etc.), and (2) social-insurance institutions whose revenues were derived in part from taxation and in part from contributions of employers and employees. According to Greek law, public corporations in existence on Feb. 20, 1928, whose own statutes explicitly designated the National Bank of Greece as their exclusive depository, and all public corporations created since Feb. 20, 1928, were obligated to deposit their funds with the National Bank of Greece. In 1938, public-corporation deposits amounted to 13.6 percent of total bank deposits. From 1945 to 1948, more than half of total bank deposits were deposits of public-corporation institutions.

29. Xenophon Zolotas, *Currency Problem and the Greek Economy*, published in Greek, (Athens: Papazessis, 1950), p. 93.

30. Ibid., p. 30.

31. Data for 1945 are not available.

32. Net national income is defined as the total net income of the economy during a given year and is equal to net national product plus income from the rest of the world minus payments made to the rest of the world.

33. Bank of Greece, *Annual Report for 1946* (Athens: 1947), p. 56.

34. Bank of Greece, *Annual Report for 1948* (Athens: 1949), p. 36.

35. Ibid.

36. Xenophon Zolotas, op. cit., p. 43.

37. Data for 1945 are not available.

38. Ministry of Financial Coordination, *National Accounts of Greece, 1946–1953* (Athens: National Printing House, 1955), p. 28.

39. Ibid., p. 35.

40. Bank of Greece, *Confidential Report for December 1953*.

41. Ibid.

42. Bank of Greece, *Confidential Reports for January 1951 and April 1953*.

43. It is estimated that the Bank of Greece sold 0.5 million gold sovereigns in 1949, 1.8 million gold sovereigns in 1950 and 1.5 million gold sovereigns in 1951. See K. Varvaressos, *The Devaluation of the Drachma*, published in Greek (Athens: 1953), p. 8.

44. Bank of Greece, *Confidential Reports for January 1951 and April 1953*.

45. Ibid.

46. Bank of Greece, *Annual Reports for 1951 and 1952* (Athens: 1952, 1953), p. 15.

47. Bank of Greece, *Annual Report for 1949* (Athens: 1949), p. 28.

48. Bank of Greece, *Annual Report for 1949* (Athens: 1950), p. 30.

49. Bank of Greece, *Annual Report for 1950* (Athens: 1951), pp. 93–94.

50. Data of the Bank of Greece indicate that 50 percent of total expenditures for housing were for new homes and that the funds came primarily from private savings.

51. Bank of Greece, *Annual Report for 1951 and 1952* (Athens: 1952 and 1953), p. 25.

52. For a detailed review and analysis of developments in Greece during the 1949–51 period see A. J. Kondonassis, *Monetary Policies of the Bank of*

Greece, 1949–1951: Contributions to Monetary Stability and Economic Development (Bloomington: Ph. D. Dissertation, Indiana University, 1961).

53. *U.N. Statistical Yearbook*

54. Ibid.

55. Bank of Greece.

56. Ibid.

57. During the 1953–62 period about $196 million was lent to Greece as part of the United States assistance program.

58. Ministry of Coordination, *The Evolution of Investments in Greece 1948–1961* (Athens: National Printing Office, 1966), p. 134–35.

59. Ibid., pp. 9, 19.

60. Ibid., p. 21.

61. Ibid.

62. *National Accounts of Greece, 1948–1962* and *Statistical Yearbooks of Greece, 1961 and 1971.*

63. *Statistical Yearbooks of Greece, 1961 and 1971.*

64. Ibid.

65. See Table 11.

66. A. A. Pepelassis and P. A. Yotopoulos, *Surplus Labor in Greek Agriculture* (Athens: Center of Economic Research, 1961), p. 22.

67. Between 1962 and 1965 about three hundred thousand Greeks emigrated to Western Europe. This was about 74 percent of the total emigration.

68. See *National Accounts of Greece, 1948–1970.*

69. See Table 13.

70. Statistical Office of the European Communities, *Basic Statistics of the Community, 1964.*

71. Bank of Greece, *Annual Reports.*

72. See Table 12.

73. Statistical Office of the European Communities, *Basic Statistics of the Community, 1964.*

74. For details on the Athens Agreement see John Komitsa and George Kontogeorgi, *The Agreement of the Association of Greece with the European Economic Community* (in Greek) (Athens: National Printing Office, 1962).

75. Data in the *National Income Accounts of Greece, 1960–69,* show that in 1960 the relative contributions of agriculture and industry to gross national income were 24.4 percent and 25 percent, respectively. In 1969 these changed to 18.5 percent and 31 percent.

76. See Bank of Greece, *Monthly Bulletin, March 1970.*

77. See European Community Press and Information, *European Community, No. 9, 1970.*

78. *Nafteboriki,* July 9, 1972.

79. For a comparative discussion of the association agreements of Greece, Turkey, Spain, and Israel, see A. J. Kondonassis, "The EEC and Her Association with Israel, Spain, Turkey, and Greece," Distinguished Lecture Series No. 3, The University of Alabama, 1972.

80. Ministry of Coordination, *Economic Development Plan for Greece, 1968–72,* (Athens: February, 1968).

81. These are government data released in 1973.

4

Yugoslavia

DENNISON I. RUSINOW

A WORLD BANK loan officer recently suggested, in a private conversation, one improbable but delightful noneconomic and nonpolitical reason why Yugoslavia has in late years done remarkably well in obtaining credits from his organization. His fellow loan officers, he said, find Yugoslavia's unique economic system and its particular problems so fascinating, especially in comparison with the more mundane capitalist, socialist, or mixed systems and the depressingly familiar problems of most other developing countries, that they actually compete for the excuse to learn more about it by processing or even inventing a loan application.

For more than twenty years Yugoslavia has been a laboratory for a series of sometimes exotic but always exciting experiments in economic and institutional development under communist auspices, but independent of Soviet direction and Soviet models. In the process, and whether because of or despite the experiments, it has in several years recorded the second highest economic-growth rate in the world and advanced from the status of Europe's second-poorest state, with a national per-capita income of less than $130, to the status of an intermediately developed agricultural-industrial society with a per-capita gross national product of $990 in 1973. Expanded or entirely new industrial sectors, sometimes producing what the natural-resource base, the domestic market, and potential comparative cost advantages suggest ought to be produced, have reduced the number of Yugoslavs dependent on agriculture, which is still largely peasant subsistence farming, from over 75 percent to under 45 percent of the total population. From a small-scale prewar exporter of agricultural products and minerals with a balance-of-payments surplus, the country has become, since the war, a medium-scale exporter of industrial, agro-industrial, and agricultural products with a relatively enormous balance-of-payments deficit.

The eclectic nature of the economic system reflects the political history of Titoist Yugoslavia, which was thrown out of the Soviet bloc in 1948 to become the world's first communist-ruled state independent of the Soviet Union, which was for some years economically dependent on the capitalist West, and which was eventually to find an international political equilibrium of sorts as a nonaligned state whose continued independence and peculiar socialism were grudgingly accepted by both blocs. System and international status are further reflected, symbolically and practically, in economic relations: 48 percent of foreign trade at the beginning of the 1970s with the Western European Economic Community (EEC), 34 percent with the Eastern Council for Mutual Economic Assistance (COMECON), participant observer status in COMECON and a special treaty relationship with the EEC, and a characteristic "Mediterranean" position as a major exporter of labor to northwestern Europe, with all that this implies for relief of domestic unemployment and of the balance-of payments through remittances.

HISTORICAL BACKGROUND

Yugoslavia, until 1929 officially called the Kingdom of the Serbs, Croats, and Slovenes, was created after World War I through the amalgamation of two previously independent Balkan states, Serbia and Montenegro, together with sizeable fragments of the former Hapsburg, Ottoman, and Venetian empires. The new political unit, with a population at birth of about 14 million, was ostensibly the fulfillment of the centuries-old aspiration of the various Slav (Jugo-Slav) peoples—who had experienced between 400 and 1200 years of foreign rule—for a united and independent state of their own.

In fact, the Yugoslavia created in 1918 brought together for the first time in history under one political roof a number of diverse if related peoples—Serbs, Croats, Slovenes, Macedonians, Muslim Bosnian Slavs, and Montenegrins, in addition to more than a dozen nonsouth-Slavic minorities—peoples whose historic experiences, religions, social and political cultures, and levels of economic development were very different. The peoples of the ex-Hapsburg lands of the north and west—Slovenia, Croatia, and the Vojvodina—had enjoyed higher living standards, most of the little industry and industrial tradition that existed, higher literacy and lower birth rates, and more complex social stratification than had the peoples of the Balkan and ex-Ottoman provinces of Serbia, Bosnia-Herzegovina, Montenegro, and Macedonia, where between 80 and 90 percent of the populations were in 1918 still dependent on peasant agriculture for their livelihood. In addition, the Slovenes and Croats of the ex-Hapsburg lands were Roman Catholic and had shared, if sometimes marginally, most of the significant developments in modern Central European history, from the Renaissance through the Enlightenment to the belated extension of modern capitalism to East-Central Europe after 1850. Their ex-Ottoman kinsmen to the south were Orthodox or Muslim in religion and had been largely isolated by non-European rule from the main currents of European history since the sixteenth century, until some of them achieved a gradual and precarious independence during the nineteenth.

An additional aggravating complication was the polarization of economic and political power in ethnically and geographically different parts of the country. While economic power was concentrated in more-developed Slovenia and Croatia, political power came to be held almost exclusively by the Serbs, who succeded in imposing a highly centralized political system on other nationalities whose leaders whould have preferred a federation, and who contributed to the new state its king, its capital city, most of the officer corps of its army and bureaucracy, and the psychological and political consequences of the former Serbian kingdom's role on the winning side in the Great War and in the founding of the new state.

The result was a system that fluctuated between instability and deadlock until, in frustration, a Serbian royal dictatorship was imposed in 1929. The dictatorship, in turn, spawned or spurred militant and sometimes fascist separatist movements, especially in Croatia and Macedonia, which were in their turn exploited by the fascist regimes in Italy and Germany for their own reasons. The country's economic history, meanwhile, was similar to that of most of its neighbors in the interwar period. There was a brief and hopeful (if modest) developmental boom in the 1920s, but this was cut short by the Great Depression of the 1930s and its social, political, and economic consequences. Then there was a reluctant but unavoidable slide into economic dependency on Nazi Germany, which alone was prepared to take Balkan agricultural and raw materials in return for growing influence and an ability to dictate terms of trade designed to keep these states in a condition that today would be called neocolonial.

The fragile vessel of such a Yugoslavia broke apart on the rocks of World War II. Under the impact of the Axis invasion in April, 1941, the state collapsed and was divided by its conquerors into a patchwork of puppet states and occupied zones whose borders and definitions emphasized ethnic differences and invited civil strife.

Out of this debris and out of the fires of an extraordinarily bloody combination of an epic national-liberation struggle, an interethnic civil war, and a social revolution there arose the phoenix of a new Yugoslavia, wearing the red star of communism. The unsolved basic problems of the old Yugoslavia remained: how to achieve effective independence for a sensitively located small country; how to achieve rapid economic and social modernization in a poor country endowed with little appropriate social infrastructure and less capital and trained manpower, and with sharply differing regional levels of backwardness that coincided with the distribution of mutually suspicious ethnic communities with significantly different histories, political and economic experience, and national ethos; and how to achieve, along with such modernization, the brotherhood and unity of these diverse peoples. The solutions were now to be sought by a group of inexperienced, dogmatically trained, but eager and frequently intelligent and flexible Balkan communists, who had just proved themselves to be motivated at least as much by patriotism as by Marxist ideology. In principle, they would seek to answer the national question with federalism, the developmental question with socialism, and the problem of independence with a rash but unsuccessful defiance of the logic of their own and their country's weakness.

FROM STALINISM TO "TITOISM"

The Yugoslav economic experiment, like the Titoist political odyssey, was born of necessity, not of conviction. Tito was condemned for ideological heresy by the Cominform before he and his close collaborators became heretics. The Yugoslav rulers' original sin was of a different order: they had refused to accept Soviet dictation and exploitation and had aspired to become an autonomous power center, under Soviet suzereignty, for the entire Balkan peninsula.

The Yugoslav system in 1948 was thus in fact a more faithful copy of the Soviet original than had been achieved in any other European state as of that date. The economic model was Stalinist in both goals and methods: extensive and rapid industrialization, concentrating on infrastructure and basic industries, financed by disinvestment and rigidly suppressed prices in the agricultural sector, and accompanied by an associated flight of cheap unskilled labor from the countryside to the factories—all on the basis of normative plans dictated by the center and administered by means of a credit system that disregarded costs and largely eliminated the use-value function of money.

By 1952, however, the methods of Stalinist economics had been abandoned in practice. The heretic *malgré lui* became a heretic in fact, and by force of circumstnces. The most important of these circumstances included excommunication and economic blockade by the Cominform, added to the burdens of awesome wartime and revolutionary destruction of capital and trained cadres, plus investment errors caused by overzealousness during the Stalinist period, all of which combined to bring the economy and the state itself to the brink of collapse. They also included a consequent dependence on Western aid for survival, a dependence carrying with it extensive contacts with the neocapitalist Western world, plus (and importantly) an urgent ideological need to criticize and deviate from the Soviet system in order to justify their independence and defiance of Soviet authority. In other words, the events of 1948 set the Yugoslavs free to experiment if they should choose to do so, and the events of the next three years made it imperative that they should so choose. The new solutions that they then adopted were tempered by all these factors, and in addition by the access to recent developments in Western economic theory and principles of business organization that their country's unique position in the early 1950s offered to Yugoslav economists, politicians, and managers.

The twin pillars of the new system, fundamentally mature in theory if not in practice by 1953, were and remain "market socialism" and "workers' self-management": autonomous enterprises making their own entrepreneurial decisions in an effort to maximize profits in a competitive market environment, with policy being made and its execution being overseen by representative bodies of workers in each enterprise. Workers' councils, elected by all the employees in an enterprise (or consisting of all of them in enterprises having less than thirty workers), took over theoretical management as trustees of "society" (the theoretical owner of the means of production). They elected management boards as their executive organs and in collaboration with the communal councils (local government) appointed and dismissed enterprise directors. In principle, these self-management organs were to decide what and how much to produce, set prices, and determine the distribution of net income into salaries and wages, investment and social funds, etc. The role of the state was to be indirect: the setting of aggregate targets by economic sector and indicative planning to be implemented by the use of the kind of fiscal tools commonly employed in the West, plus residual control over the volume and sectoral distribution of most investment funds.

An important if technical distinction between this system and the Soviet one is that in Yugoslavia after the reforms of the 1950s macroeconomic decisions were explicitly separated from microeconomic decisions. The former were to be made by government planners, working under political authorities at the federal, republican, and communal levels as the political system, too, was decentralized in tandem with the economic. Until 1965, they took the form of annual and (occasionally) five-year "Social Plans." The criteria that the planners were supposed to use were derived from an amalgam of Marxist and post-Keynesian definitions of growth, and the decisions made were reflected in a set of detailed legal rules and fiscal instruments. Microeconomic decisions, however, were to be made by enterprises acting independently and on the basis of their analysis of the market and within the framework established by the set of legal rules and fiscal instruments drawn up by the macroeconomic planners. The most important obvious result of this system, and one consistent feature throughout two decades of change and reform, is that in Yugoslavia "the state administration has the right to question only the legality of the business transactions of firms and not their opportuneness."[1] When viewed from this angle, the history of the Yugoslav experiment from the early 1950s until the mid-1960s becomes a chronicle of efforts to evolve a set of legal tools and institutions that would relate the macroeconomic decisions of the planners and the microeconomic decisions of the enterprises in the most effective and satisfactory way.

At the same time, in the early 1950s, forced collectivization of agriculture was abandoned, albeit with considerable reluctance. When the peasantry had exercised the right to withdraw from unwanted collectives, the socialized agricultural sector that remained accounted for only 9 percent of the country's arable land, an amount that grew slowly (primarily through purchase) to 16 percent by 1970. Private ownership of up to ten hectares of arable land per peasant household was guaranteed by the constitution. Until 1965, however, almost no facilities were made available to encourage the private peasant to produce profitably for the market, except in cooperation with the "social sector." The consequent backwardness of the dominant peasant sector of agriculture, with the median size of holdings about four hectares, was and is still today a major brake on economic development, limiting both the supply of agricultural products for export and domestic consumption and the growth of a domestic market for consumer industrial goods.

In its essential features this theoretical structure has remained intact for twenty years. In implementation, however, it has suffered many vicissitudes and a bewildering series of changes, one of them (in 1965) of major implications. Many of these reflected a characteristic Yugoslav impatience with, and overeagerness to change, institutional devices that display even minor defects. Others were necessitated by distortions produced by inherent contradictions in the Yugoslav model. Many, however, represented efforts to cope with the kinds of problems that are faced by anyone who sets out to undo a Stalinist-type "command economy" in a semiliterate and poor society with a continuing commitment to rapid industrialization and social modernization—and industrial democracy—but with natural, financial, and appropriate human resources all in short supply.

In such a society, for example, how can illiterate ex-peasants, only recently inducted into industry, be expected to operate the sophisticated machinery of "workers' self-management"? Poor, without capitalists or a capitalist capital market, and politically unable or unwilling to import foreign capital through normal channels, how can such a society hope to industrialize without the forced reduction of living standards and the centralization of forced savings that imply some variant of the Stalinist model? Indeed, how can one create a market economy at all, without inducing inflation and chaos, when the existing price structure is geared to the requirements of a command economy and does not, therefore, reflect real market-dictated, relative-scarcity values, with a continued commitment to communist "investomania," and when many industries either would not exist or would go bankrupt except for an artificial price structure, continued injections of "political" investment funds, or subsidies of some kind?

For the Yugoslavs in 1952, as for many others in Eastern Europe in later years, there was an additional, a political, problem. In the execution of their program, the reformers were dependent on precisely those people who were its natural opponents, i.e., the state and party bureaucracies, the holders of a monopoly of effective political and economic power in the country, who were now being told to relinquish much of that power—always a difficult order to follow—to people and institutions that they considered, with some justification, both less qualified than themselves and ideologically unreliable. Such a bureaucracy was hardly an ideal instrument for the reformers' program, but there was no other, and besides, they themselves were part of it.

Yugoslavia's hybrid economic system of the later 1950s was thus the product of an implicit compromise between these two groups, or factions, in the ruling communist elite, and between two aspects of Yugoslav reality. On the one hand, there were the protagonists of a genuine, if of necessity gradual, implementation of "market socialism" and "workers' self-management," backed by universally recognized and urgent reasons for the reform of a collapsed economy. On the other hand, there were the "conservatives" of the elite, fearful for their power, for the purity of Marxist-Leninism, for economic growth rates, and for the future of both order and socialism in a Yugoslav society still marked by primitivism, divisive ethnic particularisms, and the lack of a broad consensus supporting the values of the communist regime. For the conservatives, the limited reforms of 1950–53 might be acceptable, especially because they appeared to be producing good economic results without a dangerous diminution of party and state control, but further effective decentralization and liberalization were to be resisted.

It is in this sense that the Djilas crisis of 1954 and the return to a more orthodox conception of "the role of the party" that followed, although primarily political developments, were also of great economic significance, for they represented an implicit decision (or the consequences of a decision) not to carry through the "market-socialism" experiment to its logical conclusion at that time.

Each party to the compromise had its essential minimum demands. Workers' councils and other elective organs existed as visible tokens of the commitment to wider participation in decision making and of the need to broaden the system's base of consent through at least the illusion of shared power. Tens of thousands of Yugoslavs, both party and non-party, were gaining experience in the uses and abuses of democratic procedures, with or without real decision-making powers, through membership in these institutions. A market economy really existed to the extent that enterprises produced in order to sell what they produced, in competition with other enterprises and with profit the index of their success—in striking contrast to enterprise motivation and behavior further to the east. On the other hand, the party retained effective (if now indirect) control over decision making in all but trivial matters, while the state retained control over the basic parameters of production and economic development through its continuing control of savings and investment and through fiscal and administrative restrictions of enterprise and communal autonomy. Most important of all for the still fundamentally Stalinist concepts of economic development, these controls avoided the possibility that workers and managers in the economy, if really in charge of their earnings, could divert an undesirably high proportion from investment to raise still very low levels of consumption. Party and state could thereby ensure the continuation of a punishingly high rate of investment, with a priority to slowly maturing basic industries and infrastructure only partly abandoned in favor of consumer goods after 1956.

A series of half-hearted minireforms between 1954 and 1961 did gradually enlarge the power of enterprises (and thus, in theory, that of their workers' councils) over the distribution of their net revenue after taxes and other "contributions" to the state, payments that still included the funds that financed the larger part of gross national investment. However, the ratio of this net revenue to taxes and contributions was not significantly altered until 1964, and the former remained by far the smaller portion. Even in 1961, according to one calculation, economic enterprises retained control of only 20.9 percent of "surplus value" (roughly equivalent to "gross profit" as calculated in the West), while the state (at the federal, republican, and communal levels) took over the remaining 79.1 percent; moreover, the enterprises' share declined to 16.9 percent in 1962 and to 15.9 percent in 1963.[2] In addition, each reform's partial devolution of power to distribute wages and residual profits tended to be eroded in the following year or two. This was Yugoslav evidence in support of Gregory Grossman's axiom for socialist societies: "In general, effective decentralization in a centrally-administered economy can take place only when carried out on a very broad front all at once, which requires intervention from higher quarters and calls for big political battles. Centralization, however, can and often does proceed in little steps, virtually unnoticed but important in aggregate impact."[3]

While resistance by party and government functionaries whose power and privileges were threatened by each proposed liberalization undoubtedly played an important role, as did the first rapprochement with the Soviet Union that followed the death of Stalin, there were also strong practical domestic reasons (as already noted) for the lack of significant further reform. The technical and general educational level of enterprise directors, many of them ex-Partisan officers from villages of the mountain republics who had been appointed as a reward for their wartime service, was disturbingly low—even in the early 1960s as many as 33 percent of directors in the total of 2,400 industrial and mining enterprises with more than thirty employees had only had primary schooling.[4] Most members of many of the workers' councils were actually illiterate, and in the early days especially their notion of how to improve their economic position was often to vote for a simple increase in wages and prices.[5] The same problem of "low cultural level" also restricted the usefulness of the party cell, or the trade union, as instruments of informal central control. Even if these cadre problems had not existed, the achieved level of industrial output and the inadequacy of the agricultural base, from which savings for new investment had to be extorted, could reasonably be considered too weak to bear the combined weight of free price and wage formation plus the high growth rate demanded by the regime and the revolution of rising expectations that its program and accomplishments had invoked.

Problems of this sort had of course been anticipated, which was one reason why the power of workers' councils and communal governments had been further circumscribed by a forest of restrictive regulations and (after 1954) by the watchful eyes of a pyramid of industrial chambers and associations to which enterprises in each sector were required to belong. In the years that followed, however, instead of the step-by-step liquidation of these administrative controls, which had originally been foreseen as workers' councils learned their job and as investments and managers matured, there was a step-by-step complication of the system by the imposition of ever more or bewilderingly changing controls—each reluctantly adopted in order to keep the hybrid model functioning. Most prices were administratively regulated, at first indirectly and later directly, and the percentage of their revenue over which enterprises exercised control tended to be progressively reduced in most years by new or larger taxes and a multitude of regulations concerning obligatory reserves of various sorts.[6]

In effect, the liberalization of the economy that the 1950–52 reforms were supposed to introduce did not take place, although decentralization did. Moreover, substantive reform became more difficult with each year's additions to the complex of "administrative controls," subsidies, and debts guaranteed by political collateral that buttressed and shored up the structure at innumerable points. Even their partial removal, a basic prerequisite to a genuine market economy, would bring entire sectors into serious financial difficulties. At the same time, the existence of these props had encouraged the growth of a multitude of enterprises and sectors having both a vested interest in their retention and the political connections with which to give weight to their interest.

By the early 1960s commentators, domestic as well as foreign, were suggesting that the results had made a móckery of both "market socialism" and socialist planning, as well as of "workers' self-management." Instead of enjoying the best of both worlds, Yugoslavia appeared to be suffering the worst, with what Professor Rudolf Bićanić of Zagreb University described as "an ambivalent system, partly governed by the laws of imperfect competition, and partly administratively controlled, so that it is very difficult to make this system work."[7]

Nevertheless—and this is an additional important reason for the lack of earlier serious reform—it did work very well indeed for a number of years. A Five-Year Plan for 1956–61 set ambitious goals and reached the plan's major targets a year early. The Social Product[8] rose in four years by 62 percent, or 12.7 percent per annum at a compound rate, compared with a planned rise of 9.5 percent per annum. Private consumption of goods and services rose by 49 percent, or 10.5 percent per annum, compared with the plan's 7.3 percent per annum. Imports grew by 67 percent, twice the planned rate, and exports by 65 percent, also more than foreseen.

Yugoslavia enjoyed the highest economic-growth rate in the world.[9] Yugoslav enterprises were genuinely free of the stultifying, absolute central control and physical-production targets of Stalinism. Despite the frustrations and distortions of meaningful cost accountancy imposed by the remaining controls and regulations, and despite the misleading signals of irrational price ratios, they really could make their own effective purchasing, production, and sales decisions over a fairly wide range. At the receiving end of the economic process, the citizen as consumer was undeniably better off, getting more of the kind and quality of goods that he wanted than, for example, the citizens of the Soviet-bloc states. At the producing end, the citizen as worker (or the minority who cared) sometimes had the illusion, and occasionally even the reality, of participation in decision making through the workers' councils.

After 1961, however, the economy ran into increasing difficulties that revealed that the critics of the hybrid model had been right, if prematurely so, on economic as well as ideological grounds.

The boom of the 1950s had been achieved in part by means of an unexpectedly high rate of investment expenditure, in which productive investment in fixed assets at constant prices rose faster than total output (at 13.4 percent instead of the lower planned rate of 8.5 percent per annum), while social investment in housing, schools, hospitals, etc., also rose faster than was anticipated. Gross investment was 29 percent higher in 1960 than in 1959 and amounted to 32 percent of the Social Product. Inflationary pressures generated by this process, which still included (despite a shift in investment priorities in 1956) a high proportion of investment in major industrial and infrastructure projects having only long-run benefits, were already making themselves felt by the end of the decade. Additional pressures were imposed by a rapid rise in personal consumption permitted in the last years of the plan.

Encouraged by their recent successes and ignoring these warning signs, the Yugoslavs launched a new Five-Year Plan in 1961, one slightly more modest than their latest achievements but more ambitious than the 1956–61 plan had been. In 1960 and 1961 a further burden was added by two successive bad harvests that were partly the result of unfavorable weather but were also in part a reflection of the still-unresolved basic problem of agricultural production. At precisely this inauspicious moment there came another attempt at liberalization through a minireform that included abandoning state control of quantitative proportions in the distribution of the net income of enterprise, enlarging their power and that of communes to make their own investment decisions, and permitting rapid expansion of short-term banking credits, which were notoriously being misused for capital-investment purposes. A package of import and currency reforms, introduced under pressure from the American, West German, and other Western creditors who supplied loans in support of the reform and as a step toward full Yugoslav membership in the General Agreement on Tariffs and Trade (GATT), further contributed to instability.

Whether or not these reforms had had time to add to existing inflationary pressures, the gross investment rate, wage levels, and the foreign-trade deficit were all thoroughly out of hand. The government was forced to intervene with classic restrictive measures, including a wage freeze, a moratorium on new investment, and a partial reversal of the most recent liberalization of foreign trade. These temporary measures were succeeded by other deflationary devices, such as linking wage rises to prior rises in productivity, constituting compulsory blocked reserves to siphon off a portion of enterprise investment funds, etc.

By the second half of 1961 the boom had turned into a recession, and by mid-1962 the new plan and the hopes that had accompanied it had been discarded. The growth rate for industrial production, which had been 15 percent in 1960, declined to only 7 percent in 1961 and to an annual rate of 4 percent in the first half of 1962. Labor productivity showed a similar decline and per-capita real wages, which had risen by 13 percent in 1959 and 8.2 percent in 1960, actually declined in 1961–62. Tito, in a famous speech at Split in May, 1962, lectured the nation, the party, and his socialist entrepreneurs on their failings and summoned a Central Committee Plenum to demand a "turning point in our economic policy." The agonizing reappraisal had begun.[10]

THE ECONOMISTS' DEBATE OF 1962–64

From the analysis undertaken at that time, two conflicting opinions emerged concerning the source of weaknesses. For one group of economists, most of whom (significantly) were Serbians from the relatively underdeveloped east and south of the country, the fault was to be sought in the group of liberalizing reforms that had accompanied introduction of the 1961–65 plan. The astounding successes of the preceding period, they pointed out, had been achieved by the hybrid system left behind after the incomplete reforms of 1950–52. The compromise then struck had apparently had its virtues. The power and freedom granted to enterprise-management and "workers' self-management" organs had been extensive enough to generate the incentives and elasticity in entrepreneurial decision making that were (and are) so conspicuously and cripplingly lacking in more orthodox Marxist economic systems operating farther to the east. At the same time, residual central control over prices, wages, and especially over investment funds and their distribution had made possible the maintenance of a high growth rate without excessive inflation in a still under-developed society that lacked an agricultural base adequate to sustain such growth under conditions of a genuinely freer market. The system was far from perfect, and most of these economists were ready with lists of minor short-run changes—particularly reforms that would encourage greater cost consciousness in existing enterprises—but they clearly felt it was too early for major meddling.

In their view, therefore, the recession had been a consequence of just such meddling and of an attempt to leap prematurely into a genuine "socialist market economy" of the sort projected and then postponed in 1950–52. The inflation that followed, requiring the reimposition of strict controls and so bringing the boom to an end, seemed to them to prove that the economy was still too primitive to permit the luxury of a free market without cutting the growth rate and introducing the kind of inflation/stagnation business cycle that socialism is supposed to eliminate.

Another group of economists, among whom Slovenes and Croats from the relatively developed northwest were strongly represented, adopted a diametrically opposed position, based on a different reading of the economic history of the 1956–62 period. They could perhaps agree that the mixed system evolved during the 1950s had expedited economic growth at the time and may indeed have been necessary until the achievement of "take-off" and a certain minimum of technological and political experience by a larger sector of the population. They could also agree that the liberalization in 1961 had been imposed too quickly and without adequate short-term cushioning. But what had then gone wrong, they argued, was that liberalization had not been carried far enough.[11] Retention of administrative props and buttresses in the post-takeoff period, they insisted, introduces a series of distortions that could fatally compromise both the economic and the socio-political principles of Titoism's theoretical "socialist humanism." In the economy, where "no one wants to admit how little the market mechanism operates,"[12] these distortions maintain a model in which the structure of demand is unable effectively to influence the structure of supply, thus preventing the market from performing its automatic rationalizing function. In society, they penalize efficiency, hard work, cost consciousness, adherence to contracts, the growth of the kind of civic conscience (here called "socialist consciousness") that comprehends how communal and private gain can be served simultaneously, and similar virtues that the rulers of Yugoslavia have decided are as appropriate for "socialist man" as for his capitalist counterpart.

The most important distortions introduced by incomplete reforms, according to this group of economists, were the specific consequences of the investment system and controlled prices. The former had genuinely decentralized the initiative in making investment decisions—in 1961 exercised by a multitude of enterprises, banks, and communal governments, as well as by the federal government—but without an accompanying distribution of real responsibility for mistakes or miscalculations. It was now generally agreed that the resulting total investment demand, which in some instances reached two or three times the planned figure, was the primary source of the crisis of 1961–62. The resulting inflationary pressures were also the primary reason why price controls had to be maintained over 70 percent of industrial commodities. These controls, in turn, provided the second major source of distortions in the market; they had been set at artificial levels during the transition away from a Stalinist controlled economy and were later altered ad hoc and without planning, in response to individual needs, so that they never reflected realistic use/value ratios.[13]

The need to find a socialist substitute for capitalist techniques of mobilizing the community's savings in order to finance investment is a problem that every socialist state must solve. In Yugoslavia, as in other communist states, the most important device had been the centralization through taxation and interest charges of part of the "accumulation" (profits) of enterprises into "social funds," which were used to control the volume and redistribute and channel the use of available savings in what was considered to be a socially desirable manner. This might or might not also be an economically desirable manner, and that is one place where trouble began.

By means of such social funds, plus other sums allocated to specific major projects, the Yugoslav federal government had continued to exercise direct or indirect control over an estimated 80 percent of planned investment. The annual Social Plan made a division of these funds by sectors of the economy, and the banks were given the task of doling out money to worthy claimants in the form of interest-bearing loans. Although the banks were instructed to disburse funds only to enterprises that could use them profitably, the system broke down, it was now said, because no one was ultimately responsible for their economic employment and repayment. The banks did not care if the funds were lost because funds were not "theirs." In fact, their own income was largely dependent on the sheer volume of business they did and they had, therefore, an incentive to make as many loans as possible. Nor was the government responsible for decisions made by others. Thus enterprises in trouble could ask for debts to be wiped out, or for a moratorium, or (and this was most frequently the case) for just one more credit to get them over the hump to profitability.[14] Such possibilities bred another, more specialized form of irresponsibility: it was obviously a good thing for a commune to have a factory, paying taxes and creating employment, on its territory; with a blueprint for a nice, cheap little factory a credit could be obtained; and once the plant was started it could be discovered that costs had been drastically underestimated and that additional credits were needed. As the commitment of the commune and the bank grew, so did the difficulty of calling a halt, especially when it was not they but the federal or republican government that had to provide the subsidies to keep the unprofitable enterprise in business.

With the help of these and other abuses, actual investments always exceeded planned investments, sometimes by a multiple of the plan, unbalancing the savings/investment equation and breeding inflation. And all over the country, but especially in underdeveloped areas concentrated in Serbia, Montenegro, Macedonia, and Bosnia-Herzegovina, "political" factories of this sort sprouted up, factories so-called because of the initial "political" decision to build and subsequent "political" decisions that a factory, once there, could not be allowed to close or even to merge with a stronger enterprise located somewhere else and therefore under the control of another communal government and tax regime.

The consequences of such policies, the "liberals" concluded, involved more than an enormous waste of national income, unnecessarily low personal-consumption levels, and the creation of a vast amount of un-utilized industrial capacity that could never be used profitably. They also provided a mammoth disincentive to workers and management in profit-able factories, who had seen their profits taxed away for this purpose— the preferred critical phrase had become "fiscal 'seizure' of accumula-tion"[15]—and for redistribution as "indirect income" in the form of sub-sidized housing, holidays, travel, and social services.[16] Worst of all for the future, existing mechanisms joined with a continuing uncritical faith in Stalinist theories of industrialization to create a sort of investment syn-drome, for which the answer to almost any and every problem in the economy was "more investment!" The productivity of labor was a matter of concern, but the productivity of capital was not.

Developments in 1963 and 1964, while the economists' debate was in progress, appeared to support this analysis. What the regime did in 1962 was, essentially, to turn the clock back to 1956, with marginal improve-ments in the foreign trade and credit mechanisms. The economy re-sponded accordingly, and the last months of 1962 and all of 1963 saw a renewal of the rapid expansion of the 1956–60 period. The boom was again accompanied, however, by the same distortions that had led to the collapse of 1961: demand, in the form of personal consumption and espe-cially in the form of investments, grew more rapidly than supply, and the cost of living, which had been stable for many months, began an upward movement that picked up speed abruptly in 1964. The trade gap widened to help finance booming consumption by means of the deficit, and an-other devaluation of the dinar appeared increasingly unavoidable. News that industrial production during the first six months of 1964 was 18 percent higher than a year before, and investment levels 50 percent higher (!), was no longer considered grounds for self-congratulation.[17]

The correct answer, according to the "liberal" economists, was a further retreat from intervention in the economy by government and other political organs, not an intensification of their role. In particular, the state should get out of the investment business, except for public works and major infrastructure projects to which business/banking criteria could not be applied. Taxes and interest rates could then be lowered and "accumulation" left in the hands of the profitable enterprises that had earned it; these would presumably also know best how to invest these moneys, either in their own modernization or expansion, in subsidiaries, or in other enterprises through a banking mechanism designed to respond to economic rather than political criteria. The banking system itself should therefore be overhauled, with its depositors (the profitable enterprises) as shareholders, jointly deciding about investments and sharing in the profits from them. That is, individual enterprises, in collaboration with the banks, should be given control over a larger share of their earnings and real responsibility to prosper or perish, according to whether their judgments were sound or not.

Even the state's residual direct responsibility for underdeveloped areas, exercised through machinery resembling that of southern Italy's La Cassa per il Mezzogiorno (The Fund for the South), should be limited. Enterprises in these areas should come to depend more on partnership agreements or credits from related industries in the developed republics. Under such a regime prices, too, could be gradually freed of administrative controls. Genuinely meaningful growth rates—of profitable industries and sectors, not of "political" factories—would be little effected, the laissez-faire socialists argued, and these rather than the global growth rates of the Statistical Yearbooks were what mattered now.

With such a package of criticisms, the protagonists of a genuine "market socialism" in Yugoslavia had moved from the demand for decentralization, which had characterized the 1950s, to a demand for depolitization of the economy. The change now became explicit as the central slogan of reform shifted from *decentralizacija* to *de-etatizacija* (decentralization to depolitization).

THE ECONOMIC REFORM OF 1965

During the year 1964 several minor changes in the economic system, apparently anticipating a major structural reform, suggested that the authorities were impressed by the "liberal" case. At the beginning of the year the General Investment Fund, the principal "social fund" that earlier had handled between a third and a quarter of gross investment financing, was abolished and its assets and liabilities were transferred to the banks. Some tax rates on enterprises were lowered or abolished. In July abrupt increases of up to 29 percent were announced in the retail prices of formerly subsidized basic commodities like flour, bread, milk, electricity, and coal—a move toward a more realistic price structure. Then, at the Eighth Congress of the League of Communists of Yugoslavia, in December, 1964, it became clear that the "liberals" had indeed won the immediate political battle; they were told, in effect, to proceed with the drafting of a set of reforms incorporating their proposals.

President Tito was later to call the result a "revolution"—a dramatic and meaningful word for a Marxist to use in such a context.[18] It was launched on July 26, 1965, and included all the "liberal" demands. Fully implemented, it would genuinely establish the "socialist market economy" that had been a Yugoslav quasi-fiction for fifteen years. As the debate had anticipated, attention was focused on changes in the investment and banking systems as the key area in which decision making should be transferred to the wider arena of the economy. As a result, the government's role in the redistribution of the national income should be reduced from 51 percent in 1962 to an anticipated 29 percent after implementation of the reform. Even annual plans were abandoned; in the future there would be only middle-range five-year plans, strictly indicative in character. Direct government interventions in the economy, one senior communist official noted, would eventually be at a lower level than in most Western "capitalist" countries.[19]

To replace the old investment system and provide a socialist substitute for a capitalist capital market a novel experiment was undertaken. The banks were to be controlled by their depositors, i.e., by the socialist enterprises and local government bodies, each with voting power on the bank board proportionate to its subscription to the bank's capital.[20] The hope was that this voting power, plus interest on moneys deposited, would be a sufficient incentive to attract a large portion of the funds that used to be taken away by the state in taxes to finance investment. It was also assumed that, under such a system, bank decisions on investment loans would cease to be political, since the depositors would have the power to insist that their money be invested economically. The national gross-investment rate would be lower, easing inflationary pressures and helping the consumer, but with capital/output ratios improved by elimination of uneconomic investments, the anticipated drop in the quantitative growth rate would be more than compensated for by the improvement in the quality of growth.

Subsidies and other props were also to be drastically reduced or eliminated. The prices of raw materials, producers' goods, and agricultural products were raised sharply as a move toward genuine market prices and to invoke increased production in these heretofore often unprofitable sectors. Finally, foreign trade was liberalized, with quantitative restrictions on imports and average customs duty being reduced from 23 percent to 11 percent—all defended by a devaluation of the dinar and a pledge to move toward convertibility.

THE ECONOMY SINCE THE REFORM

With the reforms of 1965 the Yugoslav economy entered a long and difficult period of readjustment that has still not come to an end and that could be interpreted as evidence that the opponents of such a reform were right. The first three years were marked by stagnation, with many key growth rates at zero or negative, and its consequences, including growing unemployment and emigration, stagnant or declining real incomes, political unrest and instability, and a more stable currency than at any previous period since the war. The following three years were characterized by renewed, if irregular, growth in investment, production, and employment, the result of another reluctant, ad hoc, and ill-planned series of orthodox reflationary measures, and by the now familiar concommitants of a high rate of inflation, booming deficit in the balance of payments, and ill-timed devaluations of the dinar. It sometimes seemed as if the only goal of the reform to be fully realized was its politically least-desirable one, growth in individual, sectoral, and regional disparities in income, which had been reluctantly accepted despite socialist abhorrence as an inevitable side effect of an otherwise desirable genuine market economy.

The magnitude of the recession (and of the preceding one in 1961–62) can best be measured by examining the fluctuating growth rates of the Social Product and its components, adjusted to constant prices as of 1966 and with each year's output as a percentage of the preceding year's:[21]

SOCIAL-PRODUCT GROWTH RATES, 1961–67

Year	Social Product	Industry	Agriculture	Forestry	Construction	Transport	Trade & Tourism	Crafts
1961	3.1	4.3	−5.0	−0.6	21.1	4.4	8.8	7.5
1962	5.0	10.3	2.3	8.3	1.4	5.2	3.5	−1.6
1963	12.3	16.6	9.1	9.3	17.2	7.6	14.0	2.1
1964	12.0	17.4	5.9	−1.5	15.4	7.8	14.0	12.0
1965	1.4	7.0	−7.6	1.7	−5.8	6.1	3.6	9.5
1966	6.6	3.7	16.4	−1.1	−0.8	4.7	5.7	−1.8
1967	1.0	0.3	−1.4	−3.6	5.4	3.3	2.9	5.0

Thus Social Product, which had grown by 12 percent in 1963 and again in 1964, grew only 1.4 percent in 1965. It recovered to 6.6 percent in 1966 primarily because good weather and the initial effects of higher agricultural prices and associated reforms raised agricultural production by 16.4 percent. Then it slumped to a bare 1 percent in 1967, a year in which industrial output grew not at all and agriculture fell back by 1.4 percent. The average yearly growth rate for the four years 1964–67 was 2.9 percent, compared with 9.7 percent in the quadrennium 1961–64 and 12.7 percent in the 1957–60 period. By the end of 1967 the value of industrial production in constant prices was only 9.1 percent larger, and that of Social Product was only 11.3 percent larger, than in 1964—another sad comparison with the cumulative growth rates of the 1950s and with 1963–64, a two-year period during which industrial production had grown in value by 27 points and Social Product by 21 points.

One of the main goals of the reform, as has been seen, was to alter the structure of national income in two ways, first, by enlarging personal incomes at the expense of investment, and second, by changing the distribution of control over savings and investment ("accumulation") in favor of the economy itself (the socialist enterprises), all at the expense of state organs at all levels.

For a time there was impressive movement toward these goals. From

1964 to 1967 the share of net personal incomes in national income grew from 33 percent to nearly 40 percent, reducing "surplus value" (taxes and other income of state organs and investment and other funds of enterprises) from 200 to about 150 percent of personal incomes. The role of economic organizations in the distribution of national income grew from control over 45 percent in 1961, to 49 percent in 1964, and to nearly 58 percent in 1967; and of savings and investment, from 19.7 to 54.2 to 62.1 percent, in the same years. In 1967 and subsequent years, however, this trend was reversed, until economic enterprises found themselves with control over proportionately very little more disposable income than before the reform. This time, significantly, the redistribution favored the state less than it did an economic power new on the Yugoslav scene, but a power at least as independent of and as nonresponsible to the enterprises as the state had been. This was the banking system, and especially the three former federal banks in Belgrade, which had fallen heir to the assets and liabilities of the General Investment Fund when the fund was liquidated in 1964. One indicator of this trend is that between 1964 and 1968 the banks increased their investments in the economy by 87 percent, while economic organizations increased theirs (out of their own funds) by 55 percent and those of the state were cut in half.[22]

By 1967 total employment was 1 percent less than in 1964, down from 3,608,000 to 3,561,000; in the socialist sector it was in fact down by 3 percent, a reduction that was partly compensated for by a rise of 42 percent in the small private sector (largely crafts, services, and catering), which accounted for only 3 percent of the total employed. To make matters worse, this slump occurred not only in a society accustomed to rapidly growing employment in industry and, more recently, in the tertiary sector (total employment in the socialist sector had grown by more than a million in the preceding decade), but also at a moment of maximum demographic pressure on the labor market.

The postwar baby boom was now of age and seeking employment. It included, as a further complication, a far higher proportion of persons with secondary, advanced-vocational, and university training than any previous generation in Yugoslav history. In the first two years of the reform, 716,000 pupils completed the eight-year primary school, 276,000 completed secondary schooling, and 86,000 students graduated from post-secondary schools or universities. The latter two classes represented increases of 42 percent and 31 percent, respectively, over the number of graduates in the last two prereform years (1962–64). When these graduates sought jobs, however, they encountered a market in which the number of employed, which had grown by 6 percent in 1964, the last boom year, grew by only 1 percent in 1965, fell by 2 percent in 1966 and another 1 percent in 1967, and then grew again but only by 1 percent in

1968, when recovery began. The number of registered unemployed in 1968 was 47 percent larger than in 1964, despite massive temporary emigration to find work in Western Europe.[23] Serious student demonstrations in Belgrade, Zagreb, and Sarajevo, and the growth of general political unrest and particularist ethnic nationalisms in 1968 and the following three years, reflected these realities.

Important additional fuel was added to this unrest and to the dissatisfaction of even the most outspoken advocates of the reform by its greater than expected success in one field, the growth of what in Yugoslavia are called "social differences," i.e., growing disparities in individual, sectoral, and regional incomes. By 1968, while about 40 percent of the employed were still receiving incomes of less than 600 new dinars (then $48) a month, a number of classes of employed were receiving six times that amount or more. These included some senior functionaries in state, party, and related organs, but also a growing number of managerial and technical cadres, persons in the free professions, small private entrepreneurs, and most of those employed in particularly profitable economic or non-economic sectors such as banking, insurance, the state lottery (!), some foreign-trade enterprises, and the electrical-production industry. Yugoslav newspapers became fond of citing cases in which janitors in one enterprise or sector had higher incomes than highly qualified workers or university graduates in another. With the sharp cutback in state-directed redistribution of national income from richer to poorer regions, the growth of interregional differences in income, in fact only rarely reduced in earlier years, despite the massive but often ill-conceived efforts of the pre-reform period,[24] also increased in tempo. This, too, fueled the fires of interethnic jealousies and regionally based ethnic nationalisms.

The most surprising feature of the period, in view of this record, was the stubbornness with which the authorities clung to the principles of the reform, expressing continuing faith in the virtue, as well as the necessity, of a genuine market economy and an almost laissez-faire role for the state and keeping what they could of the system inaugurated in 1965.

Much of this stubbornness was of course political in origin, reflecting both an ideological commitment to a definition of socialist democracy considered unrealizable without a wholehearted implementation of the reform and the precarious political position of the reformers, who had many enemies ready and eager to replace them if they were discredited by the failure of their program.[25] Their faith was not, however, without an economic and social rationale. It could be argued that the principles of the reform were perfectly sound and in fact the only ones appropriate to a "socialist model for a more developed society." The difficulties they were encountering were to be blamed, instead, on a complex syndrome of other factors, both "subjective" and "objective."

The reform had been hastily and therefore badly drafted. In addition, and because of their haste, the drafters had left for later the resolution of several politically sensitive and disputed but important issues such as the distribution of former federal investment funds and obligations and the foreign-currency system. These questions, central to the functioning of the reform, urgently required early solutions, but for political reasons agreement on most of them had still not been reached six years after the reform was launched.[26]

Other factors included the continuing burden of major long-term investment projects, committed and often begun before the reform and now increasingly expensive—the huge hydroelectric and navigation system at the Iron Gates on the Danube, built jointly by Yugoslavia and Romania and completed in 1972, and the Belgrade-Bar railroad, still under construction in 1973, were two outstanding examples. There was also incompetence or an inability to think or do business in terms of a genuine market economy on the part of many entrepreneurs and party and government officials. There was the continuing burden of irrational investments in the past. In addition, finally, there was at least one piece of bad luck: the Yugoslavs had opened their economy to the outside world and its competition to a greater extent than ever before (and with all the optimistic zest of nineteenth-century free-traders) just when their principal trading partners, and members of the Common Market in particular, were moving back toward protectionism. Yugoslav countermeasures were slow in coming, contrary to the laissez-faire spirit of the reform, and were in any case of limited potential effectiveness in view of Yugoslavia's small share in the total foreign trade of these partners.

Among these assorted problems and deficiencies, the foreign-currency system was technically perhaps the most amenable to solution, but it became politically the most passionately disputed. The question was, essentially, how to reconcile (1) a nonconvertible currency and (2) the aspiration for free trade in foreign as well as domestic economic relations and with appropriate export incentives. The regime, committed to work for convertibility as a definitive solution but underestimating the time needed to achieve it, found a temporary device in the form of "retention quotas" to encourage exports: exporting and tourist enterprises were entitled to keep a variable, small proportion of their hard foreign currency earnings, ranging from 4 percent up to 20 percent, to be used as they saw fit. The rest had to be sold for dinars to authorized banks, which then resold these currencies at a higher rate to importers and other claimants, including the enterprises that had originally earned them, and with demand always exceeding supply, as imports always exceeded exports plus invisibles.

The device was clearly open to the charge that it was a relic of the old system of central redistribution, which took from those who earned (in this case) desirable hard currencies and gave to those who did not. This argument was pressed by politicians and businessmen in regions or sectors that earned the most foreign currency, and particularly in Croatia, whose industries, Dalmatian tourism, and many migrant workers in Western Europe produced 40 percent of all Yugoslav hard-currency earnings. In the political atmosphere of the late 1960s the dispute was unresolvable, and it was aggravated after 1968 when a renewed high rate of inflation and an explosive trade deficit made it clear that a convertible dinar was more remote than had been hoped in 1965.

Finally, after a major political crisis in December, 1971, brought about a lifting of barriers to compromise on this and other issues, agreement was reached to raise the "retention quotas" from an average of 7 percent to 20 percent in the economy as a whole and 45 percent for tourist enterprises. It was followed by the passage in June, 1972, of a new Law on Foreign-Currency Transactions (which only came into force in the summer of 1973), creating in addition to the world's first (if still limited) foreign-currency market in a communist country. Under this law, all banks authorized to engage in foreign-exchange transactions were entitled to buy and sell on this market on their own behalf or that of their clients, who still would not have direct access to it. Supply and demand would determine exchange rates, subject to certain limitations and an obligation by the National Bank to intervene with purchases or sales of its own to keep the dinar within plus or minus 5 percent of its legal parity with gold.[27]

Politically unresolved and technically difficult or in principle contradictory features of the new investment and banking system provided a final and major source of distortions and weakness. The new banking system has in consequence failed so far to evolve into the desired socialist substitute for a capitalist capital market, responsible to enterprises, presumably responsive, in turn, to market-dictated investment needs and through the banks in control of most of the gross national investment.

One problem is that in most cases, particularly where large banks are concerned, the enterprises and other legal persons who subscribed to the bank's capital and who therefore sit on its board have found it as difficult in practice to control the bank's decision making as their workers' councils have found it difficult to control that of the enterprise, and for largely similar reasons. By 1970 these banks were being accused by many of becoming independent and over-awesome powers in their own right—of being no longer responsible to the state for their operations, and not responsible to anyone else in its stead. Ironically, the leading Yugoslav business weekly, *Ekonomska Politika* (Belgrade), had anticipated such an outcome when the novel banking system was first under discussion in

1963, warning its readers that without other structural changes "the green tables in the conference rooms of the banks will only be a new terrain for the old practice" of investment decisions sometimes responsive to political factors but only coincidentally related to market-indicated output requirements.[28]

A second and quite separate major problem is that the role of the state in investment has remained, *nolens volens*, larger than intended, while another large part of the banks' funds were earmarked under the old system and so are still, all but nominally, state investments.

The particular strength of the former "federal" banks in Belgrade was initially based, as noted above, on their inheritance in 1964 of the assets of the General Investment Fund, a *faute de mieux* solution maintained in later years because of continuing political disagreements about alternatives. With these assets, however, came obligations—those expensive commitments to slow-maturing major investments, primarily in infrastructure, which had been made on the eve of the reform and on the assumption of continuing high growth rates, and which now had to be honored in a period of recession, recession-restricted availability of other investment funds, and inflation-derived cost overruns. These commitments therefore took an ever larger rather than a smaller portion of the banks' funds. In addition, the state had reserved the right to earmark future repayments by enterprises of credits granted from the former social-investment funds and used this right extensively to finance the residual federal incentive subsidies represented by a peculiar post-reform device called "extra-budgetary funds" (only partly liquidated after a major political discussion in 1971). This device, added to the trend back toward an increasing tax burden on enterprises after 1967, further limited the proportion and absolute value of the funds for autonomous investment at the disposal of either enterprises or banks. The net result was a de facto recentralization of a portion of national savings for redistribution by the state and thereby a partial reversion to, or retention of, the old system.

As a final complication, the ethnic and regional prejudices of all those involved in investment decision making—whether enterprises, banks, or state organs—continued severely to restrict interregional free circulation of capital and pooling of investable resources on a wide basis. These, too, were primary goals of the reform, essential both to the creation of a genuine, all-Yugoslav capital market and to any hope that backward regions, poor in capital but often rich in natural resources, would ever catch up with the relatively well-developed north and west.

Meanwhile, the power and behavior of the big banks and of enterprises enjoying a monopoly or oligopoly of the domestic market, like that of a handful of "socialist conglomerates," especially in the import-export business and some with foreign subsidiaries in the capitalist West, was also suggesting that in this sector, too, "laissez-faire socialism" would display most of the vices as well as some of the virtues of its capitalist counterpart.

Such behavior, but even more the prolonged recession after the reform, has led the regime back toward more interventions in the economy—again not without ironic analogies in the recent experience of some Western "capitalist" states having administrations pledged to do the opposite. The first result was a period of renewed (if uneven) growth accompanied by an unacceptable rate of inflation and an explosive foreign-trade deficit. This was followed in 1970–71 by efforts at stabilization that were only partly effective in that they restricted growth but not inflation (also a familiar phenomenon in some Western states!) and contributed to a crisis of illiquidity in many enterprises and sectors so severe that their workers suffered weeks (or even months) of payless paydays, leading to increasing industrial unrest and to a number of wildcat strikes. Finally, since the beginning of 1972, more favorable trends have been observed, especially in foreign trade, where they are no doubt helped by inflation rates in Yugoslavia's principal trading partners high enough to offset, at least in part, the Yugoslavs' failure to bring down their own rate by more than a few points.

The growth rate of the Social Product in the four years of 1968–71 again averaged 8 percent per year, with a high of 10 percent in 1969 (which preliminary data suggested would be equalled in 1972). Industrial output in these four years grew by 43 percent, compared with 20 percent in the recession years of 1965–68; it now stood at 675 percent of the 1952 level. Employment, which had continued to stagnate through 1968, the first year of recovery, began to grow again at an average annual rate of about 4 percent. The official cost-of-living index, however, increased by 5 percent in 1968, by 8 percent in 1969, by 11 percent in 1970, and by 16 percent in 1971 and the first half of 1972, while real increases were thought by most observers to be even higher. Neither a price freeze imposed in 1970 nor a "deep freeze" (sic) in 1971 proved effective. In foreign trade the gap between exports and imports grew until the balance-of-trade deficit in 1971 amounted to a record $1,437 million (out of a total turnover of $5 billon), while the percentage of imports covered by exports dropped from a high of 84.7 percent in 1965, and 73.3 percent in 1967, to 55.5 percent in 1971. Despite a growing surplus in invisibles (particularly tourism and remittances from workers abroad), the balance-of-payments deficit continued to grow through 1971, when it reached $434 million.

It was these last indices that took a remarkably favorable turn in 1972. Exports grew by about 20 percent while imports declined by about 12 percent, so that the value of exports again covered about 75 percent of the import bill. Invisible earnings did even better, reaching a record of $1.56 billion, an increase of 23 percent over 1971; $870 million of this total was remitted by Yugoslav workers abroad, and $470 million came from tourism. (As recently as 1966, equivalent figures had been $96 million from workers' remittances, $117 million from tourism, and a total of $261 million.) The net result was a balance-of-payments surplus of about $250 million, the first since 1965 (when there was a surplus of $23 million) and an all-time record.[29]

While two devaluations of the dinar in 1971 (by 16.66 percent in January and by 11.76 percent against the dollar and 18.73 percent against gold in December) and the government's renewed efforts at stabilization in October undoubtedly played a role, as did other, sometimes external factors, these trends may well be a sign that the agony of readjustment imposed by the reforms is at last paying dividends. Serious problems, both old and new, remained, however, and were enumerated by one of the party's leading economic experts, Kiro Gligorov, at a late October, 1972, meeting of the Party Presidium that was called to discuss stabilization. In addition to the still critical problem of illiquidity, Gligorov's list included "expenditures beyond possibilities, the predominance of state and bank capital in the economy, lack of coordination and equality between the market and self-management, alienation of surplus value, lack of control over economic activities abroad, and lack of responsibility."[30]

These were still manifestations of deeper structural and psychological problems, which Dušan Bilandžić, a social scientist working in the federal party apparatus, had described in 1969:

... in many environments one still thought and conducted business as formerly. The tendency toward closed enterprises and markets was still strongly expressed and an autarchic approach in the development policy of individual regions was still present, as well as insistence on large projects of doubtful economic potential, etc. Slowness, uncertainty, and inconsistency in the realization of the purposes of the reform exist. In parts of the economy there were instances of opposition to acceptance of wider responsibility and demands that problems be solved frfom the center, by the old methods.

A particular problem is the conspicuous nonimplementation of the reform in the noneconomic sphere, which increasingly imposes limits on a more rapid development of both the economy and the standard of living. Concentration of financial means in banks is not always economically motivated, nor are the banks in a position to do business under the immediate control of their depositors. Modernization of the economy proceeds more slowly than was foreseen, as does the process of creating one's own and integrating modern techniques and technology. And alongside significant results in integration into international commerce, there continue to be problems because of the growth of imports without sufficient links with production and export potential. Foreign currency reserves are unsatisfactory.[31]

On the other hand, the same author has described some significant positive results:

> The reform had given a number of new qualities, although with great delay: a new mentality and orientation on the part of producers; creation of a situation in which the basic preoccupation of the producers was how to produce goods which might sustain competition on the domestic and especially on the international market, in contrast with the former condition when virtually all production could be easily sold without regard to quality and price. The orientation of enterprises was based to a greater extent on their own forces, because the intervention of factors outside the economy in many areas were reduced in scope. A process of differentiation and economic selection had been opened. The greater influence of economic laws and a businesslike orientation based on objective economic criteria had been achieved.[32]

Perhaps this judgment is only partly true and the positive turn of key economic indicators since 1971 is still too recent and of too short duration to be taken as serious evidence. Nevertheless, it was at least too early for the kind of despair that had seized some party and business circles by 1972, when several leading personalities declared privately or publicly that Yugoslavia would never achieve the economic integration into the developed world's "international division of labor" that had been a primary goal of the reforms of the 1960s, and that they should, therefore, abandon the attempt and reorient their efforts toward the less-demanding markets of the socialist bloc.[33] Not only the trade figures of 1972, unlikely to be maintained, but also the changing structure of exports since the 1950s, and more recently the growing number of enterprises in modern, sophisticated sectors like electronics, which have successfully engaged in joint production ventures with leading Western European firms, all suggest that there are still sound reasons to carry on.

FOREIGN ECONOMIC RELATIONS AND THE EEC

The structure and evolution of Yugoslavia's foreign economic relations reflect the double "in-betweenness" of the country's status: politically in an uneasy limbo between East and West and economically poised between the categories of "underdeveloped" and "developed."

The geographic distribution of foreign trade since World War II has followed the vicissitudes of Yugoslavia's international political position. Thus the country moved from heavy and growing dependence on the socialist East (51 percent of Yugoslav exports and 46 percent of imports in 1948), through total dependence on Western Europe and the United States during the years of the Cominform economic blockade (92.6 percent of exports and 88.4 percent of imports in 1953), to the relative but fluctuating balance of recent years. By 1963 48 percent of exports and 41 percent of imports were in trade with Western Europe (and 34 and 27 percent, respectively, were with the six countries of the Common Market), the United States and Canada accounted for 6.6 percent of exports and 18 percent of imports (the latter figure still inflated by United States grain sales under Public Law 480, which ended the following year), while Eastern Europe and the Soviet Union took 27 percent of Yugoslavia's exports and provided 22.5 percent of her imports.[34]

In the following decade, while the value of trade with Eastern Europe's COMECON continued to vary, largely as an increasingly weak function of fluctuations in Yugoslavia's political relations with the Soviet Union and its allies, the growth of trade with Western Europe in volume and percentage was limited primarily by the weakness of Yugoslav exports to the convertible currency area as a whole but in part by the barriers to these exports, especially of agricultural products, imposed by Common Market tariff policies. Trade in 1971, with total exports valued at $1.814 billion and imports at $3.253 billion, showed the following pattern: EEC (including the countries then negotiating entry), 35.2 percent of exports and 44.1 percent of imports; United States, 6 percent in both categories; COMECON, 36.1 percent of exports and 21.1 percent of imports. (The non-EEC Western European states took 10.2 percent of exports and provided 14.8 percent of imports; trade with the "third world" accounted for about 10 percent of exports and 11 percent of imports.) An abrupt increase in the COMECON percentages in that year reflected a sharp rise in trade with the Soviet bloc, the result of a major Soviet trade drive.

The Soviet Union thereby moved temporarily into first place as a market for Yugoslav exports, to a total value of $268 million, followed by Italy (the traditional leader in most years), West Germany, Czechoslovakia, and Great Britain. West Germany continued to be by far the principal source of imports ($617 million), followed by Italy ($396 million), the Soviet Union, Britain, and the United States. The growth of COMECON trade, with prospects for further increases after an agreement on Soviet investment credits of up to $450 million was signed in October, 1972, was also in part a function of difficulties of cost and quality besetting exports to the West and worries about excessive dependency on a Common Market with unpredictable impulses toward protectionism. Yugoslav businessmen and most leading politicians have made it abundantly clear in recent years that they would prefer to trade with Western Europe if possible, the former because they know and prefer the quality of Western goods and currencies, and the latter because they are wary of Soviet intentions.

The total volume of foreign trade, though still relatively small as a percentage of GNP in a small country at Yugoslavia's level of economic development, has also grown impressively from a mere 115,509 million dinars (then about $385 million) in the dark days of 1950 to 443,757 million dinars in 1961, and 90,233 million new dinars (equals 9,023,300 million old dinars) one decade later in 1971, before the 20 percent jump in 1972 exports.

More significant as an indicator of general economic development and of the success of postwar industrialization is the qualitative structure of exports. Yugoslav statistics look at trends in this sector in two ways. The first examines "exports by stage of production." By 1961, on this reckoning, raw materials had declined to 24.7 percent of all exports, semifinished goods accounted for 37.6 percent, and highly finished goods for 42.8 percent. Ten years later, in 1971, the equivalent figures were 11.2 percent for raw materials, 31.8 percent for semifinished goods, and 57 percent for highly finished goods. Alternatively, grouping exported goods in accordance with standard international commercial classifications reveals the following changes (as percentages of the total value of exports) between 1962 and 1971:

YUGOSLAV EXPORTS, 1962 AND 1972

(In Percentages)

Class of Goods	1962	1971
Livestock, foodstuffs, beverages, tobacco	27.6	17.6
Raw materials, other than mineral fuels	13.8	8.1
Mineral fuels, lubricants	2.6	1.0
Animal and vegetable fats	.1	.2
Chemical products	3.1	7.1
Classified manufactured goods[a]	22.6	27.2
Machinery and transport equipment	22.8	24.5
Other manufactured goods[b]	7.3	13.9
Miscellaneous goods	.2	.1

[a]Especially basic metals, metal products, textiles, nonmetallic mineral products, wood products (except furniture), and leather products.
[b]Includes, of significance, furniture, outer wear, and footwear.

(On the import side in 1971, machinery and transport equipment constituted about 31 percent of total imports, classified manufactured goods 28 percent, of which over half consisted of basic metals, and chemical products, raw materials for processing, and foodstuffs just under 10 percent each.)

Finally worth examining is the list of principal exports, by value, and their principal buyers. The 1971 list, with its total value of 27,217 million new dinars, is headed by shipbuilding (in which Yugoslavia now ranks tenth in the world), to a value of 2,045 million new dinars and with Britain and the Soviet Union the leading buyers. Other export leaders include copper and zinc products (1,836 million new dinars, with the United States, Italy, and the Soviet Union as leading customers), machinery and electrical equipment (1,601 and 1,438 million, respectively, principally sold to COMECON, Egypt, India, Indonesia), fresh meat (1,384 million, of which 778 million to Italy) and canned meat (411 million, principally to Great Britain and the United States), footwear and outerwear (1,052 and 994 million, diverse markets), rail and road vehicles (986 million, diverse markets led by East Germany), and furniture (765 million, principally to the United States and West Germany), followed by such products as cables and wires, steel products, tobacco, and cotton cloth.

The assortment is certainly no longer that of a producer of primarily agricultural products and raw materials, while the distribution of markets contradicts at least in part the critics who argue that Yugoslav industrial goods are competitive only in the socialist bloc and possibly in the underdeveloped world. This last is not to say, however, that these goods are necessarily or always really cost-competitive in the West without subsidies and other favoritism. So long as Yugoslav producers cannot honestly calculate their "real" costs of production, because input prices are still distorted by administrative controls and only partly dictated by supply and demand on the market, this is virtually an unanswerable question. A more significant weakness is in the very high proportion of industries that are heavily dependent on imported components, raw materials, or both, making it impossible to increase exports or output for domestic consumption without also increasing imports by at least the same rate.

Meanwhile, Yugoslav economic integration in, and dependence on, Western Europe in general and the Common Market in particular, already evident in trade statistics, is further increased by the fact that these same Common Market partners are the principal sources of the employment abroad of over 800,000 Yugoslavs (3.5 percent of the total population, more than half of them in West Germany), otherwise largely unemployable at home; and of licensing, joint-production, and (recently) joint-investment agreements that bring them modern technology and management, marketing techniques, and, in the joint-investment variant, needed capital, as well. These countries are similarly the chief sources of the workers' remittances, the foreign tourism, and a large share of the commercial and investment credits that together have replaced American and other Western aid as the balancing factor in Yugoslavia's international economic relations. It should also be noted that it is income from these sources, as a substitute for $2.6 billion in Western aid received in earlier years, 1949–64, that still permits the Yugoslavs to go on enlarging their cake and eating it too, i.e., maintaining high investment and growth rates, despite inefficiency in many sectors, without the suppressed living standards (to extort savings from a poor population with a high marginal propensity to consume) and the ubiquitous coercion by a harsh authoritarian regime that have been characteristic of most other underdeveloped states (and all communist ones) that have had similar growth-rate success stories in the contemporary world.[35]

Recent trends in the value of workers' remittances and foreign tourism have been examined in the previous section. In both fields the Common Market countries are dominant, with Austria and Sweden the only significant employers of Yugoslav labor and suppliers of hard-currency tourism outside the EEC. Most licenses for the manufacture of foreign products inside Yugoslavia also have been bought from and provide links with Common Market firms—158 out of a total of about 200 in 1964, when this device began to go out of fashion with the discovery that it usually means the importation of obsolescent technology. Joint production and marketing agreements and direct foreign investment under a 1967 law permitting foreign companies to own up to 49 percent of the capital of a Yugoslav enterprise have more recently intensified this kind of commitment to the EEC. Most of the meager $64 million that was invested under the 1967 law in its first four years (a disappointing result that has led to two liberalizations favoring the foreign investor, so far without significant effect) came from Italian or West German firms, though Austrian, Swedish, and East German enterprises were also on the list. The most visible sector involving such cooperation is the automobile industry, in which Yugoslavia's largest manufacturer (Crvena Zastava) has evolved from a licensee to a joint-investment partner of Italy's Fiat, while competing Yugoslav producers engage in joint-production arrangements with French or British automobile manufacturers.

The intensity of these links has induced the Yugoslav government to seek a formal relationship with the Common Market as a whole. The effort was begun in the early 1960s—participant observer status in COMECON was achieved in 1964, for largely analogous reasons—but was frustrated, first, by Yugoslavia's lack of diplomatic relations with (and the consequent hostility of) West Germany (relations were reestablished in 1967), and then by French reluctance to contemplate liberalized entry to the EEC for Yugoslav agricultural products, particularly beef and baby beef for Italy. It was thus only in March, 1970, that a Yugoslav-EEC agreement was finally signed, bringing concessions to Yugoslav meat exports, a Yugoslav ambassador to Common Market headquarters, and the establishment of a mixed commission to investigate other possibilities.

Uncertainty about the future of all aspects of the EEC-Yugoslav relationship, and Yugoslav concern over being so heavily dependent on the good will as well as the economic stability of a trading bloc that is both a demanding market and subject to powerful protectionist pressures, have played an important role, as already noted, in the nervous reappraisal of foreign political (as well as economic) policy recently going on in Belgrade. Ideologically pulled to the East and economically tied to the West, wary of the power ambitions of the former and uncertain of their ability to cope with the demanding market and unpredictable tariff policies of the latter, conscious of the fragility of heavy dependence on emigrant workers and tourism for domestic prosperity, but fearful of being left out between two great trading blocs, the Yugoslavs have reason to be nervous.

Meanwhile, already-achieved levels of economic and social integration with Western Europe, a token of accomplishment as well as a source of new or larger problems, would be costly to undo—economically, socially, and politically. Barring a major political upheaval, the future of socialist Yugoslavia's road to modernization seems indissolubly linked to the future of the European Economic Community.

NOTES

1. Rudolph Bićanić, "Interaction of Macro- and Micro-Economic Decisions in Yugoslavia, 1954–1957," in Gregory Grossman (ed.), *Value and Plan* (Berkeley: University of California Press, 1960), p. 347.

2. Dušan Bilandžić, *Management of the Yugoslav Economy (1956–1966)*, (Belgrade, 1967), p .127.

3. Gregory Grossman, "Economic Reforms: A Balance Sheet," in *Problems of Communism*, vol. 15, no. 6 (November/December 1966), p. 54.

4. *Ekonomska Politika* (Belgrade), Feb. 16, 1963.

5. George W. Hoffman and Fred W. Neal, *Yugoslavia and the New Communism* (New York: The Twentieth Century Fund, 1962), p. 243.

6. For one good summary of the consequences of these policies, see a series of articles on the background to the 1965 reforms by Krešo Džeba in *Vjesnik* (Zagreb), Aug. 5–31, 1965.

7. In a 1957 article quoted by Ljubo Sirc in Margaret Miller et al., *Communist Economy Under Change* (London, 1963), p. 149 n.

8. Yugoslav "Social Product" is a concept that excludes "nonproductive" activities like health, government activities, and many services. It therefore underestimates gross national product (GNP), as calculated in the West, by at least 10 percent.

9. According to most standard measurements. See Branko Horvat, *Note on the Rate of Growth of the Yugoslav Economy* (Belgrade: Jugoslav Institute of Economic Research, Paper and Monograph No. 4, 1963).

10. D. I. Rusinow, *Yugoslav's Problems with Market Socialism*, American Universities Field Staff Reports, Southeast Europe Series, vol. 11, no. 4 (May 1964).

11. The evolution of the "liberal" position during the debate that became

public in 1963 can be traced in many sources, including the weekly *Ekonomska Politika* (Belgrade), two Belgrade dailies, *Borba* and *Politika*, and the Zagreb daily *Vjesnik,* which was evolving into a significantly outspoken advocate of the interests of Croatian entreprenuers. Of special interest is *Ekonomski Pregled* (Zagreb), nos. 3–5, 1963, a 324-page special issue devoted to the materials presented and the discussion at a meeting of economists in Zagreb in January, 1963, which was the most important single forum for the general economic debate.

12. A Belgrade economist in private conversation, 1964.

13. An early complaint in these terms was voiced by *Ekonomska Politika* (Belgrade), May 25, 1963, with a table of prescribed prices as a percentage of total income by industrial sectors; by this method of calculation, 97 percent of prices were controlled at that time (cf. 70 precent of *commodities,* the figure normally cited).

14. For a helpful general discussion of the history and institutions of the banking system in this period, see Milós Vuckovič, "The Recent Development of the Money and Banking System of Yugoslavia," *The Journal of Political Economy* (Chicago, August 1963), pp. 363–77.

15. Edward Kardelj, in a series of articles on "Productivity of Labor and Tasks of Work Collectives and Public Organs," *Borba* (Belgrade), June 9–12, 1963.

16. An analysis of the extent and disincentive effects of this last aspect in a series entitled "Clouded Earnings" in *Vjesnik* (Zagreb), Feb. 12, 13, and 15, 1964.

17. *Borba* (Belgrade), July 15, 1964. For the evolution of prices in this period see Petar Krasulja *et al.,* "Kretanje cena 1962–65," in *Jugoslovenki Pregled* (Belgrade, January, 1966), pp. 5–9.

18. Speaking at the Zagreb Autumn Fair (*Borba,* Sept. 10, 1965), and again in talking with representatives of twenty enterprises in December (*Borba,* Dec. 26, 1965; cf. *Komunist* (Belgrade), Dec. 30, 1965.

19. Bogdan Crnobrna, secretary-general to President Tito, in *Borba,* Feb. 20, 1966.

20. For a normative description of the new system, see J. J. Hauvonen, "Money and Banking in Yugoslavia: Since 1965," in *Finance and Development,* no. 1, 1972.

21. From Dušan Bilandžić, *Borba za samoupravni socijalisam u Jugoslaviji 1945–1969* (Zagreb, 1969), p. 127, who takes his figures from *Privreda u godinama reforme,* published by the Federal Institute of Statistics in Belgrade, 1968. In the same official Institute's *Statisticki Godisnjak* (Statistical Yearbook), 1972, slightly to significantly higher values are given to almost all the same data.

22. Ibid., pp. 126–28, for all these figures. Other calculations differ in detail (see the preceding footnote), but show the same trends.

23. Ibid., pp. 130ff.

24. Mary B. McDonald, *Economic Development in the Backward Regions of Yugoslavia, 1953–64* (University of Oxford, Unpublished D.Phil. thesis, 1968).

25. A leading reformer in the party's highest organ told the present writer in 1969 that the authorities were perfectly aware of the shortcomings of laissez-faire economics in contemporary Yugoslavia ("We are not economic illiterates") but reform-induced economic stagnation, instability, and undesirable

"social differences" had to be tolerated for some time to come, until political and interest groups seeking a return to the old system had been destroyed or demobilized, "lest we go back to Stalinism."

26. For the political side of this story, see D. I. Rusinow, *The Price of Pluralism*, American Universities Field Staff Reports, Southeast Europe Series, vol. 18, no. 1 (1971), and *A Note on Yugoslavia: 1972*, ibid., vol. 19, no. 3 (1972).

27. The law appeared in the *Službeni list* (Official Gazette), Belgrade, no. 36, July 13, 1972. Opening of the foreign currency market, originally to take place in October, 1972, was still being repeatedly postponed "for technical reasons" in the spring of 1973.

28. Loc. cit., Nov. 16, 1963. Since the present essay was completed a new Yugoslav constitution, promulgated in 1974, responded to some of these criticisms by requiring a further reform of the banking system designed to make business banks genuinely responsible to their "stockholders."

29. These figures are from Zdenko Antić, "Yugoslavia's Invisible Earnings Increase Considerably," *Radio Free Europe Research Reports*, Jan. 24, 1973. The statistics in preceding paragraphs have been compiled from the *Statistički Godišnjak Jugoslavije 1972* (see warning in the footnote above) and other publications of the Federal Institute of Statistics, Belgrade.

30. Quoted from *Vjesnik* (Zagreb), Nov. 1, 1972, in a *Radio Free Europe Research Report* on the Presidium meeting, Nov. 2, 1972.

31. Bilandžić, *Borba za samoupravni socijalizam* . . . (op cit.), p. 135.

32. Ibid.

33. See, for example, Edward Kardelj's warning to his fellow Slovenes, who have come closer to the goal than any other Yugoslavs: "People who think that the solution is a one-sided link-up with Western Europe or Bavaria and similar ideas spread under the slogan 'our place is in Western Europe' do not at all accept the fact that, despite the economic progress achieved, this type of economic relations could turn Slovenia into a province exploited by Western European capitalism. It must also be asked, to what type of political dependence would such a solution lead and how would the East European countres react to such a separatist and antisocialist orientation." (*Borba*, Belgrade, Sept. 23, 1972).

34. All statistics for the period up to 1964 in this section are taken from D. I. Rusinow, *Trade and Aid at the Halfway Point in Developing Yugoslavia*, American Universities Field Staff Reports, Southeast Europe Series, vol. 11, no. 2 (February, 1964); those for later years are from the *Statistički Godišnjak 1972* (op cit.).

35. A Serbian economist told the present writer in 1964: "Having rejected the harsh accumulation techniques of both early capitalism and Stalinism, we must find a third way; I sometimes fear that our major success so far in this field has been in 'finding' American aid!" His estimate was that foreign aid during the 1950s had approximately equalled net new domestic investment in most years. If such a calculation is valid, it may be worth noting, as a very crude approximation, that net new investment (gross investment less depreciation) in 1971 was almost precisely equal to the $1,560 million earned from "invisibles" in 1972, most of it—as noted—from workers' remittances and tourism.

5

Malta

DALE DOREEN AND MICHAEL BARTOLO*

THROUGHOUT HISTORY, Malta's strategic geographical location
has made her important as a military base and as a commercial port,
and the Maltese economy has relied upon external sources of income
derived by providing services for foreign military operations and for
commercial shipping.

One might presume that this long history of dependency upon external
sources, coupled with a severe lack of national resources, would have
created some difficult times for the Maltese. Strangely enough, this has
not been the case. Relatively few years in Malta's history could be considered as economically difficult. In fact, Malta has always been a reasonably prosperous country. Throughout Malta's long history the world has
experienced many social, economic and political changes, most of which
have had favorable repercussions on the importance of Malta's strategic
location. As a result, Malta has never been forced to develop a self-
sufficient economy.

At present, however, there is pressure on Malta to create just such an
economy. The British, who for many years have maintained a large military base on the island, are gradually winding up their military operations
there. This fact, coupled with Malta's having gained political independence from Great Britain in 1964, is forcing the Maltese to consider
"going it alone" economically. Whether future changes in the world's
political and economic affairs will again be favorable to Malta remains
the supreme question in the minds of her citizens.

Thus, we find Malta today in a period which might be termed "economic transition," which involves planning for eventual economic self-
sufficiency.

---

*The views expressed by Michael Bartolo are his own and are not neces-
sarily those of the United Nations.

BACKGROUND

The Land

Individuals unfamiliar with the Southern Mediterranean area often mistakenly believe that Malta is a single island isolated in the middle of the Mediterranean Sea. In fact, however, Malta is but one of a group of three inhabited and two uninhabited islands known as the Maltese islands.

The archipelago lies approximately 58 miles due south of Sicily, 220 miles due north of Tripoli, and 180 miles east of Tunis.[1] In size, Malta is the largest of the Maltese islands, followed by Gozo, Comino, Cominotto, and Filfla, respectively.[2] Malta is 17.5 miles long and 8.3 miles wide, with a total area of approximately 93 square miles. Gozo, located five miles off the northeast tip of Malta, has a length of nine miles and a width of 4.5 miles, totalling approximately 26 square miles. Comino, which lies in the five-mile-wide Comino Strait between Malta and Gozo, has a total area of one square mile. Cominotto and Filfla are uninhabited tiny islets.[3]

In 1969, approximately 296,854 persons were estimated to be living on Malta, 25,915 on Gozo, and about 30 on Comino. The Maltese islands total only about 121 square miles, making them one of the most densely populated countries of the world, with approximately 2,661 persons per square mile.[4]

The Maltese islands are composed almost entirely of sedimentary, or water-laid, rock. These rocks are basically in the form of a sandwich. The top and the bottom layers of rock are composed of a hard bed of limestone with softer rocks in between. The order of sequence from top to bottom of the layers of rock which form the geological sandwich is as follows: Upper Coralline limestone, Greensand, Blue Clay, Glasigerine limestone, and Lower Coralline limestone.[5]

The limestone is a particularly important natural resource of the Maltese islands, for nearly all buildings in the country are constructed with limestone. Likewise, the blue clay is very important because it is impervious to water. This characteristic of blue clay has effectuated the development of a fertile soil upon it in addition to contributing to the formation of springs that help to relieve the historic deficiency of fresh water on the islands.[6]

The terrain of the islands is quite varied, often consisting of a succession of ridges and depressions. The ridges have eroded over time and, together with the downwashing of debris, have filled the depressions with soil. At its highest point, the terrain does not rise more than 800 feet above sea level.[7]

New visitors to Malta are often surprised at the extreme rockiness of the land, and by the apparent lack of trees and green vegetation. Though there are few trees and little natural green vegetation, extensive cultivation does take place in some parts of the island. To clear the land for cultivation, farmers have built walls with the many rocks that cover the soil. Since such an abundance of rocks exists, an amazingly extensive network of walls about five feet in height, runs all through the cultivated areas. Thus, most of the agricultural production is derived from the many tiny plots of land enclosed by these stone walls.

Gozo's land contains a greater percentage of blue clay and her soil, therefore, is more fertile than that of Malta. In addition, the land is less rocky than Malta's. Thus vegetation is much more plentiful and cultivation more extensive. A large part of the agricultural production of the Maltese islands takes place on Gozo.[8]

"Healthy" is a characterization of the Maltese climate often observed in various printed sources. This healthy climate can be roughly broken into two seasons: summer (May through October) and winter (November through April). Summers are hot and dry, while the winter months can be generally described as mild and rainy.[9]

A Brief History

Charles Owen has summarized succinctly what is in many ways the most important aspect of Maltese history—the interest in, the domination by, and the influence of a variety of foreign powers over the centuries:

> The strategic position of the Maltese islands astride the sea lanes of the central Mediterranean, coupled with the main island's superb natural harbors and a terrain favoring the defender, have long made these islands a coveted possession and during much of their history, a pawn in Mediterranean political politics.[10]

Recorded Maltese history begins about 800 B.C., at which time the Phoenicians were the most influential people in the Mediterranean area.[11] Although the earliest remains in Malta attributed to the Phoenicians date back to only the ninth century B.C., there is a good possibility that the Phoenicians arrived in Malta much earlier.[12] After the Phoenicians, the Greeks were next to occupy the islands, and they were followed, in their turn, by the Carthaginians and then by the Romans.[13]

The Romans are known to have gained definite control by 146 B.C.,[14] and they remained in control until about the sixth century A.D., at which time the Byzantines assumed control of both Malta and Sicily.[45] Probably the single most important historical event to occur on Malta during Roman rule was the shipwreck in A.D. 60 of St. Paul, who was en route to Rome to appeal a charge of heresy; while stranded on Malta for three months, he laid the basis for Christianity in the islands.[16]

In 870 the Byzantines were succeeded by the Arabs, who remained in power for approximately 200 years, introducing Islamic architectural styles and exercising an influence on the islands' language that persists to the present day.[17] From the Arabs, control of Malta passed to the Normans under Count Roger, and after the death of the last Norman King, to the Swabians (1194–1266), the Angevins (1266–83), the Aragonese (1283–1410), and the Castillians.[18]

In 1522 the Turks drove the Knights of the Order of St. John of Jerusalem from Rhodes.[19] To give the knights a home and a base of operations, Emperor Charles V gave the Maltese islands and their protesting inhabitants to the Sovereign Military Order of St. John of Jerusalem. This order, which became known as the Knights of Malta, was a powerful group of celibate nobles from all over Europe who were dedicated to helping the sick and the poor and to fighting Islam.[20]

The Knights of Malta maintained control of the islands until May 11, 1798, when Napoleon Bonaparte took possession of them for the Republic of France.[21] Because of religious persecution (and a variety of other reasons) the Maltese were not happy with French rule, and on September 2, 1798, they rebelled against the French troops in the city of Mdina. Unable to put down the rebellion, the French withdrew into Valletta while the Maltese appealed to the king of Naples for help. The British fleet, under the command of Lord Nelson, came to the aid of the Maltese, and together they eventually drove the French from Malta in November, 1800.[23].

On June 15, 1802, the Maltese National Congress issued the Declaration of Rights stating their acknowledgment of the king of Great Britain as their legitimate sovereign.[24] The Treaty of Paris in 1814 reaffirmed the Maltese allegiance to His Britannic Majesty and received recognition from the other European powers.[25]

The British, soon after acquiring Malta, began to perceive just how valuable her strategic location and natural harbors could be in helping increase Great Britain's influence in Mediterranean affairs. Lord Nelson wrote in 1803: "I now declare that I consider Malta as a most important outwork to India, that it will give us great influence in the Levant and indeed all the southern parts of Italy. In this view I hope we shall never give it up."[26] Similarly, a writer in 1888 stated that Malta was the strongest link in the chain that linked Great Britain and her possessions in the East.[27]

From the time when Britain first came to Malta, the Maltese were periodically granted increasing responsibility for controlling the affairs of the islands. Since World War II, moreover, the importance of Malta as a British military base has decreased with the advent of strategic bombing forces, nuclear weapons, and NATO. The diminished importance of the islands to Great Britain and the ability of the Maltese to control their own affairs were two significant conditions that led to Malta's eventual political independence—within the Commonwealth—from Great Britain on September 21, 1964.[28]

The attainment of independence in 1964 gave Malta the opportunity to be heard on the international level, particularly at the United Nations. In this respect Malta is credited with having initiated, in 1967, one of the most timely activities of the organization, which called for the declaration of the seabed and the ocean floor beyond the limits of national jurisdiction as the common heritage of mankind. It was this activity that eventually led to the convening of the Third United Nations Conference on the Law of the Sea. Other activities, further demonstrating Malta's keen interest in the marine environment, include the establishment at the University of Malta of an International Ocean Institute, which has been active in a number of research and study fields. Its director has also served as adviser on the Scientific Subcommittee of the Malta Pollution Control Committee, on the Malta Fisheries Policy Committee, and to the Malta delegation to the four-power talks (Italy, Libya, Malta, and Tunisia) concerning the central Mediterranean.

The People

The Maltese way of life has been greatly affected by the cultures of the many different peoples who have controlled Malta over the centuries, most notably the Arabs, the Knights of Malta, and the British.

The Arab influence is reflected in the architecture and in the Maltese language. The Maltese language of today is basically Semitic, and although it has been influenced in varying degrees by French, Italian, Spanish, and English, the Maltese can communicate quite well using their own language in Tunisia and other Arab countries.[29]

The Order of St. John of Jerusalem gave the Maltese for the first time a feeling of sovereignty. Although the Maltese people were completely subservient to the knights and had no authority to rule their own land, they were not responsible to a foreign government. The order was a community of foreigners living largely in Malta. Thus, the island became a self-governing state under the knights.[30]

The British gave the Maltese considerable freedom to govern the affairs of the islands to suit themselves. Indeed, the present form of government in Malta is modeled after the British.[31] The school system is also very similar to that of Great Britain.

The structure of the Maltese government, as specified in the Constitution of 1964 requires a parliament composed of fifty-five members elected from ten electoral districts on the basis of a proportional representation. Initially a governor general was appointed by Queen Elizabeth II, in her capacity as queen of Malta, on the advice of the prime minister. The governor general represented the queen and was therefore the head of state in Malta. Though executive authority was constitutionally vested in the queen, it was actually exercised by a cabinet headed by a prime minister responsible to the parliament.[32] The constitution was recently changed by an Act of Parliament to provide for a republican system of government replacing the above mentioned monarchical system. The change *inter alia* entails that the head of state of Malta will henceforth be a president instead of a governor general, said president to be elected by Parliament.

The Maltese are practicing Catholics, for the most part, and the Catholic church exerts a great influence on their lives.

THE ECONOMY

Historical-Institutional

Little is known about the economy of Malta prior to Roman rule except that during the period of the Phoenicians and Carthaginians the islands were believed to be famous for production of textile fabrics.[33] The Romans encouraged commerce and manufacturing, and cotton and linen cloths of very high quality were produced in Malta during this period (beginning in 146 B.C.) and were regarded as a luxury in Rome. Historians believe that Malta was probably economically prosperous under the Romans.[34]

Under Arab rule, too, the Maltese economy was a prosperous one. For one thing, the Arabs introduced advanced agricultural methods and new crops. In addition, the Arabs appear to have dominated the trade in the Mediterranean area at that time, and this probably benefitted the Maltese economy. The islands' prosperity continued during the period of Norman rule that followed the Arab period. Under the Normans, agriculture was improved still further, new industries were established, and trade was carefully regulated.[35]

The prosperity that had existed for so long during the Roman, Arab, and Norman periods did not continue after the downfall of the Normans. From the middle of the thirteenth century to the end of the fifteenth century, war, disease, and other problems beset the islands, and numerous records indicate that extreme poverty and insecurity were the rule during much of this period.[36]

When the knights of the Order of St. John came to Malta in 1530 they found very poor economic conditions and a declining population. These conditions were soon improved by the Knights of Malta, who promoted economic development in several ways. First, they helped establish relative security in the islands and thereby created a safer place for investment. In addition, they established Malta as a base for piracy, which brought large sums of capital to the islands.[37]

Because of the lack of natural resources, Maltese economic development necessitated large-scale imports and these, naturally, required foreign capital for payments, as exports were not nearly enough to offset the imports. The knights supplied much of the foreign exchange necessary for development, obtaining the capital in a variety of ways.

Firstly, all the Knights of Malta came from noble European families, many of which were very wealthy. As a result, many knights either received substantial allowances from their families or had personal fortunes that they spent in Malta to maintain lavish living standards. Secondly, noble estates were frequently donated or willed to the order by sympathetic nobility or by members of the order, which provided a continuous flow of capital to Malta. Finally, the order occasionally received contributions from various European governments. As long as there existed a threat from the Turks, Western European powers could be encouraged to contribute to the order.[38]

A large percentage of the knights' income was devoted to military expenditure, and such expenditure encouraged the establishment of new manufacturing concerns that were linked to military activities. One important industry developed to aid the military was shipbuilding. The knights helped finance the first shipbuilding facilities in Malta. These facilities were the progenitor of the present Malta drydocks, which currently employ more people in Malta than any other industry.[39] The cotton industry continued to provide an amount of foreign capital throughout most of the eighteenth century, though a decline had commenced by the time the British took possession of Malta.[40]

The economic rehabilitation that followed the arrival of the Order of St. John was certainly lopsided and was aimed at satisfying as much as possible the efficient operation of the order as against that of the country as a whole. During the three centuries that the knights remained in Malta there was gradual expansion of the services sector at the expense of the other sectors, particularly manufacturing. There was no hope that the Maltese economy, as it was then developing, could ever achieve self-sustaining growth.

The overall increase in the prosperity of the islands during the rule of the Knights of Malta was coupled by an equally significant increase in population. The increase was so great, in fact, that in spite of the impressive economic development of the islands large numbers of people were unemployed.

After examining the population figures for this period, the fact becomes obvious that the knights of Malta must have imported vast sums of money into the islands. To support such a great number of people in relative prosperity with several limited resources could only have been possible with considerable infusions of outside wealth.[41] Understandably, long before the British took control, demographic pressures on the islands' limited resources were noted, and emigration was being suggested as a solution as early as the eighteenth century.[42]

By the end of that century the primary sources of wealth in Malta were drying up. For example, the markets for Maltese cotton, by far Malta's biggest export at the time, were no longer available at the beginning of the nineteenth century. In addition, the income that the Knights of Malta had derived from their foreign estates and gifts from European royalty had completely ceased by the time of the French occupation of Malta in 1798.[43] Furthermore, Malta suffered economically by the introduction of iron hulls, which revolutionized shipping in the early 1800s; these hulls not only made Malta an unnecessary port of call, but also made Malta's wooden shipbuilding and transporting industry obsolete. The conversion to iron hulls by Maltese shipbuilders and transporters was ruled out, owing to the lack of necessary capital.[44]

The loss of income attributed to the declines in cotton exports and in the shipping industry, however, was made up by a boom in civil port activity during the last half of the nineteenth century. With the protection and encouragement of the British, mercantile enterprises and a large labor force, concerned with entrepôt, developed around the harbor areas.[45] Port activity was further aided by the introduction of steam-powered ships and the opening of the Suez Canal. The introduction of steam-powered ships enabled Malta to become a coaling station, while the opening of the Suez Canal in 1869 greatly increased the traffic in the Mediterranean. Furthermore, British trade with the Levant increased considerably during the same period, which further expanded traffic in the Mediterranean.[46] For two decades after 1870 the shipping business and port activity in Malta increased at a faster rate than did world trade.[47]

This expansion of port activity, however, had ended by 1891 for a variety of reasons, including increased competition from other ports and Malta's inability to make the right investment decisions. Moreover, the size of ships being built increased greatly and this fact, together with the introduction of the triple-expansion engine, meant that the newer ships could travel for longer distances without refuelling. Thus, stops at intermediate coaling stations such as Malta were unnecessary for an increasing number of ships.[48] The decrease in income that resulted from the fall-off in Malta's port activity was partly cushioned by an increase in British military expenditures in building up the naval and military garrisons. This build-up, however, ended in 1902.[49]

A census of population was taken in Malta on April 2, 1911. The results of this census were published in 1912 and included a statement that between 1901 and 1911, "productiveness has not risen in proportion to the increase in population."[50] Evidence of an economic slump during this period is clearly shown by the increase in the unemployment rate as well as by a decrease in personal incomes for the same period. The poor economic conditions that existed during this period led to the setting up, in 1911, of a royal commission to investigate the problem. The commission heard testimonies from a variety of knowledgeable persons in Malta between November 13, 1911, and January 2, 1912, and published its report in May, 1912. The following passage from the report summarizes the general problems underlying the Maltese economy at that time:

> For centuries the people of Malta have never been a self-supporting community. Their own agriculture, industries, and commerce have never supported them. They have always been able to rely on a large expenditure in the island of revenues drawn from outside sources. This has by no means produced a pauperized and parasitic population, but it has diverted industry from production for internal consumption and external trade to work for the Government and the foreign governing class. Before the British occupation, the Knights of Malta drew revenues from the world of Western Christendom, and the splendid and numerous public and private buildings of Valletta remain as evidence of the magnificent scale of their public and private expenditure. From the beginning of the British occupation a similar system has existed. The Government expenditure has more than made up for that of the Knights, and has diverted more of the labour of the population to the service, direct or indirect, of the foreign government, which applied it to purposes entirely imperial and unconnected with the special interests of the colony. Doubtless this expenditure has led to immediate prosperity, to an increase of activity, wealth and population, but the basis of the prosperity is artificial and precarious. A sudden withdrawal of the British fleet and garrison would reduce a large section of the population to idleness and starvation. To a partial extent this is what has already happened. In 1905, 9175 men were employed in the Naval Establishments, as compared with 5181 in 1911. We have no figures as regards the reduction of employment under the War Department, but this has also been considerable.[51]

The lack of local investment by local capitalists was perhaps one of the most significant findings of the commission. As the report put it:

> While capital is not wanting in the island to start new industries which promise a good return, yet, from the lack of initiative and from an exaggerated fear of local competition, capitalists decline to risk their money and prefer to invest in foreign securities—the more so as capital so invested escapes all taxation.[52]

The problems of the Maltese economy in 1911, as stated above, are

strikingly similar to current economic problems in Malta, and the commission's suggestions for improving the economy are likewise very similar
to the suggestions currently being advanced by developmental economists
concerned about present-day economic ills. In the main, these include
improving agriculture, developing tourism, and creating various incentives
for investment in local industry, including loans, grants, and guaranteed
monopolies.

The period of World War I was characterized in Malta by high inflation and a severe general dissatisfaction on the part of the Maltese with
the economic conditions in the islands, a dissatisfaction that culminated in
riots in June, 1919. The British reacted to the riots by allocating considerable monetary aid to the islands, which helped revive the economy
somewhat in the early 1920s.

At the same time, considerable attention was again devoted to the idea
of diversifying the economy by various means. Efforts were made to
bring about some diversification, including the establishment of some small
industries, encouraging agricultural improvement, and creating a tourist
bureau in 1924. These steps brought few material results, however, and
the economy continued to remain heavily dependent upon British military expenditure.[53]

General prosperity again swept the islands between 1923 and 1926, but
by 1927 world economic pressures had begun to bear unfavorably upon
the Maltese economy. Malta suffered depression and high unemployment
until about 1934, when world trade improved somewhat and the British
began to rearm and to build up their military strength in the Mediterranean. This military expenditure helped maintain prosperity in Malta
until the start of World War II.[54]

During the war Malta suffered considerably as a result of extensive Axis
bombing, which destroyed many buildings and disrupted large sections of
the islands' commercial life, but unemployment did not occur. In addition,
large amounts of capital accumulated in Malta during the war primarily
because of relatively high wages paid by the service departments and the
small amount of imports.[55]

To aid the Maltese in reconstructing the many buildings destroyed
during the war, the British government established a 30-million-pound
War Damage Fund. In sum, despite the extensive damage caused by the
war, the economy of Malta generally prospered during it, albeit on the
basis of a continuing dependence upon British military expenditures. But
in the postwar years, with growing political independence from Great
Britain and declining British military spending, the Maltese would find
themselves in a historically familiar situation: the need to diversify their
economy.

PLANNING AND STRUCTURAL CHANGE

Need for Development Planning

Postwar Malta has maintained a relatively prosperous economy. Evidence of this prosperity was cited, for example, in the introduction of the First Five-Year Development Plan published in 1959:

> The visible signs of prosperity cannot be mistaken. Sterling balances total more than 70 million pounds (including some 50 million pounds of Bank deposits). There is no public debt, except a minor amount of short-term Treasury Bill borrowing for working capital needs, and there has been no resort to long-term borrowing for development nor indeed any contribution from the recurrent budget to capital investment. This is an enviable situation not repeated in any of the developing countries of the world, save only those on wealth accruing from oil fields. Taxation levels are not duly high; compulsory primary education is free, as is medical treatment for those who cannot afford to pay, and there is a comprehensive social insurance scheme covering all the usual benefits of old age pensions, unemployment benefits and the like. Consumption of consumer goods is high and there are 20,000 vehicles on the roads (or one per 16 persons).[56]

Indeed, the Maltese could be thankful for their obvious prosperity. By late in the 1950s, however, they had begun to realize fully that the structure of their economy would have to be radically altered if they were to maintain it. The need for change became plainly evident when the British government announced its intention to decrease its military spending in Malta (a cutback that actually began in 1958).

The former importance of the British military to the Maltese economy becomes startlingly evident when one examines employment and income statistics for Malta. In 1957, 20.4 percent of the Gross National Product was contributed by the military sector,[57] while 27.1 percent of all persons employed in Malta were engaged in servicing the British military.[58] In addtion, the British services provided Malta with a great deal of foreign-exchange earnings (even as late as 1961, the British services provided 55 percent of such earnings).[59] These percentages have all been gradually decreasing each year since 1957.

To cushion the effects of the decrease in British military expenditure in Malta, the Maltese government, with technical and financial assistance from the United Kingdom, introduced economic-development planning. The long-term objective of such planning in Malta was (and still is) to diversify the economy by gradually building up the private sector to take up the slack being created by the run down of the British military in Malta.

The First Development Plan, for the five-year period from 1959 to 1964, clearly notes (in the introduction) the primary difficulty with economic-development planning in Malta: her very limited natural resources. "There are, in fact, only three: its natural harbor, and general geographical position on an air and sea communications crossroad in the Mediterranean; the skill and industry, and thriftiness of its peoples; and its equitable, sunny Mediterranean climate."[60]

In a report entitled *Economic Adaption and Development in Malta*, prepared by a team of United Nations technical-assistance experts headed by the eminent economist Wolfgang F. Stolper, the problem of the lack of natural resources in Malta is also appropriately stated. The report explains that the biggest problem with the Maltese economy is that the value of its major resource—its strategic position—has declined greatly. Thus, the problem in Malta is not exactly one of economic development as generally understood, but it is rather the problem of adapting to technological obsolescence. Malta's resources are not unique, nor have they previously been exploited to the degree that they have in surrounding areas. For instance, Malta's good climate can attract tourists, but it must compete with other tourist areas with similar or better locations. Malta has an excellent harbor, but so do Palermo, Naples, and a number of Northern African ports. Malta's brine and limestone supplies are not unique: many other places have adequate supplies of both and are in as good or better locations with respect to markets. Finally, if the relatively large population of Malta is to be considered as a major resource, then the skills and attitudes of the people will have to be modified if they are to contribute to the diversification of the economy.[61]

The First Development Plan (1959–64)

Realizing the limitations of economic development resulting from the lack of natural resources, the architects of the First Five-Year Development Plan stated the following aims: (1) establishing full employment and (2) maintaining (or possibly improving) the standard of living.[62]

To accomplish these aims, the plan listed four areas of primary concern: (a) to convert the naval dockyard to a privately owned commercial ship-repair yard, (b) to bulid up industry in areas with high export potential, (c) to develop the tourist industry, and (d) to further develop and exploit the agricultural sector.

To assure some significant development in the four areas of concern stated above would, naturally, require some incentive. The incentive was induced primarily in two ways: (1) by establishing a capital investment program to expand and improve the infrastructure of the economy, which would enable the manufacturing and tourist industries to develop, and (2) by designing policies that would encourage private capital investment in specified growth areas.[63]

The plan projected a capital-investment program that would total 32.25 million pounds over the five-year period. This investment was financed to a large extent by loans and grants from the British government. The British parliament allocated a total of 24.25 million pounds in grants, including 1.4 million pounds from the War Damage Fund and a 5-million-pound exchequer loan. Three million pounds were raised from a local government loan.[64]

The First Development Plan failed in its goal of obtaining full employment; in fact, unemployment actually doubled (to 8,000) during the five-year period. This increase can be attributed primarily to the accelerated run down of the British defense establishments in Malta and to the private sector's unwillingness to invest in local industry and tourism to the extent that the plan had envisioned. On the other hand, the plan was successful in accomplishing its goals in the public sector: its infrastructural programs were generally carried out, the legislative programs were accomplished, and its stated fiscal and financial policies were initiated.[65]

The Second Development Plan (1964–69)

In view of the less than total success of the First Five-Year Development Plan, the United Nations mission that visited Malta in 1964, as mentioned previously, recommended several goals that the Second Five-Year Development Plan should seek to achieve.

To summarize a few of the mission's recommendations, it first emphasized the necessity of organizing an economic structure that would be favorable to the development of a viable export-oriented economy that could eventually support its own growth. This, it predicted, would take between fifteen and twenty-five years to accomplish. In addition, such an accomplishment would require increasing productive efficiency relative to the wage levels at the time. This in turn would help Malta overcome the often relatively high costs of production and distribution arising from Malta's disadvantageous position with respect to markets. The mission suggested that efficiency would be increased by lowering import duties so as to help keep production costs low relative to Malta's international competitors.

Furthermore, the United Nations mission warned against maintaining employment in enterprises that were no longer profitable. Future investments should be directed towards profitable, workable schemes, aided possibly by interest-free loans but not by grants. Establishing a development corporation to include all agencies of the Ministry of Development and Tourism, which aids industries, and creating a central bank to help build up a capital market, were also recommended.

The United Nations mission stressed the importance of improving the efficiency of Malta's administrative machinery. Reorganization and increased planning by some government departments and decentralization of decision making were all suggested.

Finally, the mission recommended that emigration should be increased to 10,000 persons per year in order to keep unemployment low. They estimated that a public-investment program of 38 million pounds would be necessary during the next five years to keep income and employment at the 1964 levels. They felt, however, that such an investment could not be absorbed by the economy and thus recommended an investment of 26 million pounds.[66]

The recommendations of the United Nations mission, together with the anticipation of an accelerated British defense run down between 1962 and 1967, heavily influenced the objectives of the Second Five-Year Development Plan. Fortunately, Malta's political independence, which commenced at essentially the same time as the launching of the Second Five-Year Plan, established a much more stable political climate than had existed during the time span of the first plan.

The proposed accelerated run down of the British military in Malta provided some very ominous estimates of the income and employment levels that would result if immediate steps were not taken to counteract the run down. These rather pessimistic projections led to limiting the primary objective of the second plan to simply helping the economy to adjust to the accelerated run down, and in turn preventing a decline in living standards. The methods outlined for accomplishing the overall objective as stated above were essentially the same as those for the first plan: to build up an export-oriented economy by developing the industrial, agricultural, and tourist sectors.

The Second Five-Year Development Plan, like the first, was largely financed by loans and grants from the British government. Shortly after achieving political independence in 1964, Malta established a financial agreement with the United Kingdom to receive a total of 50 million pounds in loans and grants from the latter over the ten-year period from 1964 to 1974. In addition, the agreement specified that all moneys expended from the 50-million-pound fund during the first five-year period would be considered as three-fourths grants and one-fourth loans. Late in 1970, the same agreement was reached on the ratio of grants to loans for the second five-year period.

Total expenditure for the second plan amounted to 33.5 million pounds, of which 24.6 million were extracted from the funds supplied by the United Kingdom. In addition, 4.5 million pounds were raised locally by issuing a government-development stock. The electricity board contributed 4.6 million pounds, which it secured from its own resources and drawings on loans it received from the International Bank for Reconstruction and Development and the Italian government. Finally, the gas board used 200,000 pounds of its own resources to help finance the plan.[67]

The Second Five-Year Development Plan was an overwhelming success in respect to the objectives that it originally established. Over the five-year period the objectives of the plan, as previously stated, were to keep income as high and unemployment as low as 1964. The plan projected the 1969 unemployment level to equal the 1964 figure of 8,000, providing a high emigration rate could be achieved. In actuality, though, the economic conditions at the time of completion of the plan were considerably better than the plan's predictions. For example, emigration decreased and, in spite of the larger working force available, unemployment decreased to less than 4,000 persons.

The Third Development Plan (1969–74)

The Third Five-Year Development Plan established somewhat more optimistic objectives than the second plan:

> The immediate task of the present Plan is to achieve a rate of economic growth high enough (a) to provide jobs for virtually all who seek them; (b) to build up those areas of activity within the economy which can be efficiently developed and which contribute to the achievement of Malta's planning objectives; (c) to raise standards of living in line with increasing productivity of labour. It will be Government's endeavor to ensure that the required investment is made, in the right amounts and in the right areas and that no constraints develop in the investment programmes for lack of resources.[68]

Like its predecessors, the third plan emphasized the importance of development in the areas of tourism, agriculture, and manufacturing. To aid development in these areas, the plan projected a government investment of 49.2 million pounds and an investment of 21.9 million pounds by public corporations. The combined public investment intended for this plan, therefore, would equal about 71 million pounds, which is nearly double the 38.4-million-pound investment for the Second Five-Year Plan.

A large percentage of the plan's intended investments was again expected to be financed by loans and grants from the British government. A small percentage was also to come from a loan from the Italian government, while the remaining funds were to be raised locally.

In June, 1971, when the Labour party took control of the Maltese government from the Nationalists, it demanded that the terms of the United Kingdom Defence Agreement be renegotiated. On March 26, 1972, after painstaking negotiations, a new seven-year agreement involving a substantial increase in the sum paid by the United Kingdom and the other NATO countries as rent for their military bases in Malta was signed. The Labour party is also actively seeking assistance from other quarters to ensure that by the end of the present defense agreement (1979) the economy of the country will be earning enough foreign exchange to become economically independent. For the present, the new Malta-United Kingdom Defence Agreement provides some of the money needed to finance the current five-year plan. Whether these political developments will also affect the development strategy is still unclear.

The Labour government replaced the third plan with its "Malta Development Plan, 1973–80." The objectives of this plan do not seem to vary much from the objectives of the previous plans, but they are more forcefully stated. The question of national debt, the magnitude of which has been noted, is given much more importance in this plan, and the figures given above, which were calculated on the basis of financing arrangements for the third plan are reduced considerably, although the problem of national debt is by no means solved.

The national debt amounted to over 40 million pounds by the end of 1974. In 1969, i.e., at the start of the Third Five-Year Development Plan, the national debt was only about 20 million pounds.[69] This 100-percent increase in just five years shows the magnitude of the borrowing the government had to do to obtain the necessary financing for development. This increase in national debt indicates that although planning is making economic development possible it has not brought Malta closer to economic viability. The current balance-of-payments account confirms this. Total imports in 1970, for example, amounted to just over 67 million pounds. This accouunted for about 75 percent of the debit side of the current account. The credits to finance this and the other 25 percent of the payments side of the current account were made up as follows:[70]

Exports	19 percent
Tourism	13 percent
U.K. Services Expenditures	18 percent
Grants and Remittances	25 percent
Others	25 percent

Exports, which must ultimately become the main earner of foreign exchange, still lag behind. Moreover, other extraordinary factors like the end of the temporary boom in tourism (caused by the United Kingdom's restriction of foreign exchange to nonsterling areas) are already having adverse effects on the Maltese economy.

Since Malta is a very small country, investment is readily reflected in visible economic activity, whether such investment takes place in infrastructural projects or in other sectors of the economy. It is no surprise that a ten-year public-investment program would change the economic structure to the extent shown above. However, it must be pointed out that the aim of the program is not just to change the economic structure but to change it in a way that makes the country self-sustaining and export-oriented.

It is clear, however, that "self-sustaining" in this context, does not mean that Malta must plan to produce locally all that it needs, but that it must plan to earn enough foreign exchange to enable it to obtain what it cannot produce locally. The performance of the economy, therefore, has to be seen more in terms of how much of the GNP it could transform into foreign exchange than in terms of total local production.

As pointed out above, Malta has hardly ever had any serious difficulties in meeting its international payments. However, the economy will be self-sustaining only when the credit side of the current balance-of-payments account shows visible exports and tourism as the main earners of foreign exchange. This is clearly not the case now, and it is just as clear that it will not be the case for some time to come.

The main obstacles to fulfilling the goals set in the Malta development plans are to be found in various administrative problems, the military-services run down, and other structural factors. In the Maltese experience, the development of institutions like the Development Corporation and the Central Bank, and the timely adoption of corrective policies may help overcome these shortcomings. A series of such five-year development plans should achieve, after overcoming the above-mentioned obstacles, the desired economic transformation.

There is no doubt, as will be shown below, that the economic structure is visibly responding to planning. But it should be emphasized that simply changing the structure is not an end in itself. The ultimate aim is to make this changing economic structure *work*.

Structural Changes

As indicated above, in the discussion of the Second Five-Year Development Plan, Malta's overall economic growth has been quite favorable in recent years. Table 1 indicates the total GNP in current prices, 1954 prices, and at factor cost, the yearly change in each series by amount and percent, which shows that between 1964 and 1969 GNP at current prices actually increased 54.9 percent, while at 1954 prices it increased 53.6 percent.

Table 2 shows the relative importance of the various industries which contribute to the GNP. The most dramatic change in the percentage contributed by a single industry is, as previously mentioned, that of the military services. The percentage of GNP contributed by the military service has steadily decreased from 20.4 percent in 1957 to 7.1 percent in

TABLE 1
GNP AND THE ABSOLUTE AND PERCENTAGE CHANGE IN GNP
OF MALTA AT CURRENT PRICES, 1954 PRICES, AND AT
FACTOR COST FOR 1960–69
(In Millions of Malta Pounds)

	1960	1961	1962	1963	1964	1965	1966	1967	1968	1969
Current Prices:										
GNP	51.5	53.2	52.4	52.2	53.3	57.0	63.0	68.2	76.5	88.3
Amount Change		1.7	–.8	–.2	1.1	3.7	6.0	5.2	8.3	11.8
Percent Change		3.3	–1.5	–.4	2.1	6.9	10.5	8.3	12.2	15.4
1954 Prices:										
GNP	43.1	42.6	41.7	41.3	42.2	45.0	49.3	52.8	58.1	64.8
Amount Change		–.5	–.9	–.4	.9	2.8	4.3	3.5	5.3	6.7
Percent Change		–1.2	–2.1	–1.0	2.2	6.6	9.6	7.1	10.0	11.5
Factor Cost:										
GNP	46.8	47.7	47.0	47.6	47.7	50.9	55.9	60.2	67.3	77.2
Amount Change		.9	–.7	.6	.1	3.2	5.0	4.3	7.1	9.9
Percent Change		1.9	–1.5	1.3	.2	6.7	9.8	7.7	11.8	14.7

Source: Central Office of Statistics (Valletta, Malta)

1969. Also significant is the increased importance of manufacturing as a contributor to GNP. Manufacturing contributed 7.6 percent of the total GNP in 1957 and rose to 21.3 percent in 1969.

Employment figures also reflect the changing importance of the various sectors of the economy. Table 3 again shows the increasing importance of manufacturing, which absorbed 22.7 percent of all persons employed in 1969, compared with 17.0 percent in 1961. Similarly, construction and quarrying have employed a large percentage of the labor force in recent years, while the British-services employment has dropped dramatically from 17.6 percent of the total persons employed in 1961 to the corresponding figure of only 7.7 percent in 1969.

The increase in the relative importance of manufacturing can be at least partially explained by the investment-incentive programs designed by the Maltese government in recent years. These incentives and assistance programs are managed by the Malta Development Corporation. The amount of the assistance depends on the size of the proposed enterprise and on its ability to increase employment, exports, and import substitutes. The form of government assistance to private industry includes grants and interest-free loans as well as exemptions from customs duties on raw materials, machinery, and equipment. Also, many industries are given a ten-year income-tax holiday on all profits.

A large portion of Malta's manufacturing output is contributed by the Malta drydocks. From the time the British took control of Malta in 1803

TABLE 2

PERCENTAGE OF GNP AT FACTOR COSTS CONTRIBUTED BY THE VARIOUS SECTORS OF THE MALTESE ECONOMY
1957–69

	1957	1958	1959	1960	1961	1962	1963	1964	1965	1966	1967	1968	1969
Agriculture and Fishing	5.6	6.6	6.5	6.4	6.9	6.9	6.8	6.7	6.9	6.4	6.5	6.8	6.8
Construction and Quarrying	7.4	8.4	6.9	7.2	6.3	5.6	5.5	4.9	5.0	5.3	6.1	5.8	5.9
Manufacturing	7.6	7.5	15.1	14.9	14.6	14.7	15.2	16.5	17.7	20.5	18.2	18.7	21.3
Transport and Communications	3.9	3.8	3.5	3.3	3.8	4.1	4.1	4.3	4.2	4.0	4.0	3.9	3.5
Wholesale and Retail Trades	23.9	22.2	21.4	20.4	20.1	19.9	19.2	19.2	18.4	18.3	17.5	16.5	15.3
Insurance, Banking, and Finance	2.2	1.9	1.7	2.5	2.8	2.7	2.8	2.6	3.0	3.5	3.9	4.5	5.4
Government Enterprises	2.6	2.7	2.6	3.0	2.9	3.4	3.3	3.0	3.5	3.5	3.8	4.1	4.2
Total Production and Trade	53.2	53.2	57.6	57.8	57.5	57.3	57.0	57.2	58.8	61.5	60.1	60.2	62.8
Public Administration	8.5	8.9	9.8	10.0	11.5	11.5	11.5	12.4	12.2	12.3	13.3	13.4	12.7
Military Services	20.4	19.5	15.1	15.3	14.7	14.0	13.4	12.0	10.8	9.2	8.3	8.4	7.1
Property Income from Domestic Sources	5.4	5.1	5.1	5.1	4.9	4.9	5.1	5.0	5.0	4.8	4.9	4.6.	4.2
Private Services	5.0	5.0	4.8	4.6	4.8	4.2	4.6	4.8	4.9	4.6	6.0	5.6	6.2
GNP at Factor Cost	92.6	91.7	92.5	92.8	93.4	92.0	91.5	91.3	91.6	9.3	92.5	92.2	93.0
Net Income from Abroad	7.4	8.3	7.5	7.2	6.6	8.0	8.5	8.7	8.4	7.5	7.5	7.8	7.0
Gross National Income at Factor Cost	100.0	100.0	100.0	100.0	100.0	100.0	100.0	100.0	100.0	100.0	100.0	100.0	100.0

Source: *National Accounts of the Maltese Islands for 1966 and 1967* (Valletta, Malta: Central Office of Statistics), p. 8.

TABLE 3

PERCENTAGES OF PERSONS EMPLOYED IN MALTA BY THE
VARIOUS SECTORS OF THE ECONOMY
1961–69

	1961	1962	1963	1964	1965	1966	1967	1968	1969
Government	18.8	19.5	19.1	19.7	19.9	19.9	19.9	19.8	19.3
Services	17.6	16.9	15.2	13.6	12.7	11.4	10.5	9.3	7.7
Private:									
Agriculture	8.2	8.4	8.0	7.8	7.3	6.9	6.7	6.2	5.7
Fishing	.7	.7	.8	.8	.8	.8	.8	.6	.6
Construction and									
Quarrying	10.1	8.1	7.7	7.3	8.4	10.8	11.1	11.0	12.3
Wholesale and									
Retail	12.9	13.2	13.8	14.1	14.0	13.2	12.8	12.8	12.5
Manufacturing	17.0	17.9	19.2	20.1	20.6	20.7	21.0	21.3	22.7
Transport	4.2	4.4	4.6	4.5	4.2	3.9	3.9	4.1	4,1
Personal Services	7.2	6.9	7.1	7.3	7.1	7.1	7.9	8.9	9.0
Other	3.5	3.9	4.6	4.9	5.1	5.2	5.5	6.0	6.1
Total Employed	100.0	100.0	100.0	100.0	100.0	100.0	100.0	100.0	100.0

Source: Central Bank of Malta Annual Reports for 1968 and 1969 (Malta: Central Bank of Malta), p. 24 and 14 respectively; and Third Development Plan for the Maltese Islands—1969–1974 (Valletta, Malta: Office of the Prime Minister, revised October, 1970), p. 51.

until 1959, these docks served as a shipyard for the British navy. In 1959 they were converted to a commercial ship-repair yard (this helps explain the large increase in the percent of GNP derived from manufacturing in 1959, as well as the large decrease in the percent of GNP derived from the British defense departments in the same year, as shown by Table 2). Many problems plagued the drydocks after their conversion to a commercial ship-repair yard, including a long-drawn-out dispute between Bailey Ltd., the company leasing the drydocks, and the British government. Eventually, the drydocks were nationalized in April, 1968, at no expense to Malta, while the United Kingdom granted the Maltese government 3 million pounds to aid the drydocks in further development and diversification.[71]

The closing of the Suez Canal in 1967 seriously injured the output of the drydocks. Considerable efforts to win additional industrial work for the docks have yet to prove very successful. This lack of additional work, plus high labor costs and rumored inefficient management, have led to heavy losses. In 1969, the drydocks lost 1.99 million pounds on a turnover of 4.6 million pounds. The drydocks are, however, very important to the economy, for they employ some 4,700 full-time and up to 700 part-time workers, which is equivalent to about 5 percent of the gainfully occupied persons in Malta.[72]

The growth in the construction industry arises from a sharp increase in the demand for dwellings by tourists, settlers, and the local population, in addition to an urgent need for factories and commercial buildings.

The strong demand for construction during the past few years has resulted in a sharp increase in building costs, which were 50 percent higher in 1969 than in 1967. Wages of construction workers have similarly risen by 50 percent for the same period, owing mainly to the shortage of skilled workers. Finally, the demand for new building sites has led to a massive land speculation, driving land prices up by as much as 200 percent between 1967 and the end of 1969.[73]

Although the construction boom continued to expand throughout 1969, latest statistics from 1970 show that there has been a decrease in construction activity. Both the number employed in the industry and the number of new building starts decreased significantly in that year.

Table 4 clearly indicates the growing importance of the tourist industry in Malta. The number of tourists visiting Malta increased from 19,664 in 1960 to 186,084 in 1969.

The importance of the British to the Maltese tourist industry is also immediately evident when one examines Table 4. Each year since 1960, between 65 and 76 percent of all tourists visiting Malta were British citizens. Italy, the United States, West Germany, and Scandinavia claim the next highest percentages, respectively. The importance of the British to the tourist industry in Malta partially helps to explain the rapid increase in the number of tourists between 1966 and 1969, as well as the decrease in 1970. In November, 1966, hte United Kingdom placed a 50-pound limit upon British holiday spending in nonsterling countries. Naturally, this restriction encouraged many more British to take their vacations in Malta, which is part of the sterling area. This restriction was lifted in January, 1970, which may partially explain the decrease in the number of tourists in that year.

The government has introduced various incentives to encourage private investment in the tourist industry. The construction of many new hotels in recent years, for example, has been partially financed by government grants. The results of this aid are clearly expressed by the increase in the number of hotel beds in Malta. For the years 1959, 1964, and 1968, the number of such beds available in Malta increased from 1,300 to 2,360, and to 6,100, respectively.[74]

The expansion of the tourist industry has had a very favorable effect upon employment, national income, and the balance of payments. Employment in hotels and in jobs indirectly related to tourism increased by about a third between 1964 and 1968: from 7,350 to 9,810 persons. Similarly, the total expenditure by tourists increased from 1.5 million pounds in 1964 to 8.0 million pounds in 1968. This expenditure as a percentage of GNP at factor cost increased for the same period from 3.2 percent to

TABLE 4
NUMBER OF TOURISTS ARRIVING IN MALTA, BY COUNTRY OF ORIGIN
1960–69

	1960	1961	1962	1963	1964	1965	1966	1967	1968	1968
United Kingdom	12,846	15,800	16,327	22,758	25,750	32,021	52,368	74,054	104,428	140,230
Italy	1,968	1,802	1,671	2,065	3,048	3,651	7,197	7,573	9,141	12,901
United States	2,223	2,267	2,363	3,351	4,238	5,404	5,459	6,681	8,671	11,221
West Germany	644	763	754	827	1,315	1,362	1,385	1,711	1,994	3,363
Scandinavia	195	205	153	341	358	469	466	436	817	3,921
Canada	255	247	237	322	369	500	618	824	1,622	2,238
Others	1,532	1,696	1,849	2,535	2,495	5,319	8,616	10,142	9,851	12,210
Total	19,664	22,780	23,354	32,199	37,573	48,726	76,109	101,421	136,524	186,086

Source: Central Bank of Malta Quarterly Review, December, 1970, vol. 3, no. 4 (Malta: Central Bank of Malta), p. 39.

11.9 percent. The increase in tourist expenditures also significantly increased Malta's foreign-exchange earnings and thereby helped relieve the loss of foreign exchange resulting from the British forces run down.[75]

The total number of persons employed in Malta decreased between 1961 and 1963, and then increased gradually from 1963. Similarly, the percentage of persons unemployed increased from 4.67 percent to 8.19 percent between 1961 and 1965 and then decreased each year thereafter to 3.66 percent in 1969. Obviously, one of the most important factors in the decrease in total employment and the increase in the percentage of unemployment in the early 1960s was the rapid run down in the British services.

Emigration per year reached a peak of nearly 6,000 in 1964 but has since decreased to a level of 2,648 in 1969. The decrease in emigration can be attributed to the increased employment opportunities available in Malta during recent years.

During most of the 1960s, wages generally remained remarkably stable. It was not until there existed a strong demand for skilled and semiskilled workers in the building and catering trades that wages increased significantly. Wages at the Malta drydocks increased an average of 16 percent in 1969, while those in the metal industries increased 12.5 percent, with promises for future increases of 7 percent. Wages in the textile industry in 1969 increased an average of 10 percent, while those of the 20,000 civil servants rose by about 20 percent for the same year.[76]

Prices also remained quite stable during most of the 1960s. With the increases in personal income in late 1968 and 1969, however, prices also rose considerably. The composite consumer-price index in Malta rose a mere 0.5 and 0.6 percent in 1966 and 1967, respectively. During 1968 and 1969 though, the index rose 2.1 and 2.4 percent, respectively.

THE MONETARY SYSTEM

Before 1949 British sterling was the only legal tender in Malta. The monetary system was dominated by Barclay's Bank (DCO), with its head office in London. Therefore, the National Bank of Malta and other local banks were influenced to a large extent by the Bank of England.

A local currency at a rate of exchange at par with sterling was established by Ordinance (1) of 1949.[77] Specifically, the Currency Notes Ordinance of 1949 established a Board of Commissioners of Currency, known as the Malta Currency Board, to be responsible for issuing and controlling the currency.

Furthermore, the 1949 Currency Notes Ordinance required the Malta Currency Board to issue upon demand Malta currency notes with a total value equal to the sterling held by the board with the crown agents in

London. Similarly, the board had to pay on demand sterling through the crown agents equivalent to the amount of Malta currency notes the board held in Malta. This provision of the Currency Notes Ordinance thus required local currency to be backed 100 percent by external resources, as was the case during World War II.

All transactions completed by the Malta Currency Board were recorded in the Note Security Fund, which was credited with the sterling value of all local currency issued (excluding issues made for replacing previous issues) and debited with payments of sterling made for currency notes lodged with the board. The Note Security Fund was held by crown agents in London, and according to the 1949 Currency Notes Ordinance, could be invested in securities of, or guaranteed by any part of Her Majesty's Dominions, excepting Government of Malta Securities. Ordiance XVII of 1959 amended this particular provision by allowing the currency board to invest in local government-registered stock up to the amount of 3 million pounds. This figure was increased to 4 million pounds by a second amendment in 1961.[78]

The Malta Currency Board had no banking functions and exercised no control over the quantity of currency it supplied. Its sole function was to guarantee the convertibility of the Malta pound into sterling at a known rate of exchange.

Given this monetary structure, the local financial system was largely oriented towards foreign investment. An individual had three possible ways of utilizing his savings. He could hold currency, deposit it in a bank, or buy securities. Ultimately, in all three cases, the banking system would probably channel the savings abroad. In 1965 over 100 million pounds of accumulated Maltese savings were estimated to be invested abroad.[79] This is a significant amount, considering that in 1965 the GNP at factor cost was about 50 million pounds.[80] Personal savings are normally about 18 percent of GNP and for the period 1954–58 nearly 85 percent of the personal savings flowed out of the economy.[81]

Such a monetary system could never play a major role in financing the development of Malta. A monetary system that encouraged most local savings to be invested abroad to the extent that it exceeded the flow of foreign direct investment into Malta was certainly not compatible with economic development. For example, in 1959, the year of the launching of the First Five-Year Plan, private investment abroad exceeded foreign direct investment in Malta by over 4 million pounds.[82]

Furthermore, under the old monetary system, the supply of money could not be regulated by monetary policy. Money supply was determined more or less automatically, as a function of the balance of payments and bank advances. If the banks reached their minimum "foreign-reserve ratio" additional money supply could have come only from a favorable balance of payments. The balance of payments was, therefore, the main factor in determining money supply, and since this was automatic, neither the government, the banks, nor the Malta Currency Board could control it. With such an indeterminate monetary policy, fiscal policy was bound to take a regulatory role, at least until the establishment of a central bank, after which some degree of harmony between monetary policy and fiscal policy would be possible.

INTERNATIONAL ECONOMIC RELATIONSHIPS

One of the striking features of Malta's trade with the rest of the world is the wide gap between imports and exports (including reexports). Despite a rapid expansion of exports and reexports from 2.9 million pounds in 1960 to 11.8 million pounds in 1968 (see Table 5) the overall trade deficit grew from 22.8 million to 34.1 million pounds over the same period. These persistent and growing commodity deficits, however, must be viewed within the framework of Malta's total balance of international economic transactions.

The source of foreign exchange to pay for the enormous trade deficit was mainly the United Kingdom's military expenditure reflected in the balance of payments as invisible exports by the government, consisting mainly of payments to Maltese civilians and servicemen, sales to non-Maltese servicemen, and costs of materials and contracts. This source was supplemented by international-investment income, income from tourism, and transfer payments.

As can be seen from Table 5, the main source of foreign exchange is changing. International-investment income, income from tourism, and transfer payments are compensating for the reduction of the United Kingdom's military expenditures. The bulk of international-investment income is made up of interest received by private individuals for their investment abroad (mainly United Kingdom Defence Bonds, National Savings Certificates, and gilt-edged securities) and of income received by the government from the Note Security Fund. Private transfer payments consist of emigrants' remittances and the capital imports by foreigners residing in Malta. Most of the official transfers are development grants.

The inflow of long-term capital is primarily utilized for development projects and the outflow represents Malta's financial investment and reserves abroad. The main feature of the capital account is that private investment abroad generally more than offsets foreign direct investment in Malta.

Though it seems that Malta is meeting her international-payments commitments, the absolute trade gap is bound to continue to widen. The growth in manufacturing will continue to require imports of capital goods

TABLE 5

MALTA'S BALANCE OF INTERNATIONAL PAYMENTS, 1960–68
(In Thousands of Malta Pounds)

	1960	1961	1962	1963	1964	1965	1966	1967	1968
A. GOODS AND SERVICES – BALANCE CURRENT ACCOUNT (1+2+3)	4,848	4,767	2,677	1,697	− 267	2,198	5,853	3,142	1,457
VISIBLE TRANSACTIONS									
Imports	−25,686	−25,700	−25,109	−26,695	−30,461	−30,516	−33,940	−36,053	−45,865
Exports and Reexports	2,928	3,648	3,151	3,802	5,378	7,097	8,680	8,288	11,778
Trade Balance (1)	−22,758	−22,052	−21,958	−22,893	−25,083	−23,419	−25,260	−27,765	−34,087
INVISIBLE TRANSACTIONS (2)	20,741	21,376	20,117	19,929	19,241	18,665	21,335	20,241	22,227
Government	20,066	20,713	18,983	17,276	15,288	13,934	13,494	11,986	12,802
International-Investment Income	3,392	3,169	3,769	3,955	4,132	4,261	4,184	4,513	5,249
Tourism	53	196	274	503	576	770	2,002	3,288	6,622
Other	− 2,664	− 2,702	− 2,909	− 1,805	− 755	− 300	1,655	454	− 2,446
TRANSFER PAYMENTS (3)	6,865	5,443	4,518	4,661	5,575	6,952	9,778	10,666	13,317
PRIVATE									
Current (Emigrants' Remittances)	1,438	1,287	1,344	1,168	1,159	1,913	2,720	3,986	5,738
Capital (Transfers by Immigrants)	523	516	482	542	471	649	1,300	1,395	2,336
OFFICIAL									
Transfers	800	1,126	686	381	872	1,910	2,381	1,211	1,380
Grants	4,104	2,514	2,006	2,570	3,073	2,480	3,377	4,074	3,863
B. CAPITAL	− 4,713	− 4,099	− 3,059	− 1,407	− 780	− 1,555	− 9,125	− 5,920	− 4,939
Foreign Direct Investment	+ 2,981	+ 1,351	+ 1,721	+ 2,636	+ 3,329	+ 3,418	+ 4,128	+ 4,221	+ 4,804
Private Investment Abroad	− 7,390	− 3,144	− 504	− 3,283	− 4,422	− 4,494	− 5,511	− 4,433	− 2,822
Long-Term Public Loans	—	—	—	+ 1,200	+ 1,259	+ 1,664	+ 1,988	+ 866	+ 1,700
Commercial Banks	+ 1,280	− 2,075	− 3,197	+ 625	+ 907	+ 659	− 3,834	− 2,139	+17,130
Central Monetary Institution and Government	− 1,584	− 231	− 1,079	− 1,335	− 1,853	− 1,484	− 5,896	− 4,455	−25,751
Errors and Omissions	− 135	+ 668	+ 382	+ 290	+ 1,047	+ 643	+ 3,272	+ 2,778	+ 3,482

NOTE: The negative sign in capital account shows increases in total assets abroad; a positive sign shows decreases in total assets abroad.

Source: *National Accounts of the Maltese Islands—1969* (Central Office of Statistics, Malta), pp. 38-45.

and raw materials, while the tourist industry will increase its demand for, among other things, imported foodstuffs. Furthermore, the most disquieting factor is that the main source of foreign exchange, namely British military expenditures, has continued to decline and will eventually disappear. However, the Anglo-Maltese defense agreement (approved in March, 1972) with the United Kingdom should guarantee adequate foreign exchange (from the United Kingdom and from NATO) until at least 1979, thus easing the international-payments problem to some degree.

MALTA AND THE EEC

Realizing the size and limitation of the local market and considering the importance of increasing visible exports, the Maltese government signed, on December 5, 1970, an agreement that aims at achieving a customs union with the European Economic Community. A customs union abolishes tariffs and other trade restrictions among its members and maintains a common external tariff. In addition, a common market abolishes restrictions on factor movements and, with some coordination of national economic policies, would become an economic union. There is no doubt that international trade is crucial in Malta's efforts to achieve self-sustaining growth, and in this respect help from the EEC is essential.

The customs union is planned in two phases.[83] During the first phase, to last five years, Malta will be allowed to retain the present quantitative restrictions for protective purposes and will, subject to certain important exceptions aimed at protecting local industries and government revenues, accord a phased linear reduction in its general tariff of 35 percent in three stages. The EEC would, on its part, from the date the agreement came into force,[84] remove quotas and other restrictions and reduce the common external tariff by 70 percent on all exports originating in Malta, with the exception of agricultural and petroleum products, and with the further provisions that certain textile exports would be subjected to tariff quotas.

During the course of the second phase, which is also likely to be of five years duration, Malta will be required to phase out her tariffs against the EEC, to dismantle her protective policy by the end of the period, and gradually to adopt the common external tariff. The EEC, on the other hand, will eliminate all tariffs against Maltese industrial exports at the very start of the second stage. By the end of the second stage a customs union will have been established.

This association has become all the more significant with the entry of the United Kingdom into the Common Market, since it involves a significant amount of Malta's exports and the bulk of its imports. It is still too early, however, to see how the agreement will affect the country's development, since being a partner in Europe may also have adverse effects. One adverse effect is that Maltese exports to the United Kingdom would suffer owing to the probable elimination by the latter of the Commonwelath preference. In other words, Maltese exports would have to compete for the British market with goods from the rest of Europe. However, the lowering of the common external tariff by the Common Market countries by 70 percent may increase the Maltese exports to the EEC, since most industrial exports would then qualify for concessions without the need of a change in the source of supply.

Curiously, the agreement does not include any assistance from the European Development Fund. Protection of various local industries would have to be completely eliminated by the end of the second phase. This is certainly a controversial point, since some of the new industries may not be able to survive the competition. The advantages that may accrue from closer cooperation with the EEC are great, but it should quickly be pointed out that the risks may also be equally great. What the outcome of this agreement will be is far from clear. What is clear, however, is that a country such as Malta, with such a high degree of dependence on international trade, should attach much importance to its terms of trade. The aim of the partnership, therefore, should be not only to increase exports but also to improve the terms of trade, i.e., the net barter or commodity terms of trade defined as the ratio between the prices of exports and imports. By means of a gain in the terms of trade, Malta would receive a higher volume of imports for a certain volume of exports, or conversely, be obliged to export a lower volume to pay for a certain volume of imports.

In other words, if the agreement failed to increase Malta's international competitiveness it would not be advantageous to all. Malta's problem is not, as in many developing countries, the deterioration of its terms of trade as a result of the price disparity between the exports of primary commodities and imports of manufacturers. It is the problem of competitiveness.

While having to keep low costs of production Malta has to look for markets, preferably in Europe, that are ready to buy at a price and volume adequate to give Malta favorable terms of trade. This Malta could easily do when its exports were mainly services rendered to the United Kingdom military base, the island having been more or less in a position of a monopoly. Now, however, with Malta having to go looking for buyers in the "free" competitive markets of Europe, it will not be easy to compete, and assistance from the European Economic Community will be essential. The EEC agreement was signed with this aim in mind. Whether this aim will be achieved, however, is another matter.

Malta's immediate objective is to obtain enough foreign exchange to effect the economic changeover as envisaged in the five-year plans. In the longer run, however, the objective is to create an economic structure that would be able to increase production and to produce enough foreign exchange to guarantee full employment and an adequate standard of living.

It is very doubtful that the present EEC agreement can contribute significantly toward this end. On the other hand, to negotiate a more meaningful association (as the present government is trying to do) Malta will have to prove that it can make a special contribution to the European Common Market. Malta is ideally situated to serve as a center of entrepôt trade—a bridge to the African continent—and this could well be its contribution to the EEC. At all events, it is only by making a valuable contribution that Malta may induce EEC members to allow her important concessions for an indefinite number of years, while at the same time allowing her to maintain a certain degree of protection for her industries and agriculture.

There is no doubt that international trade is of extreme importance to Malta. The gap between the imports and exports has to be closed if the economy is to become really self-sufficient. This will be no easy task if Malta has to compete for markets at a stage when all its trading partners have a commanding superiority in whatever commodities are to be traded.

The problems that are peculiar to Malta owing to its unique economic structure and stage of development are not the real problems. Such problems can be and are being overcome by planning. The other problems are the ones that depend not only on Malta but also on the "outside" world. The increase in total production, for example, becomes meaningful only when the excess over local demand finds markets abroad and earns foreign exchange. The alternative to exports in this case would be a decrease in production and therefore a reduction in employment. Malta's association with the EEC should ensure such export outlets. Moreover, assistance from the European Development Fund should aim, as much as possible, at strengthening export-oriented industries and at improving agriculture to facilitate substituting domestic food production for imports.

The size and position of Malta makes its economy highly vulnerable. Assuming that the renegotiated agreement with the EEC will aim at assuring Malta of markets for its exports at favorable terms of trade, the prospects of creating an export-oriented, self-sustaining economy are encouraging. However, as a protective measure against external fluctuations arising from the openness of the economy, Malta should never allow itself to depend too much on any one sector, no matter how promising the one sector appears to be at the moment.

The bridging of the trade gap (by increasing exports and by substituting some of the imports), the increase in tourism, and the "nursing" of agriculture, fishing, and local handicrafts should enable Malta to develop an economic structure diversified enough to adjust to external fluctuations and thus to reduce her economic vulnerability.

NOTES

1. H. Bowen - Jones, J. C. Dewdney, and W. B. Fisher, *Malta—Background for Development* (Department of Geography, Durham Colleges, 1961), p. 25.

2. J. D. Evans, *Malta* (New York: Fredrick A. Praeger, 1959), p. 31.

3. Ibid.

4. *Annual Abstract of Statistics—1969* (Malta: Central Office of Statistics, 1970), p. 11.

5. Brian Blouet, *A Short History of Malta* (New York: Fredrick A. Praeger, 1967), p. 18.

6. Ibid.

7. Ibid., p. 20.

8. Blouet, p. 21.

9. Nina Nelson, *Your Guide to Malta* (London: Alvin Redman Ltd., 1969), p. 175.

10. Charles Owen, *The Maltese Islands* (New York: Fredrick A. Praeger, 1969), p. 25.

11. Ibid.

12. Blouet, p. 38.

13. Maturin M. Ballou, *The Story of Malta* (Boston: Houghton, Mifflin & Company, 1893), p. 6.

14. Owen, p. 26.

15. Blouet, p. 40.

16. Owen, p. 26.

17. Nelson, p. 23.

18. Jeremy Boissevain, *Saints and Fireworks* (New York: Humanities Press, Inc., 1965), p. 4.

19. Nelson, p. 24.

20. Boissevain, p. 4.

21. Christopher Kininmonth, *The Brass Dolphins* (London: Secker & Warburg Ltd., 1957). p. 192.

22. Blouet, p. 160.

23. Kininmonth, pp. 193–94.

24. Nelson, p. 32.

25. Blouet, p. 174.

26. Ibid., p. 166.

27. Ballou, p. 2.

28. Blouet, p. 219.

29. Ibid., p. 41.

30. Kinninmonth, p. 161.

31. Owen, p. 21.

32. Edith Dobie, *Malta's Road to Independence* (Norman: University of Oklahoma Press, 1967), p. 238.

33. Ballou, p. 82.

34. Louis de Boisgelin, *Ancient and Modern Malta*, I (London: Richard Phillips, 1805), p. 7.

35. Blouet, p. 43.

36. Ibid., pp. 44–48.

37. Ibid., p. 123.

38. Ibid., p. 126.

39. Ibid., p. 129.

40. Ibid., pp. 130–32.

41. de Boisgelin, p. 109.

42. Bowen-Jones, Dewdney, and Fisher, p. 136.

43. Ibid., pp. 161–62.

44. Kininmonth, p. 195.

45. Bowen-Jones, Dewdney, and Fisher, p. 119.

46. Kininmonth, p. 195.

47. Bowen-Jones, Dewdney, and Fisher, p. 119.

48. Blouet, p. 187.

49. Bowen-Jones, Dewdney, and Fisher, p. 125.

50. *Census of the Maltese Islands* (Government Printing Office, 1912), p. xxiv.

51. *Report of the Royal Commission on the Finances, Economic Position, and Indicial Procedure of Malta* (London: His Majesty's Stationery Office, May, 1912), p. 12.

52. Ibid., p. 8.

53. Blouet, p. 190.

54. Ibid., p. 191.

55. Ibid., p. 214.

56. *Development Plan for the Maltese Islands—1959–64* (Malta: Department of Information, 1959), p. 2.

57. *National Accounts of the Maltese Islands—1966* (Malta: Central Office of Statistics, 1967), p. 8.

58. *Annual Abstract of Statistics—1958* (Malta: Central Office of Statistics, 1959), p. 8.

59. "Malta Needs Ideas," *Economist*, March 18, 1967.

60. *Development Plan for the Maltese Islands—1959–64*, p. 2.

61. Wolfgang F. Stolper, Rune E. R. Hellberg, and Sten Ave Callander, *Economic Adaption and Development in Malta*, (United Nations: Department of Economic and Social Affairs, no. 64-35557, Jan. 20, 1964), p. 3.

62. *Development Plan for the Maltese Islands—1959–64*, p. 1.

63. *Third Development Plan for the Maltese Islands—1969–74*, (Malta: Office of the Prime Minister, as revised in October, 1970), p. 7.

64. *Development Plan for the Maltese Islands—1959–64*, p. 7.

65. *Third Development Plan for the Maltese Islands—1969–74*, p. 7.

66. *Development Plan for the Maltese Islands—1964–69*, (Malta: Department of Information, 1964), p. 3.

67. *Third Development Plan for the Maltese Islands—1969–74*, p. 13.

68. Ibid., p. 55.

69. Ibid., p. 106.

70. *Central Bank of Malta Quarterly Review* (December 1971), p. 3.

71. *Central Bank of Malta Annual Report—1968*, (Malta: 1969), p. 33.

72. *Central Bank of Malta Annual Report—1970*, (Malta: 1971), p. 16.

73. International Monetary Fund, Malta, Part II: *Background Material for 1969 Article XIV Consultation*, (Washington, D.C.: International Monetary Fund, Jan. 20, 1970), p. 11.

74. *Third Development Plan for the Maltese Islands—1969–74*, p. 40.

75. Ibid., pp. 41–43.

76. *Central Bank of Malta Annual Report—1969*, p. 16.

77. The Malta pound is now allowed to fluctuate within margins of 2.25 percent on either side of the central rate for pound sterling.

78. Joseph Licari, "The Malta Currency Board," *Journal of the Faculty of Arts—Royal University of Malta*, vol. 4, no. 1, (Malta: The Malta University Press, 1969), p. 4.

79. M. Abela, *Malta—A Developing Economy*, (Malta: Central Office of Statistics, 1963), p. 18.

80. *Third Development Plan for the Maltese Islands—1969–74*, p. 18.

81. *Malta* (London: Commonwealth Economic Committee, 1966), p. 12.

82. *National Accounts of the Maltese Islands—1965*, (Malta: Central Office of Statistics, 1959) p. 409.

83. *Third Development Plan for the Maltese Islands—1969–74*, p. 56.

84. Apr. 1, 1972.

6

Il Mezzogiorno:
Southern Italy

DOUGLAS LAMONT

FOR MANY centuries the Italian south has been interpreted for outsiders by the Italian north, which has even given the south its name, "*Il Mezzogiorno.*" Within the meaning of this word are understood all the pejorative ideas traditionally held by Piedmontese about Sicilians. It is through the north's eyes that conclusions have been drawn about the south's society and its impact upon economic development there. The north's conclusions have been more along the lines of moral judgments than of well-reasoned, analytical arguments, and they have led many people to believe categorically that what exists in the south is "bad" per se.

It is a mistake to follow this intellectual habit. It is true that what exists in the south *is* different. The *Mezzogiorno* does have its own distinct philosophy of life, its own set of beliefs, and its own pattern for decision making. However, these are not necessarily bad. Instead they are the "given," the context within which the process of economic development must necessarily occur. They are a part of the milieu that will be changed whenever economic development does take place there. These two ideas are important ones to remember for purposes of discussing in a rational manner the south's chances for integration within the larger international community.

What follows is a description of the south's traditional social order.[1] Then there will be a discussion of the forces at work in the post-World War II period to modernize southern society. This interplay between tradition and modernization will be evaluated to see what has been accomplished in the south in the decade of the 1960s. Has the south become a viable economic asset to the European Economic Community? This is the question that underpins all that is said in this essay. It will be answered as the story of the south unfolds here.

THE HISTORICAL PEASANT

The *Mezzogiorno* conjures up strange, oriental visions in the mind of the outsider. To Italians from northern Italy, the people who live south of a line that could be drawn from Pescara on the Adriatic to Aprilia on the Tyrrhenian Sea are viewed as people who are of Mediterranean origin and are therefore unlike their conationals in Turin or Milan, who view themselves as Europeans. The people of the *Mezzogiorno* are considered to be quarrelsome, fatalistic peasants who are suspicious of all strangers. They are known to have a tendency to procrastinate and to accept with a patient resignation the repeated disappointments that occur throughout life. These peasants fear only some all pervasive, mysterious evil eye (*mal' occhio*), which can bring bad luck if traditional ways are not carefully followed.

Loyalty to their extended family has their highest priority. Status is gained by one's membership in that family. The father is the head, but the mother interprets the father's wishes to the children. She keeps the family purse, and she selects her sons' wives. When the father dies, the eldest son takes on his father's responsibilities and moves his family into his father's home; however, his wife remains subordinate to his mother until the mother dies. Should both parents die while the eldest son is still a child, then the godparents (the father's eldest brother and the latter's wife, or powerful neighbors) take up the responsibilities of the dead parents. In this way, the respect for authority that binds the southern family together is maintained and passed on from one generation to the next.

These kinship relationships are strongly supported by all the other families in the village (or commune) because almost all families are related to one another through blood or through marriage. There are very strong taboos against marrying some stranger from another commune. Thus individuals are bound together into a ritualistic web of social obligations that is exceedingly difficult to escape. The men live by a code of behavior that requires them to protect their family's honor and to avenge any sullying of that honor. In Sicily, in particular, this behavior pattern and its supporting ingroup solidarity are maintained by a brotherhood of silence about quasi-governmental functions that are performed by the *Mafia*.[2] The loyalty of these men to their extended kinship relationships (*i parenti*) gives them the ability to build up some personal power to counter a competitor's challenge. But since this is not enough of itself, they must secure additional power by gaining new vassals, by doing favors for more influential friends, and by getting one of their kinsmen accepted into the official establishment as a member of the *carabinieri*. They cement these sources of additional power by becoming godparents to children of weaker families and by seeking godparents for their own children from stronger families. These fictitious kinship roles, or the process of *comparatico*, give skillful men the power to intimidate their rivals and give weaker men the power to prevent outsiders from encroaching on their land. Only in western Sicily (Palermo) does this power sanction the *mafia* to kill rivals when the latter are too stubborn to make an accommodation. In eastern Sicily (Catania) and on the southern mainland the local *mafie* have not been sanctioned to kill their rivals, even though familial loyalty is strong there, too. In these two areas, more subtle means must be used to bring a transgressor back into line.

Loyalties do, however, become unraveled. In the south, there is strong intrafamily and intracommunal competition over property rights to water and land. Though such properties yield only very small returns, the rights to these returns are jealously guarded. The arguments over who owns a particular hedge, bush, or stone boundary marker are carried on from one generation to the next. Because such arguments have tended to become personalized, they have led to real and implied insults in which one side must avenge the other side's action on an eye-for-an-eye basis. These feuds have denuded villages of their men and have forced the remaining peasants to seek out the protection of their local *mafie* against those who have belligerent claims against them. Thus, the absolute quality of southern familial loyalty, which one finds so often in books about the *Mezzogiorno*, should be tempered by the realization that the competition for survival is also a strong force in southern society.

For most southerners survival means long hours of toil in the fields, where men and women work side by side with an occasional draft animal. (This is not true, however, in Sicily because Muslim customs are still in evidence there. Women and girls do not work in the fields; they stay at home, where they sew and carry out other household chores.) The work day is long; for those who have to walk several miles to their fields, the day can begin as early as three in the morning. Of course, during the middle of the day, when the sun is at its high, the peasants stop their toil and take an afternoon siesta. This routine is broken up by holidays that take up about a fourth of the days of the year. All in all, given the low state of mechanical technology that is available to the peasants and the slowness with which they work, the productivity of the land throughout the *Mezzogiorno* is very low.

Some men work as traveling artisans, as peddlers, or as small shopkeepers. Each is a specialist. Some peddlers, for example, sell only drinking water. They go out early in the morning to get snow from the mountains and bring it back to their village. These barrel-men, as they are called, set up a portable stand upon which there are glasses, a pitcher, and a bottle of anise for flavoring, and sell their water to the villagers. Other specialists sell herbs, leeches, and old clothes. Some are cobblers, locksmiths, or dressmakers. A person who shows that he is ambitious soon finds that he is hemmed in by the traditions that pervade all these occupations. If he presses his case, he is looked upon with suspicion by the commune because his new ways upset the way things are normally done.

This lack of employment opportunities for the ambitious person shows up in the abysmal poverty in which the overwhelming number of peasants live. Some live in a single narrow room.[3] Its floor is unpaved. In it are some chairs, two beds, a stove, a manger for the donkey, and a heap of manure in the corner. This is the poorest dwelling. One step above this is the room with a paved floor and a loft. It has a table and other rustic furnishings. Both dwellings have only one doorway, which serves also as a chimney flue for the smoke from the wood fires.

The poorest eat a breakfast of wheat or rye bread and a pepper or onion, a lunch of bread and greens or some cheese, and a supper of soup made of greens and beans. Those with more income eat some form of pasta without cheese and tomato sauce. Those with still more income eat their pasta with cheese and sauce, and may also have some meat. Wine and *caffè*, which is made from any grain available, are drunk as beverages by most peasants.

Their clothing is made of sheep's wool, which is woven in the home and sewn into clothes by tailors and dressmakers. Their shoes are wooden soles with a three-tie strap across the instep and another about the heel and ankle; during the winter they wrap hemp sacking around their feet.

Though poor, these peasants participate in games of chance such as the lottery and *morra*, or "the throwing of the fingers." On holidays they spend their time participating in religious festivals, listening to *contastorie* (or public storytellers), and watching puppet shows. Many of these shows are carryovers from ancient Greek, Roman, and Islamic stories. The religious practices, in which there are a multiplicity of saints and feast days, are also carryovers from the past. The evil eye and the black-magic practices associated with it can be traced back to pre-Christian times. Anyone in the commune could be possessed with the evil eye, and each peasant has a lingering suspicion of all others, because one who possesses the evil eye could hurt him intentionally. Amulets are used to ward off the acts of those who possess the evil eye and to correct organic health disorders that are thought to come from these same people. Sometimes the barber or the herbalist is called in. The physician and the hospital are looked upon with suspicion even when contagious diseases, such as cholera, are rampant. When the physician is called in or a peasant is taken to the hospital, it is only because death is near. In death, the relatives of the deceased destroy their furniture and prepare a loaf of bread on which the departed relative may feed himself as he moves from this life to the next. These, then, are some of the traditional customs still current in southern society.

In summary, the peasants are bound up into a web of social obligations that tend to use up whatever savings they may have set aside. A man cannot refuse to "throw the fingers." A family cannot refuse to prepare its dead for the next life. A commune cannot refuse to decorate the village for the feast days of the Virgin Mary and the local patron saint. A refusal to carry out any of these traditional customs would bring swift retribution. A man's stone boundary markers would disappear and his land would be encroached upon. His wife could no longer join the other women when sewing lessons were being given in someone else's home. His children would not be able to find suitable marriage partners. His family, having dishonored itself by not following the mandatory customs, would deserve no help from other families in the commune when the local *mafia* took action against the recalcitrants. This certain knowledge, together with the fact that most families were interrlated, has kept the traditional social order in existence through centuries of outside attacks from many foreign lands.

THE HISTORICAL OUTSIDER

The society described above took a long time to penetrate the south as a whole. As part of the Roman Empire and later, as part of the Eastern Roman Empire, Byzantine Italy's cities were centers of commerce and trade. They shipped the wheat, olives, and timber produced in the countryside to other areas of the empire; in return they received cloth, wax, oil, jewels, and spices for distribution within the cities and throughout the countryside. Although the south continued to be prosperous even during the Lombard conquests of northern Italy, by the sixth century it was beginning to suffer a long-term decline in population, as the center of imperial activity shifted further eastward.

In the eighth and ninth centuries, the Arabs came, and Amalfi, Naples, and Gaeta—though nominally owing allegiance to the Eastern Empire—were quick to expand their commercial activities with them. Amalfi was one of the key links in the triangular pattern of trade that involved southern Italy, Arab North Africa, and the empire. The goods mentioned above were the staples of this trade; and although the volume of trade did not permit a large amount of functional specialization, the skills handed down by painters, smiths, and decorators passed from the eastern Mediterranean into Western Europe through the trade carried on by Amalfi.[4]

In the eleventh century, the Normans drove out both the Greeks and the Arabs and Sicily became the staging point for attacks on the heartland of the Byzantine Empire. Sicily's Norman kings brought her prosperity, and the cities of Messina, Catania, Siracusa, and Palermo flourished once again, as they had in the days of the old Roman Empire. In the thirteenth century, under Frederick, king of Sicily and emperor of the Holy Roman Empire, southern Italy was used as a manpower reserve in Frederick's wars to unify Italy and Germany under his rule. The imperial troops were victorious against the papacy and the Italian city-states. The papacy called in the French to oppose Frederick, but although the pope "gave" southern Italy to Charles of Anjou, he never conquered Sicily, and he had to content himself with the southern mainland. After 1442 southern Italy passed under the long-term continuous influence of Spain. It was ruled first by the house of Aragon and then by the Spanish monarchy itself. This rule was interrupted early in the eighteenth century by two decades of rule by the Austrian Hapsburgs. The Spanish crown then passed to the house of Bourbon, and in 1735 southern Italy became the personal kingdom of a younger branch of this royal house. The *Mezzogiorno* remained as the Kingdom of the Two Sicilies until its unification with northern Italy in 1861.

Throughout all these successive changes in foreign rulers the south was experiencing a long-term decline in the amount of rainfall that it received. This condition brought about deforestation, which led to increased erosion of the hillsides and the creation of malaria-infested swamps in the valleys. As the land became less fertile, the south produced fewer and fewer exportable agricultural products. Coastal trade and interregional commerce declined, and foresighted merchants emigrated to areas in the Greek-dominated East, and later to areas in Western Europe that were in the ascendancy. Thus centuries of economic decline saw the south's cities become shells of their former selves, as the remaining middle-class population and the poorer classes sought economic subsistence as peasants in the countryside. Over the centuries, under foreign rulers, the south had reruralized itself.

Although the peasants worked the land, they did not own it. During the centuries of foreign rule, land had been grouped together into *latifundi* (large estates) whose owners, together with local *mafie*, controlled access to the south's very limited supplies of fresh water. The owners of these estates were the landed gentry, who maintained elegant homes—in the French tradition—in Naples and in several Sicilian cities, and the Roman Catholic church. The owners rented out their land to the peasants under a sharecropping system known as the *mezzadria*. The owners provided acreage, a home, some stock animals, chestnut trees, grape vines, olive trees, and some fruit for the peasant's table. In return, the owners received half the food crop. The peasants used their share to feed themselves and to barter the surplus for material to make clothes, for gambling during the holidays, and for meeting the costs of family deaths.

Unification with northern Italy brought in the Piedmontese, under the house of Savoy, and new laws that would affect both the landowners and the peasants. Church lands were redistributed to the existing landed aristocracy, the bourgeoisie, and some northern Italians. Because of this, and because of the liberal educational reforms of the Piedmontese, the church forbade its members to participate in the new national government. Since most southerners chose to obey the church rather than the Piedmontese, southern interests were not protected by the new regime as they had been by previous ones.

The Bourbons, for example, had not taxed food or other necessities. Instead, they raised the revenue needed to support their government services by placing high tariffs on all imported manufactured items. This had the additional effect of protecting the local industries that had been built up since 1825 with the aid of foreign capital and technicians. These industrial activities were in metallurgy, machine products, ship-building, silk, wool, linen, cotton, paper, glass, hides, gloves, and soap.

When the Piedmontese took over they eliminated all tariffs between the fledgling industry in the south and the robust industry in the north. Within four decades after unification the south's industry had ceased to function. It no longer had the Bourbon regime to protect it and to subsidize it by buying southern-made military goods. Moreover, it had lost virtually all its small southern market to northern industry, which produced better-quality goods. Finally, in 1887 it lost its foreign-export market in silk and other products, when France retaliated against the protectionist policies of the Piedmontese with tariffs that hurt southern industry more than northern industry.

Tied in with this was the fact that the Piedmontese used taxes on food and other necessities, such as the grist tax, to finance government services. Because of these higher taxes and because northern grain producers were now protected from both French and American competition, bread prices went up substantially in the south. Higher taxes and increased protection by the Piedmontese for all of Italy also caused rises in the prices of manufactured goods throughout the south in the four decades following unification. All in all, southern peasants found that the few things they bought or bartered for, such as materials for clothes and fish from the coast, had substantially increased in price. Given their obsolete methods of cultivation, they had little ability to increase their production of food and hence could not maintain their preunification standard of living. Thus under the Italian Piedmontese southern peasants were relatively worse off than they had been before under the Bourbons. Many peasants emigrated. Others stayed at home to fight these new outsiders. They became the "brigands" who were so famous for thwarting the Piedmontese government in the nineteenth century and the early part of the twentieth.

In 1922 the Piedmontese liberal democracy was replaced by the facism of Mussolini's "corporate state." The south became the place where wheat would be planted everywhere so that Italy would be self-sufficient in grains. This policy failed. All it did was to increase the historical tendency for the thin topsoils to be run off in heavy rains, reducing the productivity of the land still further. Though some attempts were made to build factories in the *Mezzogiorno*, the south remained fundamentally the peasant society that it had always been. Finally, during World War II, the Allied invasion and the fierce German resistance to it destroyed almost all that remained of the infrastructure that had existed in the south. Thus, nothing in the historical experience of southern Italian peasants gave them any reason to believe that outsiders—Bourbons, Piedmontese, Germans, or the Allies—could be trusted. Each in their turn had taken something from the south, and each had given back little if anything good.

In the post-World War II period, the new republican government of Italy decided to commit substantial portions of its revenues to the industrialization of southern Italy. It was forced into this because Sicily and some of the other areas of the south were talking about separating themselves from Italy. Investments were to be made under the auspices of a newly created La Cassa per il Mezzogiorno (The Fund for the South). Government funds would go into agriculture, electricity, water, transport, and new industry. Funds also were to come from Italian public-sector firms, Italian private-sector firms, and foreign private-sector firms. The Cassa was given the mission of promoting the economic development of the south. This meant that the peasant society would have to give way to a new middle-class society that would be tied to outward-looking forces in the international economy. The public- and private-sector firms were to be the means by which industrial jobs were created for the peasants so that they would have income to spend in a new urban-oriented market economy. Since the work of both the Cassa and these firms was to transform the peasants into new kind of men, the former were viewed by the latter with distrust and suspicion. The Cassa and these firms were perceived as simply a new set of historical outsiders who would take something else from the south, as others had done in the past. Were these new outsiders able to do what other historical outsiders had not been able to do, namely, change the historical southern peasant into an urban-oriented, middle-class man? This question will be answered below.

LA CASSA PER IL MEZZOGIORNO
AND STRUCTURAL CHANGE

As can be seen from Table 1, the south's economic situation did not compare favorably with that of the rest of Italy in 1951. Although the south made up 40.8 percent of the land surface of Italy and held 37 percent of her population, the south's gross domestic product at factor costs was only 24.1 percent. As if this overall picture was not bad enough, the south's contribution to industry, a mere 15.6 percent, was proof that the south lagged far behind the rest of Italy in a key sector of the economy. Why was this so? Again, the figures in Table 1 provide an answer. The south received only 15 percent of all new industrial investment. It had only 11.7 percent of Italy's manufacturing capacity. Its value added per employed in industry was substantially below that of the rest of Italy. Thus its income per capita was only 62.7 percent of that which the whole of Italy enjoyed. Clearly, the *Mezzogiorno* was economically backward. It had been so conditioned by the abuse of its land, by the traditional ways in which work was carried out, and by the lack of investment in both new industry and infrastructure that no short term solutions could make it fully integrated within the Italian economy or, for that matter, within the European Economic Community.

TABLE 1

THE SOUTH AND THE REST OF ITALY COMPARED BY
INDICATORS OF REGIONAL DISEQUILIBRIA, 1951 AND 1970
ITALY = 100

| | 1951 | | 1970 | |
	The South	The Rest of Italy	The South	The Rest of Italy
Area	40.8	59.2	40.8	59.2
Population	37.0	63.0	35.5	64.5
GDP at factor cost				
(1963 prices)	24.1	75.9	24.0	76.0
Agriculture	37.9[a]	62.1[a]	40.2[c]	59.8[c]
Industry	15.6	84.4	17.3	82.7
Services	26.0[a]	74.0[a]	25.7[c]	74.3[c]
Income per capita	62.7	121.9	62.5	121.2
New Industrial Investment	15.0	84.3	26.0	74.0
Value added per employed in agriculture	89.3[a]	108.9[a]	84.0[c]	115.0[c]
Value added per employed in industry	76.9[a]	106.9[a]	70.4[c]	109.1[c]
Total employment	33.0	67.9	30.6	69.4
Employment in agriculture	42.2[a]	57.8[a]	47.9[c]	52.1[c]
Employment in industry	22.5	77.5	23.2	76.8
Manufacturing capacity	11.7[b]	88.3[b]	12.9[d]	87.1[d]

[a]1951–53 average.   [b]1960.   [c]1967–69 average.   [d]1969.

Source: ISTAT Yearbook of National Accounts, ISTAT Statistical Yearbook; *OECD Economic Surveys—Italy* (July, 1971, and November, 1972); and Francisco Forte, "It Takes More Than Industry to Stamp Out the Mafia." *Successo*, 13: 6 (June, 1971): pp. 109–120, 159. Reprinted with permission from Douglas F. Lamont, *Managing Foreign Investment in Southern Italy* (New York: Praeger, 1973), p. 21, Table 3.1.

The Cassa was given the authority to spend $2 billion from 1951 to 1957, $3 billion from 1957 to 1961, $4.8 billion from 1961 to 1970, and $10.9 billion from 1970 to 1975—a total of $20.7 billion.[5] Between 10 and 25 percent of this amount has not been spent because of the bureaucracy's inability to do so. This so-called *residui passivi* is hopelessly lost somewhere in the ministries of the Italian government.

With about $16.5 billion, the Cassa had to accomplish the following during this period:[6]

    (1) to increase the livestock/cereal ratio within total agricultural production;

    (2) to raise the proportion of industrial to agricultural activity;

    (3) to increase the proportion of larger-scale industry relative to small industry;

    (4) to raise the proportion of more technologically advanced industry relative to light industry; and

    (5) to increase the region's dependency on foreign trade.

The results achieved by the Cassa from 1951 to 1972 can be observed more clearly if this twenty-two-year period is divided into four periods of time that reflect accurately the changing investment pattern followed by the Cassa. From 1950 to 1957 the Cassa spent most of its funds for land reclamation, irrigation, flood control, and the transformation of large landed estates into small peasant-owned farms. Southern peasants were encouraged to form cooperatives so that they could better market their citrus fruits and vegetables in the north. However, the noble families of Sicily resisted the breaking up of their estates and the construction of the dams that would have destroyed their control over the supply of water. The national government was unable to find an effective force against the local *mafie's* support of these families. The industrialization program, though a very small part of the Cassa's investment plan, had a limited amount of success and some industry was brought into the south. However, the north grew only slightly faster than the south, and these investment programs in agriculture and industry were barely enough to help the south maintain its relative position within the Italian economy. Between 1951 and 1954 per-capita real income in the south increased at an average annual rate of 3 percent; between 1955 and 1957 it increased by 4.4 percent.[7] There were indications that southern peasants were spending the additional money on meat and on better furnishings for their homes.

During the years from 1957 to 1962, the Cassa introduced an incentive program to bring industrialization to the south. The following types of incentives were offered to firms that were willing to make industrial investments in the south: first, 50 percent of retained earnings, if reinvested in the south, were tax exempt; second, interest rate subsidies were made available to firms looking for additional funds; third, these firms could receive the capital grant that would cover 20 percent of the cost of constructing a new building and 10 percent of the cost of the new fixed equipment for that building; and fourth, buildings that were owned by the Cassa could be rented at a nominal cost. Between 1959 and 1962 per-capita real income in the south increased at an average annual rate of 6.9 percent.[8] The value added by the industrial sector increased from 29.5 percent to 32.8 percent, and the value added from the service sector increased from 27.2 percent to 35.3 percent.[9] And too, the percentage of the work force employed in the secondary sector increased from 23.8 percent in 1954 to 34 percent in 1963.[10] Although the south was showing some definite signs of economic improvement, it was still lagging behind the north. In 1964, for example, 45 percent of Italy's total net domestic product came from manufacturing, mining, construction, and utilities; in the same year, however, these same sectors supplied only 29 percent of the south's total net domestic product.[11]

In the period from 1962 to 1971 and especially after 1965, when the Cassa's life was extended for another fifteen years, a concentrated effort was made to industrialize only a few selected sites (or growth poles) in the region. After 1965 33.5 percent of the Cassa's funds had to be spent on these industrial projects. Agriculture's portion declined to 24 percent. These investment funds did not come from within the south itself, but came instead from taxes levied on the prosperous north by the national government. This meant that the south had been unable to provide itself with its own internal source of investment capital and that economic development in the south had not become self-generating.

The one bright spot in the economic picture is that there has been a secular decline in the percentage of the south's work force that is employed in agriculture from 47 percent in 1952, to 43.2 percent in 1961, and to 34 percent in 1969.[12] This exodus from the farm has shown up in the secular increase in the percentage of the work force employed in industrial sectors from 25 percent in 1952 to 31 percent in 1969,[13] and in the percentage of the work force employed in the services sector from 28 percent in 1952 to 35 percent in 1969.[14] In the latter sector there has been a more than average increase in the employment of the otherwise unemployable white-collar worker by the regional and national governments.

Disguised unemployment is also prevalent in the industrial sector. Capital-intensive manufacturing firms, which were financed by the Cassa, have also been encouraged to make work for the blue-collar worker. These increases in work forces at petrochemical plants, steel mills, and tire factories are almost invariably additional gardeners employed to beautify the plants' surroundings.

The decline in importance of agriculture's share of the total work force reflects the following points. First, many southern peasants have given up their age-old battle with the south's land. Instead, they have moved to central and northern Italy to take over farms that were in the process of being abandoned as their former residents became attracted to the cities. Second, the young men who would have done most of the very hard work on the south's land have opted for emigration to the north or elsewhere in Europe. Those who have remained in the region have found that they can lead a better life on the remittances of their relatives in the north than by scraping a living out of the land. Third, all the Cassa's programs for agriculture pointed towards increasing the size of the unit of land so that production could be mechanized. Those who wanted to remain on the land were indeed excess inputs to the production process. Finally, there were new opportunities in the cities of the south in industry and government service. Through nationwide radio and television the peasant was attracted not only by the slim possibility that there were jobs available but also by the "brilliance" of city life. Even if the jobs did not materialize, unemployment in the city, with all its modern gadgets, was preferable to the monotonous life of the rural countryside.

Though a long-term decline in the percentage of the work force employed in agriculture is one indicator of economic development, it should be interpreted here only as follows. The south experienced some economic growth from 1952 to 1969. This advance was sufficient to prevent it from falling further behind the north. If the south had been a separate country and we were able to calculate the average annual real increase in its gross national product there is every reason to believe that it would be no lower than one percentage point below that of Italy as a whole. From 1952 to 1958 the average annual real growth of Italy's GNP was 5.7 percent,[15] and from 1961 to 1971 it was 4.9 percent.[16] An indicated regional growth rate of 4.7 percent and 3.9 percent, respectively, is not outstanding, but it is respectable and better than the growth rates of most nations that are seeking to transform themselves into developed economies. Unfortunately, the premise of all economic planning for the south was that by coordinated public and private investment the south would catch up to the north.

Table 1 shows how unsuccessful the Cassa's programs were in closing the gap between the two. In 1970 the south's contribution to GDP at factor costs was still only 24 percent, the same share as in 1951. Moreover, the south's contribution to industrialized output at factor cost had inched up to a mere 17.3 percent of the total. Even though the south was now receiving 26 percent of all new industrial investment, it still had only 12.9 percent of Italy's manufacturing capacity in 1970. In fact, its value added per employed in industry fell compared with the rest of Italy from the early fifties to the later sixties. Thus the south's income per capita remained at 62.5 percent of that which the whole of Italy enjoyed. Clearly, the Cassa had not been able to make any dent whatsoever in closing the gap between the two regions of Italy.

In 1971 the Cassa embarked on a new incentive program.[17] Its purpose was to shift the focus on investment away from capital-intensive projects to those that are more labor-intensive. The Cassa was authorized to spend $10.9 billion from 1971 to 1975. It would offer to small investors (those who invest less than $2.5 million) capital grants of up to 35 percent for buildings and equipment; in high emigration areas, such as Calabria, the grant would go up to 45 percent. Interest charges would be a low 3 to 5 percent. Finally, the government would forgive 30 percent of the social-security benefits that are owed by the firm. Larger investors would receive reduced grants and be required to pay higher interest rates. It was hoped that these new incentives would attract investors who would employ more workers than has been the case before. It was doubtful, however, that the Cassa would be successful in closing the wide gap that still existed between the south and the rest of Italy.

ITALIAN STATE ENTERPRISES AND UNITED STATES INVESTMENTS

The Cassa was not the only organ of government that was caught up in the drive to industrialize the south. Beginning in 1957, all government-owned enterprises were required to place 60 percent of their new industrial investments and 40 percent of their total yearly investments in the southern region. To gain the Cassa's incentives and subsidies, these investments were to be highly meshed with the Cassa's plans for developing the south. From 1961 to 1970 the Istituto per la Ricostruzione Industriale (IRI) and the Ente Nationale Idrocarburi (ENI) invested $2.7 billion in the south under programs approved by the Cassa.

The IRI, which was set up in 1933 as a central holding company, controls 300 or more companies, 20 to 25 percent of the stock issued by all Italian companies, and 5 percent of the gross product of Italian industry.[18] Examples of companies that it controls are as follows: Fincantieri (shipyards); Finelettrica (electricity); Finmare (shipping); Finmeccanica (engineering); Finsider (iron and steel); STET (telephone); Alitalia (airlines); RAI (radio and television); and Motta (bread and chocolates). Its investments in the south include the Taranto steel works, new cement facilities at Maddaloni, the construction of the Alfa-Sud automobile plant near Naples, and the expansion of southern facilities to produce brakes, tires, batteries, glass, and other manufactured items.[19] These investments were designed to establish large basic industries that could provide the south with a local source of supply for steel, cement, and other items.

The ENI has sought to provide the south with a fully integrated petro-chemical industry capable of competing with industry already established in the north. By 1970 ENI had built substantial petrochemical facilities at Gela and Augusta in Sicily and at Ferrandina in Calabria. ENI employs 18.3 percent of its Italian work force in the south, and makes 13.3 percent of its sales to public and private firms in the south.

From 1970 to 1975 both Italian state enterprises were going to place about 61 percent of their new investment in the south. This would total $7.2 billion, or a little over two and a half times the $2.7 billion that was invested in the previous five-year period. Included in this would be 92 percent of all new investment in the chemical industry, 85 percent of new investment in the steel industry, 83 percent of new investment in the electronics industry, and 52 percent of new investment in the mechanical industry.[20] Although these investments by Italian state enterprises have had some multiplier effects, they must be considered failures because they do not operate at full production levels. They have not generated a sufficient number of secondary supporting firms; in fact, IRI-group companies still tend to buy from themselves rather than from local southern manufacturers. Thus, the "big-push" that was to propel the southern economy into a period of "self-sustained growth" has not come about with the forced-investment program of the Italian state enterprises.

UNITED STATES BUSINESS INVESTMENT

Between 1966 and 1971, American private investment in Italy rose from $1.148 billion to $1.860 billion.[21] Because of this, American firms gained control over 100 percent of the fine-materials industry, 51 percent of cosmetics, 49 percent of electronics, 37 percent of pharmaceuticals, 28 percent of soaps and detergents, 24 percent of nonalcoholic beverages, 20 percent of petroleum derivatives, 16 percent of photographic equipment and movie theaters, 12 percent of paper, 11 percent of foods, and 5 percent of tires.[22]

At the beginning of this period only 25 of the 600 American firms that had made investments in Italy made them in the south.[23] By the end of 1968, 100 of these firms had invested in the south. At no time between 1967/1968 and 1971/1972 did American investments there total more than $300 million for the whole period. That is, the south received almost half of the increase for American investments in all of Italy during the period from 1966 to 1971. These firms made their investments there because of the incentives offered to them by the Cassa. Most of them built their plants about fifty miles south of Rome in Pomezia, Aprilia, and Latina. Others put their plants along the Adriatic in Bari, Brindisi, and

Taranto, all cities in which the productivity of the work force is far above the average for the south and almost equal to that of the north. A few firms put their plants in Sicily.

As a point of comparison, European firms also made investments in the north of Italy. They, too, were offered the same incentives by the Cassa, in the hope that they would make their future investments in the south. The Europeans (Germans, British, Dutch, and northern Italians) did not accept these inducements. What investments they did make in the south were few in number and always on a very small scale.

In 1968 and 1969 four United States firms closed down their operations in Sicily.[24] Celanese abandoned an investment of $82 million; Raytheon abandoned an investment of $25.6 million; Rheem abandoned an investment of $4 million; and Union Carbide sold its 50 percent interest in its petrochemical plant in Siracusa, Sicily. After these disinvestments, only six American firms were left on the island.

There were no similar disinvestments on the southern mainland during the same period. However, neither were there a significant number of new investments by American firms in the south after 1969. For the most part, only replacement capital was being invested into the south by the American firms from 1969 to 1974.

Most of the firms that had proven to be successful in the south where those that had placed their plants fifty miles south of Rome. Generally, these were all small-scale investments in light industries. Goods were assembled and packaged and then shipped back to the north for sale in the large consumer markets of Turin and Milan.

The American private investments did not bring about the "big-push" that was to propel the south into "self-sustained growth." As suggested in Table 1, these investments together with those of the Cassa, IRI, and ENI had failed in their purpose. They had not closed the gap between the economies of the north and the south.

COPING WITH THE HISTORICAL PEASANT

The answer as to why these historical outsiders have not been more successful in the south than they have been lies with what has been said earlier, Both public-sector and private-sector firms and the Cassa itself have tended to remain outside the fictitious kinship relationships in terms of which southern society is organized. Because the investors' professional managers were not tied to local patrons through marriage or through godparent obligations they had little or no loyalty base. Moreover, these managers had little use for the small, reciprocal acts that put one person into another's debt. They preferred to judge their employees on the basis of efficiency and competency. Thus they lose the opportunity to cement a client/patron relationship with the powerful people in the south.

Unfortunately for the outside investors, loyalty is rarely given by southern employees without such relationships. The employee feels no personal commitment to carry out the job to which he was assigned. Without this personal commitment, the interpersonal relationship between manager and employee is in fact a relationship between two strangers. A long time is needed to overcome this antipathy toward all outsiders. Thus it is not difficult to understand why these investors were not able to remake the *Mezzogiorno* within a decade or two.

Yet these fictitious kinship relationships are not a drag on economic development per se. In Rome, for example, southern businessmen have used the financial resources of a *parentela* (an organized family clan) to expand and modernize the city's commercial wholesale-retail distribution system. Other southerners have been able to gain powerful positions in Milan's stock market and in northern banks and insurance companies. These same things could be done in the south if those with risk capital were willing to tie themselves into a *parentela*. By doing this, the investor could assure himself that he and his firm would have powerful friends who could assist him in overcoming the inherent sociocultural problems that will plague any modern corporation when it seeks to invest in a region still bound to its history.

THE EEC AND THE *MEZZOGIORNO*

Clearly, the main currents of change that have sought to impose themselves upon the south have come mainly from Italy itself. Since 1951 the Italian government has worked very hard to make the south's difficulties a problem to be resolved by all Italians. In this effort, the government has been quite successful; most Italians now accept the conventional wisdom that, for Italy to prosper, the south must catch up with the rest of the country and that, therefore, the government should have an investment policy that favors the south. This policy should include work-inducing incentives so that fewer southern Italians will migrate to the already-congested cities of the north and thereby relieve northern Italians of some of the social headaches they foresee as their schools, hospitals, and housing become even more overcrowded than they already are. In fact, some northern Italians will go so far as to encourage the use of special taxes and other disincentives to forestall further investment in the northern regions of Piedmont and Lombardy.

These attitudes have not permeated the European Economic Community as a whole. More than a million Italians work in other EEC countries, and another half million work in Switzerland. Most of these workers are from the south.[25] They add to the money in circulation in the south by remitting a part of their wages to the families they have left behind. Only

Switzerland has sought to convert this foreign work force into permanent citizens. In Germany, France, and the Benelux countries, there is evidence that the employers in these EEC countries prefer noncommunity workers such as the Yugoslavs and the Turks over southern Italians because the latter must be paid higher wages and are more knowledgeable about their rights.[26] However, there is little indication that most northern Europeans wish to stop the flow of this labor from southern Europe and the Mediterranean. They prefer this cheap labor as a substitute for deepening their capital stock. These Europeans are not convinced that it is in their best interest to support a program of special taxes and other disincentives that would encourage less investment in northern Europe and more investments in southern Europe. They have not seen it to be in their best interest to follow the pattern set by northern Italians, i.e., that of encouraging capital investment in areas away from the industrialized north and in areas where the cheap labor actually lives. These Europeans do not see the *Mezzogiorno* as a European concern.

This conclusion will become apparent once we briefly review the niggardly amount of interest shown by the EEC in the south during the 1960s. Along with all other depressed and frontier regions of the six member countries, the south received a limited amount of development benefits. These were as follows:

(1) The European Coal and Steel Community has subsidized the development of modern coal and steel industries. From 1961 to 1971 Italy received 11.3 percent of these redeployment funds, or $26 million.[27] Of this sum, $22.5 million (or 86.5 percent of Italy's share) was spent in the south: $15 million to build IRI's Taranto steelworks and $7.5 million to build the continuous-casting facility in Terni near Rome.[28] These sums are very small when compared to the hundreds of millions of dollars spent by the Cassa and IRI to build a steel industry in the south.

(2) The European Investment Bank has loaned the Cassa money to help construct the ENI-Exxon petrochemical plant at Priolo, Sicily. In 1967 the bank's loans for the south totaled $36.2 million and by 1971 they reached a high of $238 million.[29] Some of this money was channelled through the Coal and Steel Community and through other organs of the EEC to the Cassa for the reconstruction of the steel industry and for building of dams and power stations. Again the sums involved are small when compared to the billions the Cassa, ENI, and ENEL (the Italian state enterprise for electricity) have spent in the south.

(3) Between 1968 and 1970, the European Agricultural Guidance and Guarantee Fund gave Italy $140 million.[30] This was a third of the total provided to the six member countries. Some of this money was spent by the Cassa to try to make southern agriculture more competitive with vegetable producers in northern Italy, citrus-fruit producers of Israel and

Spain, wine producers of Algeria, and olive-oil producers in the Mediterranean countries of the EEC. Table 1 suggests that these efforts, together with those of the Cassa, had come to naught; the value added per employed in southern agriculture fell from 89.3 percent to 84 percent when compared to Italy as a whole in the period from 1951 to 1970. In 1969 there was some attempt by the EEC to shield the south from the impact of more efficient citrus cooperatives elsewhere in the Mediterranean, with the hope that similar marketing coopertaives would be introduced in the south.[31] Unfortunately, the Italian bureaucracy was unable to reorganize southern agriculture before the temporary preventive measures were lifted. The bureaucracy was also unable to implement the EEC's milk-subsidy scheme, and thus Italian farmers lost the use of these funds, too. Because there was a surplus of olive oil in 1968 the EEC lowered its intervention price and reduced the income that southern farmers received from one of their main crops.[32] In 1971, the EEC added Turkey to the olive-oil preferential system that already included Morocco, Tunisia, and Spain. These two actions by the EEC severely hurt southern-Italian agriculture.[33] Of all the Mediterranean regions enjoying the protection of the EEC, the *Mezzogiorno* has been the least able to transform its agriculture, even with the limited money of the fund, into a commercial-marketing system that would produce high-quality, standardized products saleable throughout northern Europe.

(4) From 1960 to 1971 the European Social Fund provided Italy with $78 million to resettle and retrain southern workers in northern Italy and in the south itself.[34] For example, the fund was used to cushion the impact of closing down Sicily's sulphur mines and to build homes for married steelworkers in Taranto.[35] But because of bureaucratic problems the fund was not made available to cushion the impact of closing down Sardinia's lead, zinc, and coal mines.[36] Most of Italy's share went to help retrain northern workers who were to be displaced when their coal mines were closed.

Clearly, the amount of resources spent by the EEC in the south was not sufficient to suggest that there was a European presence there. The development of the poorer regions, although one of the goals of the EEC, has never held a high priority in the view of West Germany. Of the six members of the EEC, Italy was always the one nation concerned with this problem. She sought unsuccessfully to link France's concern for her relatively less developed Midi and Brittany to the *Mezzogiorno* and to combine all these regions into a European program for regional economic development. With Great Britain in the Common Market, Italy fears that Mediterranean problems will cease to interest the northern Europeans altogether.

There is some sentiment to suggest that Italy's past failures were Italy's own doing. She sent ministers and bureaucrats to Brussels who were less proficient in their respective areas of competence than were other Europeans at the EEC. Her views were not made known to the others with the same technical expertise that came from the other member delegations. Moreover, when EEC decisions were made to introduce a milk subsidy program or the value added tax, the other members found that Italy's bureaucracy was unable to carry out its duties adequately. The net result of this was that the other member countries lost confidence in Italy and wrote off her problems, such as that of the *Mezzogiorno*, as among those that were (and are) unsolvable under existing circumstances.

Although there have been reports that the EEC will try again to come up with a regional economic development policy, it is evident that the West Germans are currently even more unwilling to finance such a policy than they were before. It is felt that only Great Britain could force a European policy through, and, if she wanted assistance for Wales and Scotland, because of the relative inability of the Italian ministers to function effectively within the EEC the chances that Britain would link these areas to the *Mezzogiorno* are considered to be slim.

Some Italians are prepared to quit the EEC. This would be disastrous for northern Italy, which benefitted the most from the EEC. Industrialists in Piedmont and Lombardy saw the EEC as an opportunity to move from managing family firms with Italy as their major market to creating modern, risk-oriented firms whose market was all Europe. Italian washing machines became the chief household appliance on sale in Amsterdam and Hamburg. Fiat became the largest supplier of automobiles throughout the EEC. ENI set up refineries and gasoline stations all over Western Europe. Because northern industry was able to sell its products throughout the EEC, it was able to reduce its per-unit costs of production and create mass consumer industries. These economies of scale were passed on to the Italian consumer in the form of lower prices. No doubt the ability of northern Italian industry to compete in the markets of the EEC led to the inability of the Italian government and the Cassa to narrow the gap between the rich north and the more impoverished *Mezzogiorno*.

Southern Italy is the best available example to show that the benefits of economic integration do not accrue to each region uniformly. Free trade can reduce the ability of an impoverished region to compete effectively with a wealthier region. This has happened twice to the south: first, after unification in 1861, and second, after the establishment of the EEC in 1957. In the first instance, improper taxes were placed upon the south, nothing was done to protect already existing industry, and nothing was done to encourage new industry to move into the south. A century later special capital-investment programs were established to make the south a more competitive location for industry than the north. A few

American firms have been able to make their southern factories sole-source producers (i.e., one factory produces one series of components for all the other factories) for their European markets, but most firms there, whether Italian or American, have not been able to reap the benefits of the mass-consumer market that the EEC offers. History has gotten in their way.

The conclusion is clear. The *Mezzogiorno*, unlike its counterpart Mediterranean countries, was unable to negotiate a transition period during which its industry could be protected from the full winds of economic integration. Capital grants and tax incentives were not sufficient to offset the economic forces that pulled the north and northern Europe further away from the south. It is doubtful that even with the modest increase in the interest given to Europe's impoverished regions by the entry of Britain into the EEC that the *Mezzogiorno* will even partially narrow the gap between itself and more affluent regions to the north. Rather, because the *Mezzogiorno* is only a region and cannot protect itself as a nation would, it probably will suffer a relative decline as the interest of the Common Market and the American firms turns to other Mediterranean countries, which have lower labor costs and governments better able to make their bureaucracies function. In sum, the immediate future of southern Italy within Europe is not bright.

NOTES

1. The interpretation of behavior patterns in southern Italy is based in large part upon following works: Luigi Barzini, *From Caesar to the Mafia* (New York: Bantam Books, 1972) and *The Italians* (New York: Atheneum, 1964); Francis A. J. Ianni, *A Family Business:Kinship and Social Change in Organized Crime* (New York: Russell Sage Foundation, 1972); Michele Panteleone, *The Mafia and Politics* (New York: Coward-McCann, 1966); Sydel F. Silverman, "An Ethnographic Approach to Social Stratification: Prestige in a Central Italian Community," *American Anthropologist*, 68 (August, 1966), 899–922; and Phyllis H. Williams, *South Italian Folkways in Europe and America* (New York: Russell & Russell, 1969). This interpretation is based also upon the novels of one of Italy's best novelists, the Sicilian, Leonardo Sciascia. Other first-rate novelists from the south include Verga, Pirandello, and of course Tomasi di Lampedusa, author of *The Leopard*.

2. When the word begins with a capital *M*, it refers to the generic organization; when it begins with a lower case *m*, *mafia*, it refers to the local organization in one commune; and according to the Italian convention for making plurals, two such local organizations are called *mafie*.

3. Giuseppe Pitre, *Biblioteca delle Tradizioni Populari Sicilane* (Palermo, Italy: A. Reber, 1913), vol. 25, p. 76.

4. Armand O. Citarella, "Patterns in Medieval Trade: The Commerce of

Amalfi Before the Crusades," *The Journal of Economic History*, 28 (December, 1968), pp. 531–55.

5. Shepherd Bancroft Clough, *The Economic History of Modern Italy* (New York: Columbia University Press, 1964), p. 346; Francisco Forte, "It Takes More Than Industry to Stamp Out the *Mafia*," *Successo* 13:6 (June, 1971), p. 116; Giuseppi di Nardi, "I provedimenti per il *Mezzogiorno*, 1950–1960," *I piani di sviluppo in Italia dal 1945 al 1960* (Milan: Giuffre, 1960), p. 225; *Raccolta leggi, decreti, e circolari riguardanti la Cassa per il Mezzogiorno* (Naples: Amodio, 1961); *Lo Sviluppo del Mezzogiorno nella Attivita della Cassa* (Rome: Nuova Antalogia, la *Cassa* per il *Mezzogiorno*, 1968), p. 120.

6. Vera Lutz, *Italy: A Study in Economic Growth* (New York: Macmillan & Co., 1964), p. 310.

7. *Cassa* per il *Mezzogiorno*, *Relazione per l'Anno 1963–1964* (Rome: *Cassa* per il *Mezzogiorno*, 1964), p. 4; Mario L. Belotti, "The Development of the Italian South," *Land Economics*, 42 (November, 1966), p. 497.

8. Ibid.

9. *Cassa* per il *Mezzogiorno*, *Relazione* . . ., p. 9.

10. *Cassa* per il *Mezzogiorno*, *Relazione* . . ., p. 139.

11. "Investment Conditions in Southern Italy," *The Economist Intelligence Unit* (February, 1966), pp. 24–29.

12. SVIMEZ, *Statistiche sul Mezzogiorno d'Italia, 1861–1953*, pp. 601–02. ISTAT, *X Censimento generale della popolazione 15 ottobre 1961*, III. ISTAT, *General Survey of the Italian Economic Situation*, 1969.

13. Ibid.

14. Ibid.

15. Alberto Campolongo, "Italy's 5-year Plan ex Post," *Banca Nazionale del Lavoro Quarterly Review*, 99 (December, 1971), p. 375.

16. Ibid.

17. "The New Law on the *Mezzogiorno*," *Iasmnotizie: News from the Mezzogiorno*, 4:2 (February 1972), pp. 4–6.

18. Istituto de Ricerca e Documentazione Luigi Einaudi (Turin, unpublished study), cited by "Italy's IRI: How Good a Formula?" *The Economist*, 225 (Oct. 7, 1967), p. 60.

19. IRI, *Esercizio 1968* (Rome: IRI, 1968), p. 39.

20. "Interview with Flaminio Piccoli, Minister of State Partecipations (sic.): The Kingdom of Public Enterprise," *Successo*, VB (November, 1970), p. 55.

21. Soris, *Effetti Degli Investimenti Esteri in Italia* (Milan: Etas Kompass, 1968), p. 44. The 1971 is a preliminary figure based upon book value. *Survey of Current Business*, 52 (November 1972), pp. 30–31.

22. Soris, p. 54.

23. Sergio Barzanti, *The Underdeveloped Areas Within the Common Market* (Princeton, N. J.: Princeton University Press, 1965), p. 283.

24. George Melloan, "U.S. Firms and 'Il Problema': Manufacturing in Sicily Turns Disastrous for Raytheon, Rheem, Carbide, Celanese," *The Wall Street Journal* (Mar. 11, 1969), p. 36. "Anomalies and Paradoxes: Misadventure in Sicily, *Fortune*, 79 (May 15, 1969), pp. 244, 250. Neil McInnes, "Darkness at Noon," *Barron's* (June 30, 1969), pp. 5, 14, 16, 19. Douglas F. Lamont, "American Business: Success or Failure in the *Mezzogiorno*," *Italian-American Busi-*

ness, 21 (November, 1970), pp. 38–46. Douglas F. Lamont, *Managing Foreign Investment in Southern Italy* (New York: Praeger, 1973).

25. M. Livi-Bacci, *Report of the Demographic and Social Pattern of Migrants in Europe, Especially with Regard to International Migrations* (Strasbourg, France: Second European Population Conference, Council of Europe Document CDE (71) T. IV, Aug. 31–Sept. 7, 1971), p. 7, cited by Jon McLin, *International Migrations and the European Community,* American Universities Field Staff Reports, West Europe Series, vol. 7, no. 1, p. 2.

26. Ibid., p. 3.

27. *Second General Report on the Activities of the Communities 1968,* (Brussels: European Economic Community, 1968), Table 15, p. 287; *Third General Report . . . 1969,* Table 21, p. 286; *Fourth General Report . . . 1970,* Table 6, p. 97; and *Fifth General Report . . . 1971,* Table 8, p. 168. Compilation of loans and percentage calculations made by the author.

28. *First General Report . . . 1967,* p. 216.

29. *First General Report . . . 1967,* p. 129; *Second General Report . . . 1968,* p. 132; *Third General Report . . . 1969,* p. 145; *Fourth General Report . . . 1970,* p. 386; and *Fifth General Report . . . 1971,* p. 418. Compilation of loans made by author.

30. *Third General Report . . . 1969,* Table 19, p. 165; *Fourth General Report . . . 1970,* Table 14, p. 139; and *Fifth General Report . . . 1971,* Table 18, p. 219. Compilation of aid and percentage calculations made by author.

31. *Third General Report . . . 1969,* p. 175.

32. *Second General Report . . . 1968,* p. 68.

33. *Fifth General Report . . . 1971,* p. 230.

34. *First General Report . . . 1967,* p. 241, and Table 12 (misnumbered), p. 243; *Second General Report . . . 1968,* Table 16, p. 302; *Third General Report . . . 1969,* Table 22, p. 295; *Fourth General Report . . . 1970,* Table 8, p. 107; and *Fifth General Report . . . 1971,* Table 10, p. 180.

35. *Third General Report . . . 1969,* p. 296; *Fourth General Report . . . 1970,* p. 108; and *Fifth General Report . . . 1971,* p. 181.

36. *Second General Report . . . 1968,* p. 38.

7

Spain

ERIC N. BAKLANOFF

HISTORICALLY, the Spanish genius has been manifested principally in military, religious, and cultural enterprises. Yet by the middle 1960s the world financial community had begun to discuss the Spanish "economic miracle" and to compare it with the German "*Wirtschaftswunder*" of the 1950s.[1]

The recent systemic transformation of Spain from an inward-looking "corporate state" to a European-style "capitalist market economy" has significantly increased the scope for economic freedom in that nation. Centralization of economic decision making in Spain has given way since 1959 to an increasingly decentralized market orientation; with the growth of capitalism the Falange government functionaries have been forced to relinquish economic power to industrialist, bankers, consumers, and the new "Europeanist" technocrats in the key ministries.

The political order that eventually supported the liberalized market economy was (and remains), in the words of Stanley G. Payne, "a pragmatic authoritarian system" characterized by a "limited but undeniable pluralism."[2]

Of major importance in the "opening" of Spain was a reorganization of the cabinet in 1957 that brought into prominence a new group of ministers whose vision of Spain's future was in sharp contrast to the semifascist Falange position. Broadly European in their attitudes and committed to the market economy, this group of younger men took command of the key economic ministries and the strategic planning commission. Most of these leaders are either members of or are associated with the semisecret Catholic secular institute Opus Dei. Because of their influence Spain became a member of the World Bank and the International Monetary Fund in 1958 and joined the organization for European Economic Cooperation (now the OECD) in 1959.

During the period from 1959/60 to 1970/71, Spain's real gross national product (GNP) increased at an annual rate averaging 7.2 percent, the second highest growth rate after Japan among the OECD's twenty-three member nations. In the next two years, 1972 and 1973, Spain's GNP growth rate (averaging 8.0 percent) continued to lead the growth rates experienced by the enlarged EEC (4.7 percent), the United States (6 percent), and the other OECD member nations, again with the exception of Japan.[3] During the 1960–70 decade Spanish industrial production increased at an average yearly rate of 8.7 percent, the most rapid industrial growth recorded among all the European countries.[4] By 1972 Spain was the fifth ranking European nation in terms of GNP and industrial production.

In the course of a dozen years Spain crossed the arbitrary dividing line that separates the "less-developed" from the "industrialized" nations. What factors account for the recent economic transformation of the Iberian nation?

HISTORICAL SKETCH

Spain occupies the greater part of the Iberian Peninsula, the southwestern extension of Europe. The area of metropolitan Spain, which includes the Balearic and Canary islands, is 196,607 square miles. Its total area is one-fourth greater than that of California and about a third less than that of Texas. The peninsular nation is bounded on the west by Portugal and the Atlantic Ocean, on the north by the Bay of Biscay and by France, and on the east and south by the Mediterranean Sea.[5]

The remainder of the Spanish territory comprises the Balearic Islands, in the Mediterranean; the Canary Islands, just off the coast of northwest Africa, where an important oil refinery is located; and Spanish, or Spanish-controlled, territories in Africa.

The Pyrenees, extending some 421 miles from the Bay of Biscay to the Mediterranean Sea, separate Spain from France. They form the second highest range of mountains in Europe. The Spanish-Portuguese border, about 613 miles in length, is not marked by any significant geographical barriers. Roughly 60 percent of Spain's border is sea coast, comprising the Mediterranean coastline, approximately 1,033 miles long, and the Atlantic coastline of about 422 miles. At the southernmost tip of the peninsula is the British fortified station of Gibraltar.

The Spanish landmass rises sharply from the sea with only a narrow coastal plain except in the Andalusian lowlands. Much of the peninsula forms a high plateau divided by mountains and broad, shallow depressions. "The Iberian Peninsula," as one writer observes, "cannot be called the bridge between Europe and Africa. It is a stubborn, individual place on the route."[6] Nearly three-fourths of Spain is arid, with less than twenty inches of rainfall annually. Northwestern Spain, however, resembles

England in climate, with slight variations in temperature and plentiful rainfall, while the coastal regions in the east and south enjoy a typically Mediterranean climate, with long dry spells and warmer temperatures.[7]

For centuries before Spain became a united nation the Iberian peninsula was a battleground of invasion and resistance. First colonized by the Phoenicians, the Greeks, and the Carthaginians, Spain later became part of the Roman Empire. From the Mediterranean came the Phoenicians, the Greeks, the Carthaginians, and the Moors.[8] From the European continent came the Celts, whose influence in northern Spain has been considerable, followed by the most important invasion of all, the Roman, and later the Visigoths.

The Roman influence has lasted into contemporary Spain, not only in the archaeological relics but in the present Spanish language, religion, and law. The Romans, mainly soldiers and bureaucrats, colonized Spain systematically. Roman ascendancy in Spain began with the Second Punic War (218–202 B.C.), during which the Carthaginians were finally vanquished by the Roman legions. During the six centuries of Roman rule, Spain specialized in the production of metallic minerals and olive oil for export to the greater Mediterranean economy. Significantly, Spain also contributed to Roman religion and literature, and among the Roman emperors, some the greatest were Spanish born.[9]

The Visigoths who invaded the Peninsula after the fall of the Roman Empire made little cultural impact upon Spain. The state organized by these Germanic colonizers between A.D. 409 and 711 has been aptly described as "a Visigothic veneer over a solid Roman base."[10]

In the eighth century the Moors defeated the Visigoths and for a brief period occupied all but a narrow strip along northern Spain. During their seven centuries of rule, the Moors contributed to Spain "particularly their racial characteristics, their technical skills, their social patterns and their habits of mind."[11] Spain's economic position, which had seriously declined under the inept Visigoths, was restored under Moorish influence. Hundreds of thousands of Moorish technicians migrated to the peninsula, where they introduced both modern specialty farming on a mass scale and advanced manufacturing methods. Spanish commerce and industry, integrated with the common market of the Islamic world, prospered with the elimination of trade barriers.[12]

Efforts to drive the Moors out of Spain, known as the *Reconquista* (the Reconquest), lasted for over seven centuries and culminated in Spain's becoming a unified nation in 1492, the same year in which Columbus made his celebrated voyage to the New World. The Reconquest, characterized by a series of protracted battles, was motivated by a desire for land on the part of the rulers and people of Christian Spain, as well as by religious and nationalist feelings. "The heroes of this frontier society,"

writes John Ramsay, "were the warrior, the monk, and the missionary—
not, it be noted, the trader or merchant."[13] Toward the end of the Reconquest period, the new lands acquired by the Catholic kings were distrib-
uted mainly to the nobles, the church, and the military orders.[14] The
transformation of the formerly productive lands into *Latifundia*, large
undercultivated estates, was to inhibit the economic development of Spain
up to the twentieth century.

The expulsion of the Muslims and Jews, which marked the unification
of Spain under Ferdinand and Isabella, drained the nation of much of its
scarce "human capital"—the artisan, financial, and commercial classes. The
religious zeal and intolerance that served the Spaniards so well in achieving
national independence and forging a world empire may have been a major
factor in Spain's declining fortunes, beginning in the seventeenth century.
An extremely doctrinaire religious orthodoxy served to isolate the Iberian
Peninsula from the scientific revolution of the seventeenth century. It is
interesting to observe in this context that Phillip II decreed in 1565 that
Spanish universities must cease all cultural contacts with the universities
of Europe.[15] In describing the Spanish situation from the seventeenth century onward, José Ortega y Gasset spoke of the "hermetization" of the
Spaniards from the rest of the world, "a phenomenon which does not
refer especially to religion nor to theology nor to ideas, but to the totality
of life. . . ."[16]

Spain was the "superpower" of the late Middle Ages. "It was the unique
achievement of the Spanish peoples," according to John Ramsay, "to
establish a world empire with industrial and technical equipment not
much advanced beyond that of the Romans, but covering an area many
times greater."[17] From midseventeenth century to midtwentieth century
Spain fell further and further behind the rest of the world, as much of
the nation's wealth and manpower were dissipated in colonial and civil
wars. The Iberian nation fought unsuccessively to hold her American
colonies during the first two decades of the nineteenth century and lost
Cuba and the Philippines in the Spanish-American War of 1898. Contest
for the Spanish throne after the defeat of Napoleon led to a series of civil
wars that slowed the nation's economic development until 1876.

In Spain, the Industrial Revolution made its tentative start during the
second half of the nineteenth century, as hand craftsmanship gave way
gradually to mechanization and the factory system. Early in this period
machinery was introduced in the textile and metallurgical industries by
Spanish entrepreneurs.

Foreign capital—loans and direct investments in branches and affiliates—
were decisive in shaping the formative pattern of Spain's modern economy. Between the 1850s and 1906 a favorable domestic investment climate
and rapid world economic growth combined to draw foreign investments

—mainly British, French and Belgian—to Spain. Multinational enterprises played a major role in the development of Spanish railways and public services—streetcars, telephone, water, gas, and electricity.[18] Foreign enterprise was crucial to the development of large-scale mining of copper, coal, lead, zinc, and iron ore and initiated the chemical industry.[19]

Spain's railway network grew from 423 kilometers in 1855, the year when the Law of Railways was enacted, to nearly 11,000 kilometers in 1900. During the final quarter of the nineteenth century production and export of coal and industrial metals from Spanish mines expanded at an accelerated pace.[20]

Banking, mainly in the hands of indigenous financial interests, developed in step with the nation's commercial and industrial growth. Repatriation of Spanish capital from Cuba and the Philippines after the Spanish-American War of 1898 stimulated domestic banking and led to the creation of three large banks: Hispano-Americano, Vizcaya, and Español de Credito.[21]

By 1900 the number of laborers employed in mines throughout Spain had risen to 76,000, while 706,000 workers were employed in manufacturing and 236,000 in construction. Still, at the end of the century, the labor force was overwhelmingly rural: 60 percent in agriculture, 13 percent in industry, and the remainder in services.[22]

The momentum of Spain's export-oriented economy slowed markedly after 1906, reflecting the end of the railway and mining booms. Industry continued to advance at a sluggish pace from 1906 to 1922, picked up speed between 1923 and 1929, and then stagnated during the Great Depression.

THE "CORPORATE STATE": FROM AUTARCHY TO SYSTEMIC CRISIS

The Spanish Republic (1931-36) was characterized by extreme political instability, economic decline, and the flight of capital. A bloody Civil War (1936-39) dealt heavy blows to the people of Spain and to the economic infrastructure. The nation lost about half a million of its working population through deaths; more than 200 cities and towns suffered the destruction of 60 percent or more of their buildings; the railroads lost 45 percent of their rolling stock; bridges, roads, ports, and industrial facilities were severely damaged; and Spain's gold reserves of 510 tons (with a current 1974 value of over $3 billion) were carted off to the Soviet Union.[23]

Following the Civil War, Spain became isolated politically and was treated by most nations as an international pariah. The reconstruction of the Spanish economy and its subsequent growth took place within a framework of isolation—partly externally enforced, partly in response to Spain's propensity for national self-sufficiency. In December, 1946, a pious United Nations resolution demanded replacement of the Spanish regime by one "deriving its authority from the governed" and requested its member nations to withdraw diplomatic recognition from the Iberian nation. The United Nations resolution, which was sponsored by the Soviet bloc, France, and Mexico, resulted in both economic and diplomatic sanctions against the Iberian nation. During this same post-World War II period, Spain also had to deal with a protracted guerrilla war in the northern provinces. This insurrection, under the leadership of a Communist hero of the Civil War, Enrique Lister, was finally defeated in about 1952 by Civil Guard detachments.[24]

On December 10, 1948, Winston Churchill spoke out against the continued ostracism of Spain, arguing that there was more freedom in that nation than anywhere beyond the Iron Curtain. Two years later, in October 1950, the South American countries moved in the United Nations to reverse the 1946 resolution. With the full support of the Arab states, they obtained thirty-seven votes, including that of the United States; only the Soviet bloc, Guatemala, and Mexico voted against the lifting of sanctions against Spain.[25]

A decade of economic and political isolation after the end of the civil conflict in 1939 compounded the difficulties and burdens of reconstruction. Data on Spain's per-capita real income are cited below for selected years:[26]

	(In 1953 Pesetas)
1929	9,007
1935	8,520
1940	5,789
1952	8,550
1954	9,310

Thus, Spain's per-capita income fell by a third between the years immediately before and after the Civil War (1935 and 1940); the 1935 level was not again regained until 1952; and the 1929 predepression level was not reached again until 1954. It took Spain seventeen years to recover the pre-Civil War standard of living and a quarter of a century to regain the predepression living standard.

The basic organizational makeup of the Spanish political economy from 1939 to 1958 became a variant of the "corporate state." Neither capitalistic nor communistic, the Spanish political economy was cast into a quasi-traditional mold. The ideological underpinning was similar to what evolved in the wider Mediterranean world (especially in Salazar's Portugal). As Seymour Martin Lipset has shown, the ideal political leader

in these societies "is not a totalitarian ruler, but a monarch, or a traditionalist who acts like one."[27] Indeed, the political formula of Spain's regime,
defined in the Law of Succession of 1947, is that of a "social and representative Catholic State which, in accordance with its tradition, is constituted a Kingdom." As Generalíssimo Francisco Franco approached the
end of his long rule, he designated (in July, 1969) Prince Juan Carlos de
Borbón to succeed him as chief of state. Thus, the prince would be sworn
in as chief of state and crowned king upon the retirement, incapacitation,
or death of Generalíssimo Franco.

The corporatist framework within which Spanish industry and commerce operated was inimical to rapid economic growth. Instead of de-
ploying economic resources—labor, capital, and land—to their most
productive uses, the system favored and sheltered the least efficient enterprises and workers. For example, the Law for the Protection of National
Industry (adopted in 1939) required state authorization, not only to set
up a new plant, but also to expand, transform, or relocate one. The law
enabled established firms to block the entry or expansion of competitors
and deterred investment by foreign enterprises in the Spanish economy.[28]
Furthermore, employers were generally prevented from dismissing
workers for economic (as distinct from "disciplinary") reasons. A system
of neomedieval reciprocal obligations—no strikes, no layoffs—presupposed
a stagnant economy with little flexibility or mobility. Conditions in
pre–1959 Spain conformed rather closely to development model described
as "the dynastic elites."[29] Enterprise managers were under little pressure
from any source; cartelized domestic-product markets transmitted no
strong demand for efficiency; external competition was limited by high
tariffs and quotas; there was little pressure on workers to develop industrial discipline or to become geographically mobile; and foreign enterprise was held at bay.

In the 1950s Spain shared certain common features with the less-
developed, semiindustrialized Latin American nations: a relatively low
per-capita income (estimated at around $300 per year) and low worker
productivity; landholding systems polarized between excessive fragmentation and very large estates; a high percentage of unskilled workers, and a
large fraction of the active labor force in agriculture and other primary
activities; comparative technological backwardness; and a highly stratified
society in which ascription and kinship rather than achievement continued to exercise an important influence in the assignment of economic
roles. With some notable exceptions, Spanish industry was fragmented
into small family enterprises equipped with obsolete machinery and
operating within a highly protected market.

What elements contributed to the reversal of Spanish economic policy
after 1959? Of initial importance was the resumption of diplomatic rela-

tions between Spain and the United States in December, 1950, and the incorporation of the peninsular nation into the Western defense system in 1953 under the provisions of the Pact of Madrid. As a consequence, the United States provided Spain with a substantial economic-aid package.[30] The military bases, together with economic, technical, and social assistance, served as an opening wedge for the unsettling influence of new ideas, as well as goods and services.

A growing number of Spanish economists, businessmen, and government officials came to the realization that a continuation of Spain's posture of isolation was inimical to the national interest. Their views took on a sense of urgency in the face of the movement among European countries toward economic integration.

"Spain must not be left at the margin of these integrating movements," wrote Minister of Commerce Alberto Ullastres, in 1960, "otherwise the nation would more and more become a backward province of Europe."[31] A study by Armando de Miguel and Juan Linz shows that an important segment of the Spanish business community favored some kind of association between their country and the European Economic Community.[32] They also learned that the larger the business firm, the greater the disposition of management to look with favor upon participation by foreign investment in Spanish industry.

Finally, a major foreign exchange crisis in the spring of 1959[33] strengthened the hand of those cabinet ministers who sought to end Spain's economic isolation. They prevailed upon Generalíssimo Franco to accept the conditions set up by the international creditors. As a result, in July, 1959, the Spanish government drew up, in cooperation with the Organization for European Economic Cooperation (OEEC) and the International Monetary Fund, a stabilization program designed to bring the nation's domestic and international transactions into equilibrium. The peseta was devalued, the exchange rate unified, and inflation moderated.

Subsequently, the new policymakers liberalized the conduct of international trade, promoted tourism, actively sought and received official external credits, and created favorable conditions for attracting private foreign capital.

THE "ECONOMIC MIRACLE": SOURCES AND DIMENSIONS

The rate of economic growth climbed sharply in the years after implementation of the stabilization program. For example, real GNP increased about twice as fast in 1960–64 as in the previous five year period, 1955–59, when the average annual rate of increase was 4.1 percent. Acceleration occurred in both industry and the services sectors: the average annual increase in value added (in real terms) stepped up in industry from 4.2 percent in 1955–59 to 11.5 percent in 1960–64, and in services from 2.9 to 10 percent.[34]

The acceleration in Spain's growth rate is associated with a rise in the level of investment and a fall in the Incremental Capital-Output Ratio (ICOR). Gross investment averaged 19 percent of GNP in the years 1955–58, fell in 1959 and 1960 because of the stabilization program, and rose to about 25 percent of GNP in the years 1962–64. However, the major explanation of the marked improvement of Spain's economic performance is the overall efficiency of the economy as reflected in the dramatic decline of the ICOR. In the years 1955–59 total gross investment outlays (at constant prices) amounted to 4.9 times the sum of the annual increases in real GNP that occurred in that period, but for the years 1960-64 ICOR fell to as low as 2.7.[35]

My own explanation for this dramatic improvement in the Incremental Capital-Output Ratio centers on four contributing factors:

(a) improved resource allocation;
(b) introduction of advanced management and technology through multinational enterprise;
(c) an increase in the availability and quality of capital equipment;
(d) greater competition in the commodity and resources markets.

A major concomitant of rapid economic growth, which appears to be a universal phenomenon of less-developed nations, is a reallocation of resources—capital, land, labor—in response to change in patterns of demand and opportunities for trade.[36] Since 1959 the whole armory of Spanish policy tools has been mobilized in support of a shift of resources from low-productivity toward high-productivity uses, including export-oriented industries. That Spain has indeed undergone a profound restructuring of its economy is evidenced by the changing distribution of the working population and the changing sector profile. Between 1960 and 1971 (see Table 1) the share of the labor force in agriculture and fishing fell from 42 percent to 28 percent, while that of industry rose from 32 percent to 37 percent and of the service sector from 27 percent to 34 percent. In Spain the shift of the working poulation out of agriculture involved a reduction in the number of persons working the land (a decline of about 1.4 million workers between 1960 and 1971) as well as in the proportion of farm workers in the total labor force.

Because of the slow growth of the Spanish population, and hence of its labor force, rural-to-urban migration provided the necessary elasticity of labor supply for the labor-absorbing industrial and services sectors. Manufacturing, the major component of the industrial sector, increased its share of the Spanish labor force from 22 percent in 1960 to 27 percent in 1971. The "other services" category includes most of the "invisible"

TABLE 1

STRUCTURE OF THE SPANISH LABOR FORCE, 1960 and 1971

(In Percentages of Total Active Population)

	1960	1971
Agriculture and fishing	41.7	28.4
Industrial sector	22.4	27.3
Manufacturing	22.4	27.3
Mining	1.6	0.9
Construction	7.1	8.5
Electricity, gas and water	0.7	0.7
Services Sector	26.5	34.2
Commerce	8.2	11.1
Transport and Communications	4.6	5.1
Other Services	13.7	18.0

Source: Banco de Bilbao, *Informe Economico 1971* (Madrid, 1972, p. 148.

activities associated with the nation's dynamic tourist industry. Both industry and services absorbed increasing investment and labor during the 1960–71 period and contributed growing shares of national output.

The Law for the Protection of National Industry was amended in 1962 and repealed in early 1963. The effect of these legal changes was to promote competition and to substitute market criteria for government regulation in the making of industrial investment decisions in Spain.

The Spanish economy took on a markedly changed appearance by 1973, when compared with its condition in 1960, as shown by the following production indicators: [37]

(1964 = 100)

	1960	1973
Agriculture	89.6	143.6
Industry	62.2	204.2
Services	69.7	177.0
Total Output	70.2	180.7

Total output of the Spanish economy in 1973 was over 2.5 times greater, in real terms, than it had been thirteen years before; agricultural output was 1.6 times greater; industrial production was 3.3 times greater; and the output of the services sector was over 2.5 times greater. Pacing the industrial sector were such basic industries as steel, cement, electric power, chemicals, nonferrous metals, paper, and shipbuilding. The metal transforming industries, especially those producing autos and trucks, tractors, washing machines, television sets, and refrigerators, also experienced tremendous growth from 1960 onward.[38]

Spain's agricultural output increased by an average of 3.5 percent per year during the 1960s, or about half the rate for the economy as a whole.

Thus food supplies from domestic production were maintained well ahead of population increase. The livestock industry, responding to changing consumer demand, has emerged as the most dynamic part of Spanish agriculture. Its contribution to the total primary sector rose from 27 percent in 1960 to 37 percent in 1970.[39] With rising incomes, Spanish consumers are eating less wheat, potatoes, olive oil, and wine and more meat and dairy products.[40] Despite the decline of the rural labor force, farm and livestock output grew as more and better inputs, notably machinery and fertilizers, were used on the land. Also during the 1960s, the amount of irrigated land was increased by 6.4 million acres.[41]

To summarize, rapid and accelerated growth of the Spanish economy after 1960 was associated with greatly improved resource allocation, the international transfer of modern technical and managerial methods, elasticity of labor supply, and an enormous increase in the quantity of modern equipment. The explosive increase of foreign exchange availability was a necessary condition for the expansion and renewal of the nation's capital stock in the poststabilization era.

How did the rapid economic growth and structural change translate into human dimensions? First, it should be noted that per-capita income increased from 28,075 pesetas in 1960 to 72,691 pesetas in 1972 (both figures expressed in 1972 prices), indicating that per-capita *real* income was 2.5 times greater at the end of the twelve-year period.[42] Further, the masses were acquiring an increasing share of purchasing power as the share of wages and salaries in national income rose steadily from 52 percent in 1961 to 59 percent in 1970.[43] An ever growing number of Spaniards were able to eat better, own a home, and purchase consumer durables. For every thousand inhabitants, 98 owned an automobile in 1973, compared with only 10 in 1960; 179 out of a thousand owned a television receiver in 1973, compared with only 5 in 1960; and 175 out of a thousand owned a telephone in 1973, compared with 56 in 1960. Meat consumption per capita nearly doubled in this period, from 20 pounds to 35 pounds, and the consumption of electricity per capita increased from 97 kWH in 1960 to 240 kWH in 1973.[44] During the phase of accelerated growth, differences in the level of living between rural and urban dweller were substantially narrowed, and the absolute number of Spaniards who lived in genuine poverty declined.

Compared with other less-developed countries Spain had already experienced, by 1950, a remarkable demographic transition: in that year the crude birth rate was only 20 per 1,000 and the death rate 10.8 per 1,000, resulting in a net population growth rate of under 1 percent per annum. Two decades later, in 1970, the net population growth rate was about 1.1 percent, reflecting a minor decline of the death rate compared with 1950.[45] In the 1940s and early 1950s, Spain was distinguished by a very late average marriage age, ranking in Europe second only to Ireland. From the midfifties onward fertility has been largely controlled "in other ways than merely by postponing marriage."[46]

Thus Spain, while still a very poor country, nevertheless was able to slow its population growth to a rate similar to the rates prevailing in the industrialized nations of Europe. Consequently, the lion's share of Spain's savings could be invested into productivity-increasing capital stock rather than being diverted to meet the needs of a growing population for housing, educational and health facilities, and jobs. In the trade-off between more children and improved living standards, the Spanish people chose the latter.

"INDICATIVE" PLANNING

The reports of the World Bank Mission and the Organization for Economic Cooperation and Development (OECD) helped prepare the ground for Spain's First Economic and Social Development Plan. Covering the period 1964–67, the first plan incorporated recommendations made in 1962 by a World Bank Mission led by the British economist Sir Hugh Ellis-Rees. The mission's report, published in the following year, recommended (and the Spanish government concurred with the recommendation) that planning should be "indicative" in nature. In planning of this kind, the government would have a twofold role: "first, to propose a policy for the rate of growth of the economy and to work out the implications for the future development of the cenomy as a whole, and, second, to state the actions it proposes to take, with respect both to public investment and to public policy as its own part in fulfillment of that rate of growth."[47] Thus, the plan would give a forward view of the economy that would indicate the main lines of anticipated growth and change; it would set targets obligatory for the state and its enterprises, but would merely offer guidelines for private enterprise. About two-thirds of the public investment funds committed in the first plan were allocated to improve Spain's infrastructure—highways, port facilities, telecommunications, electric power, and irrigation.

Building on the momentum already achieved by the 1959 stabilization program, the 1964–67 plan indicated that the private sector would continue to be exposed to the forces of competition in combination with incentives for modernization and for investment in selected industries and less-developed regions. It's major objectives were (1) higher living standards, (2) greater economic freedom, and (3) progressive integration into the world economy.[48] Significantly, the first plan envisioned a growth path supported by rapid advances in exports, tourist income, and inflow of foreign capital, and projected the following selected annual percentage rates of growth (see Table 2):

GNP	6.0
Imports	9.0
Gross Capital Formation	9.0
Exports	9.8
Employment	1.0

A high rate of capital formation anticipated for the planning period required rapid growth in the supply of machinery to reequip obsolescent industries and expand productive capacity generally. The solution was sought in terms of (1) accelerating the growth of imports, and (2) an average growth rate of nearly 16 percent per year in domestic production of machinery.

Table 2 summarizes target- and realized-growth rates of major output and expenditure categories for the three consecutive development plans. The table also includes projections and results of employment growth and price changes (the GNP deflator) and of the current-account deficit in the balance of international payments.

All the growth targets, with the exception of public consumption, were more than achieved in the course of the first-plan years, 1964–67. The actual growth in employment, 0.7 percent annually, fell short of

TABLE 2

SPAIN:
MAIN PROJECTIONS AND ACHIEVEMENTS IN THE FIRST,
SECOND, AND THIRD DEVELOPMENT PLANS
Average Annual Changes in Percentages

	First Plan (1964-67) Target	Achieved	Second Plan (1968-71) Target	Achieved	Third Plan (1972-75) Target	1972-73 Average Achieved
Disposable Resources						
GNP	6.0	6.4	5.5	5.9	7.0	8.2
Imports	9.0	12.9	6.8	6.5	11.0	20.5
Use of Resources						
Private						
Consumption	5.5	6.3	4.5	5.1	6.5	6.7
Public Consumption	5.0	4.4	3.4	5.3	5.3	6.8
Gross Capital						
Formation	9.0	10.7	6.9	4.0	9.9	17.2
Exports	9.8	10.6	11.8	15.6	10.0	15.5
Employment	1.0	0.7	1.3	0.9	1.0	
GNP Price Deflector		7.2	2.7	5.5	3.7	9.5
Current External						
Balance	−250	−369	−338	+50		
(annual rates in millions of dollars)						

Sources: *III Plan de Desarrollo 1972-1975* (Imprenta Nacional del Boletin Oficial del Estado, 1971), pp. 217 and 228. *OECD Economic Surveys: Spain* (Paris, January, 1972), p. 39, table 11.
For 1972-73 realized rates of growth, Banco de Bilbao, *Informe Economico 1972*, p. 50, and *Informe Economico 1973*, p. 68.

the projected 1 percent rate owing to a heavy emigration of Spanish workers to the more industrialized countries of Europe. It should be noted that a faster than anticipated GNP growth rate was achieved despite the slower than projected increase in employment. Spanish policy makers were confronted with strong inflationary pressures as workers pressed for wage increases far in excess of productivity gains—a situation that particularly characterized the years 1964 to 1966. The general level of prices, as the table demonstrates, increased by over 7 percent a year. A larger than expected current-account deficit, averaging $370 million a year, was more than covered by the inflow of private foreign capital, resulting in rapid accumulation of Spain's foreign reserves at the conclusion of the first-plan period.

The Second Economic and Social Development Plan (1968–71) continued to emphasize the central role of international economic transactions in Spain's economic future. Compared with the priorities of the 1964–67 period, the second plan focused greater attention on agriculture and education. Actual GNP growth during 1968–71 slightly exceeded the projected 5.5 percent rate; private and public consumption and particularly export growth all exceeded the traget growth rates. The devaluation of the peseta in 1967 undoubtedly contributed to the acceleration of export growth during the years 1968–71. Prices as measured by the GNP deflator increased at twice the rate projected by the planners. The larger than anticipated growth in exports of goods and services (nearly 16 percent a year), compared with a slower rate of import expansion (6.5 percent annually), resulted in a current surplus in Spain's external balance averaging $50 million a year. This current surplus, added to the large inflows of private capital from abroad, built up Spain's gold and foreign-exchange reserves to over $3 billion at the end of 1971. As was true during the first plan, the policymakers again overestimated the rate of employment growth.

The Third Economic and Social Development Plan, for the period 1972–75, seeks to come to grips with the nation's more important economic and social problems at the present juncture. As Table 2 shows, the plan sets a 7 percent target for GNP and stresses three major lines of action for improving the overall performance of the economy: (1) a strengthening of the public sector, (2) an enhanced role for market forces so as to improve competitiveness and the allocation of resources, (3) and decisive efforts in favor of regional development.[49] Because of Spain's rapid transformation since the later fifties, the economy is now faced with many of the problems confronting the industrialized countries. These new problems include increasing regional disequilibria, the social costs of rapid urbanization, the growing need for education and technical training, and the protection of the environment—all of which are documented in the third plan. Significantly, the earlier plans failed to reduce significantly regional inequality. Industry continues to be concentrated at the points of the Madrid, Barcelona, and Bilbao triangle. To extend opportunities for higher education on a regional basis, the plan envisions the building of new universities in Cordoba, Malaga, Santander, and Extremadura, as well as in Madrid.[50]

The targeted 7 percent growth rate for real GNP compares with the 5.5 percent rate forecast in the second plan for 1968–71 and with an actual rate of just under 6 percent. Considering the slower projected growth of employment for the third plan, as compared with the 1.3 percent rate assumed during the previous four years, it appears that the planners anticipate a significantly faster increase in productivity (output per employed). This improved performance probably reflects the projected acceleration of real investment, i.e., a capital formation growth rate of 9.9 percent for the 1972–75 period, compared with the 6.9 percent rate anticipated (and the 4.0 percent rate achieved) during the second plan.

The forecasts for both export and import growth, 10 and 11 percent, respectively, emphasize the continuing exposure of the Spanish economy to the influences of her international commerce.

Spain's experience during the first two years of the third plan, 1972–73, reveals that the planners had underestimated the forward momentum of the economy. The realized rates of growth for the main components, as the figures in Table 2 make clear, all exceeded the target rates, and some did so by a wide margin. For example, the actual growth rate of capital formation was 17 percent, compared with a projected rate of about 10 percent, and the realized growth rate of exports during 1972–73 (20.5 percent) was nearly twice the 11 percent rate anticipated by the planners. However, the behavior of prices indicates that the third plan did not foresee the intensity of inflationary pressures that were to plague the Spanish economy during the early seventies. Thus, the actual forward movement of the price level (the GNP price deflator), which averaged around 10 percent during 1972–73, should be compared with the projected increase of only 3.7 percent annually for the plan years.

THE BALANCE OF INTERNATIONAL PAYMENTS

Spain's new economic policy is mirrored in the nation's balance of international payments with the rest of the world. Major components of the balance for the 1957–73 period are shown in Table 3. The components that have responded most directly to official policy directives are as follows, in millions of United States dollars:

	1958	1973
Exports	486	5,040
Imports	801	8,640
Tourist receipts	69	3,150
Foreign private capital	15	795

The response of foreign-trade, private-capital inflow, and tourist receipts proved to be nothing less than phenomenal. An important consequence of this new direction has been a quickening of Spain's economic growth rate as the external impulses were transmitted to the domestic economy.

In the three prestabilization years, from 1956 to 1958, Spain incurred deficits in the basic balance,[51] with the consequence that her international liquidity position became gravely impaired. Following the 1959 stabilization program Spain's payments position improved dramatically. Except for the two years of 1965–66, Spain's basic balance during the long 1959–73 registered surpluses. The cumulative effect of these overall payments surpluses was to build up the nation's foreign reserves to their

TABLE 3

SPAIN:
SELECTED INTERNATIONAL ECONOMIC TRANSACTIONS,
1957–73
(In Millions of United States Dollars)

Year	Exports (f.o.b.)	Imports (f.o.b.)	Tourist Receipts	Emigrant Remittances	Foreign Private Capital (net)
1957	476	856	74	51	13
1958	486	801	69	53	15
1959	503	750	138	48	42
1960	745	697	296	66	40
1961	749	1,048	385	116	207
1962	800	1,438	513	211	107
1963	786	1,799	679	258	214
1964	1,005	2,076	919	319	268
1965	1,019	2,778	1,105	362	322
1966	1,308	3,300	1,292	420	302
1967	1,419	3,200	1,210	452	502
1968	1,667	3,242	1,213	463	437
1969	1,994	3,865	1,311	562	481
1970	2,483	4,357	1,681	674	697
1971	2,978	4,577	2,054	809	602
1972	3,507	6,070	2,486	905	795
1973	5,040	8,640	3.150	1,268	795

Sources: International Monetary Fund, International Financial Statistics, vol. 19, no. 11 (November, 1966). Banco de España, Informe Anual 1970, appendix 19, and Informe Anual 1971, appendix 62. Banco de Bilbao, Economic Report 1973, abridged version, p. 53.

historical peak level of $6.8 billion at the end of 1973. Spain's growing commercial deficits (the merchandise balance) have been more than covered by tourist receipts, emigrant remittances, and the net inflow of foreign private capital.

The recurrence of strong inflationary pressures in 1965–66 diverted part of the excess home demand toward foreign markets, contributing to excessively wide trade gaps (totalling $3.75 billion for the two-year period). And so, despite high levels of tourist income, emigrant remittances, and private-capital flows from abroad, Spain experienced her first balance-of-payments deficits ($130 million in 1965 and $205 million in 1966) since 1958. The nation's large foreign reserves served to cushion the effects of the external deficits without forcing either devaluation of the peseta or the imposition of trade controls in 1965–66. Spain's policy-makers were thus provided with a margin of time within which to apply restraining monetary and fiscal measures against the boom. In 1967, however, the exchange rate was devalued from about 60 to 70 pesetas per United States dollar. Subsequently, with the rapid buildup of the nation's gold and foreign-exchange holdings, the peseta was revalued upward relative to the United States dollar between 1971 and 1973.

Table 4 illustrates Spain's typical balance-of-payments position since the stabilization program. For example, in 1972 a negative merchandise balance of $2.564 billion was offset by a positive services balance of $2.31 billion and a positive remittances balance of $908 million. The net effect of these transactions resulted in a current account surplus of $653 million. In that year Spain also received an inflow of autonomous capital

TABLE 4

SPAIN'S BALANCE OF INTERNATIONAL PAYMENTS, 1972
(In Millions of United States Dollars)

A. Goods and Services	— 255
Merchandise balance	—2,564
Balance of services	2,309
Tourism and travel	2,296
Freight and insurance	— 40
Investment yield	— 174
Technical assistance and royalties	— 179
Other	407
B. Balance of Remittances	908
C. Current Account (A+B)	653
D. Autonomous Capital	822
Long term private (net)	795
Public	27
E. Basic Balance (C+D)	1,475

Source: Derived from Banco de Bilbao, *Informe Economico 1973*, abridged version, p. 53.

(mainly private long-term capital) exceeding $800 million. The combination of positive balances in both the current and capital accounts yielded a surplus in the basic balance of $1.475 billion, most of which served to increase Spain's gold and foreign-exchange reserves. The negative balances in the categories "investment yield" and "technical assistance and royalties" reflect Spain's growing dependence on foreign investment, management, and technology since 1959.

THE COMPOSITION AND DIRECTION OF TRADE

Spain's "opening" toward the world economy, as we have suggested, has taken numerous forms. The country had neither the resource base nor a large enough internal market to continue to develop in isolation. The new policymakers wanted to expose the Spanish economy to the dynamic impulses radiating from the industrial countries, particularly the European Economy Community. They have encouraged exports and substantially reduced barriers on several import categories. Consequently both imports and exports, visible and invisible, have grown appreciably in relationship to GNP since the 1959 stabilization program. The share of imports of goods and services increased from 8.6 percent of Spain's national income in 1956–58 to over 20 percent in 1973.

Spanish exports traditionally consisted of agricultural, forestry, and mineral products, particularly citrus fruits, olive oil, and wine. Since 1959, however, Spain has been eminently successful in diversifying her exports. In 1963, after four years of gradual liberalization of the economy, industrial commodities accounted for only a third of total exports; some ten years later, in 1972, industrial exports comprised nearly three-fourths of total exports. This expansion of industrial exports—on average by more than 25 percent annually between 1963 and 1972—represented a considerable penetration of Spanish industrial sales in world markets.[52] The capacity of a nation to transform its export structure toward a concentration of industrial goods is one of the most significant indices of successful development. Of the three categories of industrial exports—intermediate products, consumer goods, and capital goods—it is the last that has experienced the most notable growth. The share of capital goods in Spain's total exports rose from 3 percent in 1961 to 21 percent in 1972.[53] Leading consumer manufactures in Spain's exports list includes shoes, autos, clothes, and books. Major capital-goods exports include ships, textile machinery, generators, and machine tools. In 1970 Spain's principal market for capital goods was the group of six countries comprising the EEC, which purchased 32 percent of the exports of that sector, Latin America (32 percent), and the European Free Trade Association countries (11 percent).[54]

The Spanish capital-goods industry, once highly protected and sluggish, has been transformed into one that is aggressive and that today competes in major international biddings.[55] Camer International, S.A., an organization formed by eleven major banks of Madrid, Barcelona, and Bilbao, scouts for capital-goods business throughout the world, particularly in Latin America. With the backing of a $1-billion credit guarantee from the Spanish government, Camer has concluded major credit agreements with Latin American central banks in support of Spanish machinery and equipment exports. The bankers work in alliance with Sercobe, a syndicate of 170 Spanish machinery makers, and Techniberia, an association of 24 engineering consulting firms.[56]

The value of Spanish agricultural exports more than doubled between 1961 and 1971, but their share of total exports fell from 54 percent to 27 percent over the ten-year period.[57]

TABLE 5

SPAIN:
COMPOSITION OF IMPORTS, BY ECONOMIC CATEGORIES,
1957–58 and 1972–73

(In Percentages of Total)

| | Annual Average | |
	1957–58	1972–73
Food products	11.6	13.3
Capital goods	21.2	26.6
Raw materials, fuels and intermediate goods	61.4	51.8
Consumer manufactures	5.8	8.3
	100.0	100.0

Sources: For 1957–58, Rodney H. Mills, Jr., "The Spanish 'Miracle': Growth and Change in the Spanish Economy, 1959 to Mid-1965," Board of Governors of the Federal Reserve System, *Staff Economic Studies*, no. 14 (December 1965), p. 6, table 2; for 1972–73, Banco de Bilbao, *Informe Economico 1973*, p. 157.

The commodity structure of Spanish imports, on the other hand, did not change appreciably between the latter fifties and the early seventies. The share of food products in the total import bill (see Table 5) increased only slightly from about 12 percent in 1957/58 to 13 percent in 1972/73; the relative importance of capital goods is reflected in a rising share of the total, from 21 percent in the first period to nearly 27 percent in the latter two years. The category "raw materials, fuels and intermediate goods" showed a declining relative importance, from 61 percent in 1957/58 to 52 percent in 1972/73. Consumer manufactures increased their participation from about 5 percent to 8 percent in the latter period. More important than the growing share of capital goods in the nation's import structure has been the explosive rise in Spain's capacity to import supported by the growth of exports of goods and services, emigrant-worker remittances, and the inflow of private foreign capital. The result has been a tremendous expansion of capital-goods imports that has contributed to the modernization of Spain's industrial plant. This reequipment effort has allowed the Spanish economy to make good lost ground in world markets in the two previous decades and to approach the market share that corresponds to her skilled-labor force and her industrial capability.[58]

Finally, the low share of consumer manufactures in Spain's total imports in 1957/58 (less than 6 percent) demonstrates that the country's potential for import substitution industrialization in this category was virtually exhausted. Instead, Spain seized the opportunity to substitute the home production of intermediate goods such as steel, cement, chemicals, and fertilizer for the imported commodities previously purchased abroad.

TABLE 6

SPAIN'S FOREIGN TRADE WITH THE UNITED STATES
AND SELECTED WORLD AREAS, 1957–58 AND 1970–71
(In Millions of United States Dollars)

Area	Average 1957-58	Average 1970-71	Percent of Total 1957-58	Percent of Total 1970-71	Percent Change 1957-58 to 1970-71
		Imports (c.i.f.)			
United States	206	833.9	23.8	17.1	303.6
EEC	186.0	1,592.4	21.4	32.8	756.1
EFTA	141.7	698.9	16.3	14.4	393.2
Latin America	96.8	431.1	11.1	8.9	345.3
Others	237.6	1,298.8	27.4	26.8	446.6
Total	868.7	4,855.1	100.0	100.0	458.8
		Exports (f.o.b.)			
United States	47.6	393.6	9.5	14.8	726.8
EEC	139.5	976.5	27.8	36.7	600.0
EFTA	134.2	450.5	26.7	16.9	235.6
Latin America	56.4	293.3	11.2	11.0	420.0
Others	124.8	548.5	24.8	20.6	339.5
Total	502.5	2,662.4	100.0	100.0	429.8

Sources: 1957: *Direction of International Trade;* United Nations, International Monetary Fund, and International Bank for Reconstruction and Development (New York, 1958), Series T, vol. 9, no. 10, pp. 150–52.
1958: *Direction of Trade,* Annual 1958–1962, International Monetary Fund and International Bank for Reconstruction and Development (New York, 1963), pp. 170–71.
1970/71: Banco Exterior de España, *Hechos y Cifras de la Economia Española 1971* (Madrid, 1972), pp. 612, 615–17, 623, and 625–27.

The period under study indicates major changes in Spain's country-trade pattern. While Spain increased her dollar trade with each of the nations or areas listed (Table 6), it is evident that the Common Market's share in Spanish commerce has been expanding appreciably. Thus the EEC was the origin of 21 percent of Spain's imports in 1957/58 and 33 percent in 1970/71. Concurrently, the Common Market absorbed 37 percent of Spain's exports in 1970/71, compared with 28 percent in the earlier two years. The 756 percent expansion of Common Market exports to Spain, from $186 million to $1.592 billion, indicates that Spain has emerged as an important market for the EEC. Spain's merchandise trade with the Latin American area grew substantially between the latter fifties and early seventies. However, the share of Spain's exports going to the area remained constant at 11 percent from 1957/58 to 1970/71 and the relative importance of Latin America as a source of Spain's imports diminished somewhat.

Western Europe (EEC and EFTA) provided Spain with 47 percent of her imports in 1970/71, and the United States was the origin of another 17 percent. Taken together, these two markets were the source of 64 percent of Spain's imports and received, in 1970/71, 68 percent of her exports. The stepped-up growth of the Spanish economy in the sixties, together with the measures liberalizing commodity trade, have thus transformed Spain into a respectable market for Atlantic Community exports.

TOURISM

Foreign-exchange earnings from tourism, which averaged $70 million in 1957/58, reached nearly $3.2 billion in 1973 (see Table 3). In that year 34,560,000 travellers visited Spain, a number only slightly less than the total population of the country. Tourist receipts contributed a sum equal to about two-thirds of Spain's commodity exports during the five-year period of 1969–73.

What factors explain this tremendous growth in the nation's "invisible" exports? To begin with, there are the cultural and historical attractions provided by the remains of the graceful Moorish civilization and of medieval churches and castles. Spain combines a large land area with the longest coastline in a temperate climate—all within easy reach of 250 million Europeans. However, it is necessary to go beyond these cultural and geographical factors to explain the success of Spanish tourism. The 1959 devaluation of the peseta provided the major initial impulse to the industry. Income growth in industrial Europe has also contributed to Spain's booming tourist industry. However, it appears that the price factor was the more decisive one. In a statistical study[59] on the impact of devaluation and revaluation on tourist earnings (including Spain), an

IMF economist finds good, if imperfect, evidence that tourist receipts are very sensitive to the price factor. Following the devaluation of the peseta in July, 1959 (from 40 pesetas to 60 pesetas per United States dollar) a vacation in Spain suddenly became a bargain for foreign visitors. Frenchmen, Germans, Portuguese, and others could now get a one-third discount (in their own currencies) on Spanish hotels, restaurants, and transportation services. In 1965, six years after devaluation, Spain became the world's leading tourist country in terms of net earnings.[60]

The continuing rise in tourism infrastructure (the number of hotel rooms rose by 12 percent annually in 1968–72) also contributed to Spain's capacity to attract foreign travellers.[61] Significantly, much of the foreign investment in land was associated with tourism activities. Finally, the large increase in air transport capacity in recent years, and the fall in air fares (before the OPEC action on oil prices), relative to other prices, have placed Spanish touristic services within relatively easy access of Western Europe.[62] Of the 27 million persons who visited Spain in 1971, 22.2 million (82 percent) came from Europe. More than half of the Europeans, 13.6 million, came from the six Common Market countries (including 8.6 million Frenchmen), and 8.3 million came from EFTA countries, mainly British and Portuguese.[63] American visitors totalled only 1,162,000; however, the average expenditure by those Americans in Spain was much larger than that of the average European traveller.

FOREIGN PRIVATE CAPITAL

Prior to 1959 the role of foreign private capital in Spain was negligible. Restrictions on the repatriation of capital and on remittance of profits, an overvalued exchange rate, and a host of other factors produced an unpropitious climate for investment. In the two-year period of 1957–58 the net inflow of foreign private capital averaged a mere $14 million.

Since 1959 the Spanish government has taken a number of measures to facilitate the inflow of private capital from abroad. Restrictions on repatriation of capital for investments made after July 28, 1959, as well as restrictions on the transfer out of Spain of profits, were eliminated. And in April, 1963, the government passed a measure that removed all restrictions on the percentage of capital that nonresidents could invest for the purpose of establishing, modernizing, or expanding enterprises in a large number of specific sectors of the economy. The Spanish government also took steps to provide greater accessibility to the nation's stock market for prospective investors.

From the midsixties onward the Spanish government gradually adopted a more selective policy.[64] Official and private attitudes toward foreign ownership and control of Spanish economic activities began to show signs of ambivalance. "We hope and expect the rate of foreign investment will continue, but we would like to alter the quality," says Francisco Gallego Balmaseda, head of the foreign-investment section for the Third Economic and Social Development Plan.

Private capital has entered Spain in many forms: direct investments in subsidiaries, portfolio investments (largely via the Spanish stock market), and real-estate purchases (mainly hotels and apartment buildings associated with the burgeoning tourist industry). On top of the private investments made by foreigners in Spain, there occurred a substantial repatriation of Spanish funds held abroad. These repatriated investments averaged $65 million per year between 1961 and 1964 and contributed to the much enlarged volume of capital formation in the nation.[66]

From 1960 to 1973 Spain received over $4.3 billion in net private long-term capital from abroad, as follows:[67]

	(In Millions of United States Dollars)
Real estate investments	1,786
Direct investments	1,999
Portfolio investments	544

The above sum, it should be noted, excludes foreign loans and credits to private enterprises in Spain.

Foreign direct investments between 1960 and 1972 were attracted principally to the chemical (26 percent), commerce (10.5 percent), transport-equipment (9.8 percent), food-products (9.3 percent), real-estate (7.7 percent), electrical-machinery (5.5 percent), nonelectrical-machinery (4.6 percent), and metal-fabricating industries (3.5 percent).[68]

By country of origin, the United States was the principal source of accumulated direct investments in Spain, followed by Switzerland (a large part of whose investments probably originate in the United States), and the European Economic Community (led by the Federal Republic of Germany):[69]

	1960–72 (percentages)
United States	31.7
EEC (six)	29.1
Switzerland	23.4
Other	15.8

Major United States-based multinational corporations are well represented in the Spanish economy. This fact was revealed in a special study that considered the 400 most important industrial enterprises of the world, according to a *Fortune* classification, 200 belonging to the United States and 200 to the rest of the world.[70] Of the 200 largest United States industrial enterprises, 92 have subsidiaries in Spain, of which 61 hold majority participation.[71] Of the other 200, only 50 have subsidiaries in Spain, 29 belonging to the six members of the original European Economic Community.

A Stanford Research Institute study cited five major incentives that the United States affiliates believe that Spain offers to foreign investors.[72] These are, in descending order of importance, (1) a rapidly expanding market, (2) a favorable investment climate, (3) relatively low labor costs, (4) generally lower tax rates, and (5) political, economic, and financial stability. Spain's favorable geographic location for exports to Europe, Latin America, and the Middle East, and an eventually closer association with the EEC, were also mentioned by the affiliates.

Spain is now in its final stages of a six-year preferential trade agreement with the Common Market countries (see next section). Spanish-made industrial goods enter the original six-member EEC at a substantial reduction from the duties that existed before the 1970 agreement. Consequently, as Spain's link with the EEC becomes closer, American-based multinational corporations are increasingly integrating their Spanish operations into their overall European strategic planning.

American and European automotive companies were making new large-scale investment commitments in Spain in response to favorable changes in government regulations. The rush to set up new automobile plants began in 1972 when the Spanish government ruled that new models no longer required 90 percent local content. They could have as little as 50 percent locally made parts, so long as two-thirds of the cars were exported.[73] Spanish cars became highly competitive internationally once manufacturers could import parts that were too costly to make in Spain. A new Ford complex will produce some 250,000 cars and 400,000 engines a year, with a total investment of $1 billion—the largest single foreign investment of the Ford Motor Company.[74] The new facilities, to be located near Valencia, will employ an estimated 7,000 workers and the first car is scheduled to come off the production line in autumn of 1976. General Motors is considering building a 150,000-vehicle-a-year automobile plant at Seville and expansion plans are underway for Seat (the government firm licensed by Fiat), Chrysler, British Leyland, and two makers of French cars, Citroen Hispania and Fasa Renault.

The Spanish government is increasingly emphasizing a list of criteria for the selection of new investment from abroad. These include:[75]

(a) export potential;
(b) research and development activities to be performed within Spain;
(c) reduced requirements for payment of royalties and of technical and management fees;
(d) increased training of Spanish nationals;
(e) greater use of national partners; and
(f) investments of significance to regional development.

A new decree law issued in October, 1973, further restricts the conditions under which foreign direct investments may enter the country. The new regulation cancelled the provision of the 1963 decree law that allowed foreign investment to exceed 50 percent in eighteen specified sectors without permission.[76] The effect of the new law is that foreign participation in Spanish enterprises in any sector may not exceed 50 percent *without special authorization* of the Spanish government.

Initially, foreign direct investments were directed mainly into high-technology, capital-intensive industries. Thus the nation's excellent investment climate and rapidly expanding domestic market attracted large-scale ventures by multinational companies in Spain's automotive, chemical, machinery, and electrical-appliances industries. The foreign equity investments brought advanced technology and superior management techniques —two resources in which Spain was most deficient.

The increasingly selective criteria will probably not slow the pace of new investment significantly. In 1973 new foreign direct investments with a majority holding in Spanish enterprises reached 31.3 billion pesetas, an amount roughly equal to the total of investments of the three previous years.[77] In addition to the construction of new plant capacity by the foreign automotive firms, multinational corporations are planning large-scale aluminum, chemical, petrochemical, steel and petroleum-refinery projects in Spain.

SPAIN AND THE NEW EUROPE

Spain and the European Economic Community entered into a preferential trade agreement on June 29, 1970. The agreement was the outcome of some eight years of negotiation since Spain first tendered its application for community membership in 1962. In the view of Spanish officials, the absence of an agreement between their country and the EEC would in the long run have hindered the growth of the Spanish economy and would also have adversely affected political relations between them. Further, it was in the interest of the EEC to encourage Spain to continue the policy of ecnomic liberalization initiated in 1959 with Europe's support. At the signing of the agreement, Spanish Foreign Minister Gregorio Lopez Bravo stressed the political significance of the choice made by his country. "Spain," he stated, "ever attentive to three continents, has now taken the decision to plant its roots in Europe: our destiny is worked out. This agreement indeed only represents a first step, but the practical irreversibility of the process is present in everybody's mind, as well as the certainty of the final objective."[78]

The agreement provides for a six-year transitional period during which

Spain and the EEC will gradually abolish most of the obstacles to trade, while respecting the provisions of the General Agreement on Tariffs and Trade. The agreement does not provide for Spanish membership in the EEC, but envisages a "second stage" after the end of the six-year period, during which Spain and the EEC will seek closer relations in the form of a customs union. Significantly, a further unanimous decision by the EEC membership would be required to move on to the second stage. So far as some member states are concerned, the transition to the next stage would depend on political developments in Spain.[79]

The first stage of the preferential trade agreement, which became effective on October 1, 1970, has a solely commercial content coming under EEC jurisdiction (see chapter eight in the present volume). Unlike association agreements, the preferential trade agreement with Spain takes no account of such important aspects as labor, regional development, or harmonization of agrarian and fiscal policies. The experience against which the agreement was negotiated was one in which the share of Spain's total exports taken by the EEC was declining, i.e., from 36.7 percent in 1964/65 to 30.5 percent in 1968/69. After the agreement went into effect, the share of Spain's exports to the Community of Six was restored, averaging 36.7 percent for the years 1971–73.

When the EEC membership was expanded from six to nine members at the beginning of 1973, Spain tried to reach an understanding with the community on an adjustment to its preferential agreement that would take into account the new, enlarged situation. As a result, a protocol was signed with the community that was said to "stop the clock" in terms of the tariff arrangements between Spain and the three new members; that is to say, the preferential rates of the Spain-EEC agreement would not be applied to the United Kingdom, Ireland and Denmark, in either direction. The situation was further complicated when in the spring of 1973 the EEC and the European Free Trade Association agreed to form a European trading bloc of sixteen countries from which Spain was excluded.

The situation that Spain faced at the beginning of 1974 with the new Europe of sixteen, and more specifically, the EEC Nine, was an unfortunate impasse. Relations between Spain and the EEC operated on a "stand still" that for all practical purposes amounted to the following: the trade preference agreement of 1970 continues to function between Spain and the original Six of the Common Market.[80]

The United States supports Spain's interest in closer ties with the rest of Western Europe and a larger role for Spain in Western defense. The Spanish-United States Agreement of Friendship and Cooperation, signed on August 7, 1970, constitutes, in the United States' view, an important factor contributing to stability in the Mediterranean. The United States has favored Spain's admission to NATO since 1955. However, Denmark and Norway, on political grounds, have consistently opposed Spanish admission to the alliance.[81]

CONCLUSIONS AND PROSPECTS

Spain's new policymakers have been eminently successful in transforming an inward-oriented "corporate state" to a European-style market economy. The profound power shift from the Falange to the "Christian technocrats" of the Opus Dei signified Spain's emergence into a postideological era in which, for a time, economics had primacy over politics.

Since 1959 the Spanish economy has been characterized by a number of salient features including accelerated industrialization and urbanization, the growth of a consumer middle class, the decline of mass poverty, the participation of foreign investment through multinational enterprises, increasing scope for economic freedom and progressive integration with the world economy, particularly the European Economic Community.

Spain's current energy dependence resembles the patterns of other industrialized nations of Western Europe. In 1950 coal was the source of 74 percent and oil of 9 percent of Spain's primary energy; by 1972 the share of coal had fallen to 21 percent and that of oil had grown to 58 percent of total primary energy use.[82] Spain's shift from coal to oil has increased enormously the nation's import dependence for meeting its energy requirements. Virtually self-sufficient in coal production, Spain had to import 96 percent of her oil in 1972. In that year, the value of Spain's petroleum bill amounted to about $1 billion, or 15 percent of total imports. With the four-fold increase in the price of internationally traded crue dictated by the OPEC cartel, Spain's petroleum bill exceeded $4 billion in 1974. The consequences of such an abrupt increase in Spain's energy costs were not difficult to foresee: a balance-of-payments deficit, a slowdown of industrial and total production, and exacerbation of inflationary pressures.

Additionally, Spain's greater integration with the world economy may become in the post-1973 climate a source of economic deceleration as industrialized Europe and the United States adjust to the higher energy costs through diminished rates of economic growth. As a consequence, Spain's markets for industrial exports may weaken and income growth from tourism, a major source of foreign exchange for Spain, may also be adversely affected.

The economic future of Spain is, of course, intertwined with the outcome of the political succession. Upon the death of Francisco Franco, Prince Juan Carlos de Borbon was installed as monarch on November 22, 1975. Will Spain follow the Portuguese way of political upheaval, nationalization of industries, and severe economic dislocation associated with the regime of the Armed Forces Movement?

King Juan Carlos must tread carefully among a strong minority of die-hard Franco loyalists, the reformist movements (e.g. the Social Democrats and Christian Democrats), and the extremists (e.g., ETA, the Basque separatist group, and FRAP, a band of Maoist terrorists.) A number of factors in Spain tilt the balance in favor of stability as against political upheaval in the transitional period. First, the Spanish armed forces are a professional group who will back a moderate constitutional ruler against any extremist faction. Second, Spain has not been engaged in a protracted and inconclusive colonial war of the sort that sapped the morale of the Portuguese armed forces. Finally, new middle classes have emerged in Spain that have "a stake" in the market economy. The King's fundamental problem—decompression of the authoritarian system toward a competitive, parliamentary democracy—poses an uncertain outcome. Should he succeed, Spain will achieve its major foreign policy aim: full membership in the European Community.

Spain's continued movement toward an open, competitive market economy will depend on the capacity of the "Europeanists" in the Iberian nation to overcome the lingering resistance of the "traditionalist" groups. And in turn, the success of the Europeanists will be influenced by the response of the Common Market to Spain's desire for membership in the European Economic Community.

NOTES

1. Charles W. Anderson, *The Political Economy of Modern Spain: Policy Making in an Authoritarian System* (Madison: The University of Wisconsin Press, 1970), p. xiii.

2. Stanley G. Payne, "In the Twilight of the Franco Era", *Foreign Affairs Quarterly Review*, vol. 49, no. 2 (January, 1971), p. 343.

3. *The OECD Observer*, no. 70 (August, 1974), p. 18.

4. Banco Exterior de España, *Hechos y Cifras de la Economia Española, 1971* (Madrid, 1972), p. 67.

5. U. S. Department of Commerce, *Basic Data on the Economy of Spain*, OBR-63-157 (Washington, D.C.: Government Printing Office, 1963), pp. 1–2.

6. Sax Bradford, *Spain and the World* (Princeton, N.J.: D. Van Nostrand Co., Inc., 1962), p. 7.

7. Department of State, *Background Notes: Spain*, no. 7800 (January 1971), p. 1.

8. Loc. cit.

9. John F. Ramsey, *Spain: The Rise of the First World Power* (University: The University of Alabama Press, 1973), p. 11.

10. Ibid., p. 19.
11. Sax Bradford, op. cit., pp. 60–61.
12. Ibid., p. 83.
13. Ramsay, op. cit., p. 79.
14. Pascual Carrion, *Los latifundios en España: su importancia, origen, consecuencias y solucion* (Madrid, 1932), pp. 291–96, cited in John Ramsay, *Spain*, p. 81.
15. Jaime Vicens Vives, *An Economic History of Spain*, with the collaboration of Jorge Nadal Oller (Princeton: Princeton University Press, 1969), p. 31.
16. Julián Marías, *La España posible en tiempo de Carlos III* (Madrid: Sociedad de Estudios y Publicaciones, 1963), p. 123.
17. Ramsay, from "Foreword."
18. "Inversiones extranjeras en españa," *Boletin de Londres*, no. 241 (September/October 1971), p. 6.
19. Ramon Tamames, *Estructura Economica de España* (Madrid: Sociedad de Estudios y Publicaciones, 1960), pp. 5 and 200.
20. Jaime Vicens Vives, op. cit., pp. 657 and 660–62.
21. "Inversiones extranjeras en españa," op. cit., p. 8.
22. Derived from *Anuario Estadistico de España*, 1970, p. 51.
23. See "Foreword" by John Davis Lodge to Presidency of the Government of Spain, *Economic and Social Development Program for Spain, 1964–1967* (Baltimore: Johns Hopkins Press, 1965), pp. v–vi, and Joaquin Gutierrez Cano, "The Economic Development of Spain," *Spain–U.S. Trade Bulletin*, no. 41 (March/April, 1968), p. 17.
24. George Hills, *Spain* (New York & Washington: Praeger Publishers, 1970), p. 436.
25. Ibid., p. 267.
26. Consejo de Economia Nacional, cited in Higinio Paris Equilaz, *El Desarrollo Economico Español, 1906–1964* (Madrid: Suc. J. Sanchez de Ocana y Cia., 1964), pp. 46–47.
27. Seymour Martin Lipset, *Political Man* (Garden City, N.Y.: Doubleday & Co., 1963), p. 130.
28. International Bank for Reconstruction and Development, *The Economic Development of Spain* (Baltimore: John Hopkins University Press, 1963), pp. 344–88.
29. Clark Kerr et al., *Industrialism and Industrial Man* (New York: Oxford University Press, 1964), pp. 97–105.
30. Including an initial $63 million credit from the Export-Import Bank, the United States provided Spain with $1.6 billion in economic assistance in the period 1950–65, as follows:

	(millions of U.S. dollars)
Defense support	507
P.L. 480 loans	527
Social assistance	188
Export-Import Bank credits	393
	1,615

(See Banco Hispano Americano, *La Situacion Economica en 1965* [Madrid, 1966], pp. 243–44).

31. Francis Canavan, "Spain and the Common Market," *America* (July 7, 1962), p. 462.

32. Armando de Miguel and Juan J. Linz, "El Mercado Comun, El Capital Extranjero y El Empresario Español," *Productividad*, no. 26, 1963. The authors show that the disposition to integrate with the EEC varies directly with the degree of industrialization of the provinces.

33. Fed by growing public deficits, wholesale and retail prices accelerated during the 1960s. Exports reflected an overvalued exchange rate and failed to increase between 1951 and 1958, while the value of imports doubled. Consequently, the trade balance was transformed from a surplus of $70 million in 1951 to a deficit of $360 million in 1958, and by June, 1959, Spain's net official reserves registered a $4 million deficit.

34. Rodney H. Mills, Jr., "The Spanish Miracle": Growth and Change in the Spanish Economy, 1959 to Mid-1965," Board of Governors of the Federal Reserve System, *Staff Economic Studies*, no. 14 (December, 1965), pp. 8–10.

35. Ibid., p. 10.

36. See Hollis B. Chenery, "Growth and Structural Change," *Finance and Development Quarterly*, vol. 8, no. 3 (September, 1971), pp. 16–28.

37. Banco de Bilbao, *The Spanish Economy in Figures* (Madrid, July 1974).

38. Ministerio de Industria, *La Industria Española en 1972* (Madrid, 1973), pp. 19 and 231.

39. "La Ganaderia en España," *Boletin de Londres*, no. 1972 (December, 1972), p. 8.

40. James Lopez, "Spain's Agriculture in the 1960's," *Foreign Agriculture* (May 8, 1972), p. 7.

41. Ibid., p. 6.

42. Contabilidad Nacional, cited in Banco de Bilbao, *Informe Economico, 1972* (Madrid, 1973), p. 251.

43. Contabilidad Nacional, cited in Banco de España, *Informe Anual* (Madrid, July, 1971), p. 119, appendix 5.

44. Derived from Banco de Bilbao, *Informe Economico 1973* (Madrid, 1974), p. 274.

45. Instituto Nacional de Estadistica, *España en Cifras* (Madrid, 1972), p. 2.

46. Charles F. Gallagher, *Religion, Class, and Family in Spain*, American Universities Field Staff, West Europe Series, vol. 9, no. 4 (February, 1974), p. 3.

47. International Bank for Reconstruction and Development, *The Economic Development of Spain* (Baltimore: The Johns Hopkins Press, 1963), p. 48.

48. Presidency of the Government of Spain, *Economic and Social Development Program for Spain, 1964–1967* (Baltimore: Johns Hopkins Press, 1965), pp. 31–34.

49. *OECD Economic Surveys: Spain* (Paris, January, 1972), pp. 37–39.

50. *Third Plan of Economic and Social Development*, Monografia Informaciones (Mar. 19, 1972), p. 1.

51. The *basic balance* registers the algebraic difference between autonomous credits and autonomous debits. *Autonomous* transactions are independently

motivated credits and debits; they exclude compensatory (or induced) transactions, which respond to a disequilibrium in the balance of payments.

52. *OECD Economic Surveys: Spain* (Paris, March, 1973), p. 20.

53. Derived from Banco de España, *Boletin Estadistico* (February, 1970), p. 72, and Banco de Bilbao, *Informe Economico 1973*, abridged version, p. 47.

54. "The Spanish Capital Goods Industry," Banco Central, *Boletin Informativo*, no. 264 (April, 1972), p. 68.

55. "The New Conquistadores," *Barron's* (Nov. 18, 1968), p. 9.

56. Loc. cit.

57. James Lopes, "Spain—A Thriving Commercial Customer," *Foreign Agricultural Trade of the United States*, U. S. Department of Agriculture (April, 1973), p. 48.

58. *OECD Economic Surveys: Spain* (Paris, March, 1973), p. 22.

59. Andreas S. Gerakis, "Economic Man: The Tourist," *The Fund and Bank Review: Finance and Development*, vol. 3, No. 1 (March, 1966), pp. 47–48.

60. IMF, *International Financial News Survey* (Sept. 2, 1966).

61. *OECD Economic Reports: Spain* (Paris, March, 1973), p. 11.

62. Loc. cit.

63. Banco de Bilbao, *Informe Economico 1971* (Madrid, 1972), p. 220.

64. Antonio Garriguez Walker, "The Emerging Trends for Foreign Investment in Spain," *Spain–U.S. Trade Bulletin*, no. 72 (June/July, 1973), pp. 21–28.

65. "Foreign Industry Pours into Spain," *Wall Street Journal* (Apr. 27, 1973), p. 34.

66. Derived from Banco de España, *Informe sobre la Economia Epañola en 1965* (Madrid, 1966), p. 56.

67. Derived from Banco de España, *Informe Annual 1970*, appendix 19, and *Informe Annual 1971*, appendix 62; Banco de Bilbao, *Informe Economico 1973*, abridged version, p. 53.

68. Banco Exterior de España, *Hechos y Cifras de la Economia Española 1972* (Madrid, 1973), p. 755.

69. Ibid., p. 756.

70. *Informe sobre Inversiones Extranjeras en España* (Geneva: Common Market Business Reports, 1969).

71. Ibid., p. 5.

72. Stanford Research Institute, *American Investments in Spain* (Barcelona: American Chamber of Commerce in Spain, 1972), p. 15.

73. *Barron's*, July 21, 1973.

74. Diplomatic Information Service, *Spain 74*, vol. 2, no. 10 (May, 1974).

75. Stanford Research Institute, op. cit., p. 19.

76. *Spain–U.S. Trade Bulletin*, no. 75 (November/December, 1973).

77. Diplomatic Information Office, *Spain 74*, vol. 2, no. 8 (March, 1974).

78. *Europe*, no. 600 (new series), (June 29, 1970), p. 6.

79. The Benelux countries object to Spanish membership in the EEC on political grounds. On the other hand, West Germany and France would apparently welcome Spain's association with the Common Market. See Sidney F. Wexler, "Franco's Peace: Spain Thirty Years After the Insurrection," *The Yale Review*, vol. 56, no. 7 (October, 1966).

80. Banco de Bilbao, *Informe Economico 1973*, Madrid, 1974, p. 185.

81. *Atlantic Community News* (August 1970), p. 3.

82. Banco Central, *Estudio Economico 1971* (Madrid, 1972), p. 49, and Banco de Bilbao, *Informe Economico 1973* (Madrid, 1974), pp. 50–51.

8

Europe and its Mediterranean Littoral: One Club or Two?

JON McLIN

BY THE moment of its enlargement to nine members on January 1, 1973, the European Economic Community had become a significant participant in its own right in international economic relations. Numbers are suggestive: even before enlargement, the combined exports of EEC members—excluding their exports to each other—had come to exceed those of the United States, which had previously been the world's largest trading unit. In 1970, the total exports of the United States amounted to $43 billion. With internal trade excluded, the exports of the six original EEC members were valued at $45 billion in the same year, and those of the nine members of the expanded EEC amounted to approximately $64 billion.

Such figures can also be misleading, however, and in general it is well to be skeptical about the implication, which all too frequently characterizes the impressive presentation of aggregate community figures, that there is a unity of policy to match the unity of statistics. For most sectors of activity, the EEC countries are not as one. As of early 1973, that is true, e.g., of monetary policy—notwithstanding the existence of the jointly floating "snake"—of macroeconomic policy, of energy policy, and of most aspects of the legal and fiscal environment in which businesses operate.

However, foreign economic relations, and trade policy especially, are areas where for most questions the community's legal and effective competence exceeds that of the member states and where it has continued to grow since the EEC negotiated as a unit in the Kennedy Round of tariff negotiations. One consequence has been the inexorable involvement of the community in foreign-policy issues (e.g. the Arab-Israeli question), with which foreign-trade questions are often linked. A logically possible outcome of this process, which has interested many EEC-watchers, is the prospect that the necessity of managing foreign-trade policy in a collective way could induce the member countries to unify other aspects of their foreign policies, especially in those regions where their trade relations are intense or where most foreign-policy questions are economic in content.

This kind of rationale explains in part the keen and somewhat glamorous interest observable in the early 1970s in the community's rapidly developing network of special relationships with the countries of the Mediterranean basin. Advocates of a community "Mediterranean policy," as well as critics of the existing relationships, such as the United States government, appear at times to share the judgment (1) that the Mediterranean region constitutes an organically evolving system, and (2) that the preferential trade agreements with the community are significant instruments that encourage consolidation of the system. Some support can certainly be found for this appreciation, but the evidence is not one-sided. A strong prima facie impression is unavoidable that what characterizes the Mediterranean is not unity but diversity, a diversity exemplified by the political, psychological, and economic gulf that divides the European north from the predominantly Muslim and non-Western littorals in the East and the South, and by the division between European countries that do, and those that do not, belong to the EEC. These conflicting interpretations, which have not been resolved by the community itself, should be borne in mind as we explore the nature of the economic interests and relations of the community and its member states in the region.

THE ECONOMIC GIVENS

Trade

The overall trade figures for 1969 between the six members of the EEC and the seventeen nonmember Mediterranean countries[1] reveal the importance of the commercial relationship. Exports of the Six amounted to $6.3 billion, which exceeded their exports ($5.9 billion) to the United States. Imports were $5.3 billion, compared to $7.3 billion from the United States. If one adds the four candidate countries (i.e. the three new members plus Norway, which elected not to join at present), the figures look like this, for the same year (1969):

	(In Billions of United States Dollars)		
	The Six	The Ten	
Exports to Mediterranean Countries	$6.3	8.0	
Share of Total Exports of the Ten			16.5 Percent
Imports from Mediterranean Countries	5.3	6.8	
Share of Total Imports of the Ten			12.9 Percent

These totals are the result of a decade of rapid growth. From 1960 to 1969, the imports of the Ten from the area grew at an average annual rate of 10.7 percent and exports at a rate of 7.9 percent.[2]

About 40 percent of the 1969 imports of the Six from the area represents crude petroleum, mainly from Algeria and Libya; the rest is roughly
equally divided between manufacturers and agricultural/primary products. Of the 55 percent fo the energy requirements of Western Europe
that is covered by oil, almost all is imported and about a third of the
imports comes from North Africa.[3] Much of the rest comes via pipelines
ports, and tankers in the Mediterranean regoin. This is clearly the most
sensitive item in the trade accounts from the EEC's standpoint.

The key role of petroleum is also apparent when one looks at trade
flows from the perspective of nonmembers of the EEC. The leading
Mediterranean exporters to the enlarged community are the leading oil
producers: Libya and Algeria. They are followed by Spain, Yugoslavia,
and Morocco. The leading importers of community goods are Spain,
Yugoslavia, Greece, Algeria, and Israel, in that order.[4] Dependency of
Mediterranean exporters on community markets is generally high and is
especially so for some countries and some products. In 1968 the Ten
took over 52 percent of the exports of the region as a whole, including the
following percentages for specific countries: Algeria, 83 percent; Cyprus,
72 percent; Libya, 86 percent; Morocco, 69 percent; and Portugal, 60
percent. Agricultural commodities are the most acutely dependent on
Community markets. Eighty-eight percent of the fresh tomatoes, 82 percent of the canned fruit, 89 percent of the potatoes, and 68 percent of the
wine exported from the Mediterranean countries is sold to the Ten.[5] This
dependency in part is the legacy of colonial structures that have been
inherited by newly independent countries, especially in the Maghreb.
Their wine and citrus production was established in large part to serve
markets in the metropole—markets that under present conditions of glut
tend to disappear, leaving the producers with an adjustment problem as
well as the necessity to import more necessary types of agricultural produce, in which they are not self-sufficient.

In the nonmember countries of the northern littoral, the trade dependency on the EEC is both less acute and historically different, but it is
not dissimilar in fundamentals. The community's share of the exports of
these countries, based on the latest available statistics in each case, was as
follows, stated in percentages (the percentage share of the country's next
most important trading partner is given in parenthesis):

Greece	45.9% (U.S., 9.8%)
Turkey	40.6% (U.S., 9.6%)
Portugal	18.3% (U.K., 20.4%)
Spain	36.1% (U.S., 14.1%)
Yugoslavia	32.9% (U.S.S.R., 14.4%

Source: Statistical Office of the European Communities, *Foreign Trade Monthly
Statistics,* 1972, no. 1.

As these figures cover only the present Six, one can infer that for the enlarged community the dependence would not be far below the 52 percent average for the region as a whole. Similarly, the heavy dependence of some of these countries on agricultural exports means that they share a common concern with their southern neighbors about the community's Common Agricultural Policy.

AGRICULTURE IN THE TOTAL EXPORTS OF SOUTHERN EUROPEAN COUNTRIES

	Production in 1965–67 (1959–61=100)		Value in 1965–67 (In Millions of United States Dollars)		
	Total	Agriculture	Total	Agriculture	(as Percentage of Total)
Portugal	201	179	632	162	25.6
Spain	186	164	1202	578	48.1
Yugoslavia	221	173	1188	321	27.0
Greece	196	180	410	293[a]	71.5
Turkey	144	132	491	395[b]	80.4

[a]Including $30 million of cotton and wool
[b]Including $130 million of cotton and wool

Source: OECD, Agricultural Development in Southern Europe, (Paris, 1969), p. 28.

The obviously heavy dependence on agricultural exports of Spain, Greece, and Turkey may be merely noted here; it will enter our discussion again when we discuss the trade arrangements between these countries and the community.

Movement of Persons

One of the strongest economic and human bonds tying the Mediterranean region to trans-Alpine Europe is the immense two-way flow of persons: Mediterranean workers and their families going north, and European tourists heading south for the sun. Both movements have an immense impact on employment patterns, the one filling jobs in the north, the other creating them in the south, and both serving to diminish the widespread unemployment and underemployment that is endemic in the Mediterranean countries. Their economic significance is reinforced by the fact that both movements are accompanied by sizable financial flows.

In 1972, the last year before enlargement, there were at least 3.8 million foreign *workers* in the Six, and virtually all of them came from Mediterranean countries, including EEC-member Italy.[6] If one adds to that figure estimates (entirely reliable figures on this issue do not exist) for non-working members of the migrants' families, and for the new member countries, the total is in the neighborhood of 10 million persons in

Western Europe who are living the migrant pattern.[7] The economic importance of this phenomenon is enormous in both the sending and the receiving countries. For the former, it is a substantial source of foreign exchange and an employment-escape valve that helps keep their demographic boilers from exploding: between 1950 and 1965, roughly half of the increase in working-age population in the European Mediterranean countries (plus Ireland and Finland) was absorbed by emigration. For the latter, it has provided a precious increment to the labor force that embattled governments have found useful in their attempt to combine high and sustained rates of economic growth with acceptable rates and patterns of social change for their indigenous populations. While foreign workers represent only 5 percent or so of the total work force of the EEC, at the margin they are much more important. In individual community countries in the 1960s the ratio

$$\frac{\text{annual increase in migrant work force}}{\text{annual increase in native work force}}$$

has ranged from 20 percent to 100 percent, and OECD projections suggest that it may be on the order of 50 percent in the 1970s.[8]

Nevertheless, the social and political costs of absorbing culturally different minorities on this scale have become increasingly evident to governments of the immigrant countries. In the years around 1970 there was considerable public discussion in Britain, France, and the Federal Republic of Germany (among other countries) about the conditions in which the immigrants lived and the desirability of imposing some kind of limits on the movement. In Switzerland the question became an important political issue, momentarily resolved only by a decision in effect to freeze the total number of immigrants in the country at about the 1970 level or below.

Pressures on governments are such that the issue is likely to be increasingly critical in the coming years. On the one hand, demographic and economic projections indicate that there will continue to be sizable and even growing labor surpluses in certain of the countries of emigration —especially Turkey and Yugoslavia—and that in economic terms, the countries of Northwest Europe will continue to be short of labor. On the other hand, the social acceptability of even higher levels of immigration is quite doubtful, especially in view of the changing ethnic composition of the flow. The government of Italy, whose nationals have been displaced by the Turks and Yugoslavs as the most numerous migrant recruits, has already begun using its legal (the nondiscrimination provisions of the Treaty of Rome) and political (its veto power over new international agreements by the community) powers to press for limits on the recourse to extra-EEC migration so long as Italy has a problem of unemployment and underemployment.[9]

Tourism

Figures for tourist movements, like those for migration, leave much to be desired, with respect both to totals and to countries of origin. The following table, the result of an OECD survey of member governments, nonetheless gives an idea of the order of magnitude of north-to-south tourist movements in Europe.

TOURISTS FROM EUROPEAN COUNTRIES OF OECD (1969)

Countries Visited	Arrivals	Nights
Recorded at registered tourist accommodation		
Greece	881,337	3,588,129
Italy	8,144,557	54,698,983
Portugal	689,996	2,736,586
Spain		39,726,947
Yugoslavia	3,624,802	17,858,755
Recorded at frontiers		
Greece	661,426	
Italy	6,307,800	
Portugal	808,300	
Spain	19,297,029	
Turkey	219,437	

Source: OECD, *International Tourism and Tourism Policy in OECD Member Countries, 1971,* (Paris, 1971).

Resource Flows

The four channels for transferring financial resources from the EEC to nonmember Mediterranean countries are workers' remittances, tourist expenditures, public aid, and private investment. There is, unfortunately, little documentary evidence available on the reverse flow: expatriate capital in search of secure havens in Northern Europe.

Workers' remittances are difficult to estimate for a variety of reasons, the most important being that only those that pass through official channels are recorded. Thus understated, it has been estimated that the total of the remittance income for the Mediterranean region was about $2 billion annually at the end of the 1960s. The sums involved represent the following share of the import bills of the various countries: Portugal, 24.5 percent; Spain, 10.2 percent; Italy, 6.9 percent; Yugoslavia, 13.5 percent; Greece, 17.9 percent; and Turkey, 15.9 percent.[10]

Foreign-exchange earnings from tourism have been estimated to be about $3 billion per year for the entire Mediterranean region, for tourists from all destinations. The following data from the OECD shed some light on the global importance of these earnings and on the degree to which they come from intra-European tourism, which originates largely from the countries of the enlarged community.

INTERNATIONAL TOURIST RECEIPTS AND EXPENDITURES IN 1970

(Rounded Figures in Millions of United States Dollars)

Reporting Country	Total Receipts From All Sources	Tourist Receipts as Percentages of Exports (1969)	From European OECD Countries	
Greece	194	14.3	Receipts	73.1
			Expenditures	39.4
Italy	1,639	9.7	Receipts	688.7
			Expenditures	39.4
Portugal	222	22.3	Receipts	118.0
			Expenditures	63.0
Spain	1,681	33.6		na[a]
Turkey	64	2.9	Receipts	38.3
			Expenditures	30.7
Yugoslavia		10.3	Receipts	212.6
			Expenditures	—

[a]na = not available

Source: OECD, *International Tourism and Tourism Policy in OECD Member Countries, 1971*, (Paris 1971).

The total public and private aid of the Six to all regions—lumped together in the quasi-authoritative figures of the OECD's Development Assistance Committee (DAC)—amounted to approximately $5 billion in 1970. Just over $1 billion of this, plus $148 million from the United Kingdom, went to the countries of the Mediterranean basin. Of that, 46 percent—mainly from France and Italy—went to the countries of the greater Maghreb, and 48 percent—mainly from Germany and Italy—went to the developing countries of Southern Europe.[11] Other DAC figures suggest that perhaps two-thirds of these totals represent public grants, loans, etc., and that one-third is private direct investment.[12]

THE POLITICAL "GIVENS"

The kind of EEC response that can be, and to some extent has been, imposed on the pattern of ecnomic relations just described depends on two groups of factors yet to be described. The first is the political interests of the member countries of the community; the second is the instruments available to the community itself.

Although the first of these is too vast a subject to be treated fully here, one cannot fail to mention a handful of factors which have been critical in determining community policy. (1) Most agricultural commodities produced in Mediterranean nonmember countries are competitive with goods from Italy and, to some extent, France. (2) For complex reasons, France has chosen since 1967 to follow a pro-Arab position in the latter's dispute with Israel, while for historical reasons that option has been foreclosed to Germany. (3) In several countries—the Netherlands, Italy and Denmark, at a minimum—political realities inhibit governments from assenting to any community action that could be construed as approving or accepting as legitimate nondemocratic regimes such as those of Spain and Portugal. (4) Out of neoliberal conviction as well as from a security-related concern to preserve good relations with the United States, Germany—as well the Netherlands—is more committed to the maintenance of the General Agreement on Tariffs & Trade (GATT)-most-favored-nation (MFN) system of international trade than is, say, France. (5) Colonial legacies have given France special interests to defend or represent in the Maghreb, Italy in Libya, and the United Kingdom in Cyprus, Malta, and Gibraltar. (6) As a corollary of its commitment to maintaining an autonomous defense industry, the French government has given a high priority to winning arms orders from the area, especially from Spain and Greece, and has cultivated potential customers by defending their interests—or at least by refraining from opposing them—in organs such as the EEC, NATO, and the Council of Europe. (7) National policies have reflected the sometimes divergent interests of "national" (whether publicly owned or not) oil companies such as Shell, British Petroleum, Compagnie Française de Petroles, and the Ente Nazionale Idrocarboni.[13]

This catalogue of particularities could be extended, but the short list is sufficient to make comprehensible the main point—that EEC policy toward Mediterranean countries has been the result less of a coherent strategy than it has been the more or less random outcome of political trade-offs reflecting the special interests of the member states. Since divergent interests would have made impossible any abstract definition of a community policy, the approach was to let the Mediterranean countries take the initiative and then to deal with them separately. The negotiating process served as a kind of forcing house requiring the member countries to sort out their differences and find a minimum of common ground. The pace has been slow, and more than one negotiation has been delayed by virtue of a political bargain linking it to another issue.

The Italian role provides a good example. Following Charles de Gaulle's first veto of the British application in 1963, Italy linked its material interest to a widely shared political goal. It proposed (in the so-called Saragat

Memorandum) that economic and institutional concessions to Mediterranean countries should go apace with progress in the European integration process—a euphemism for the admission of Britain and the other applicant countries. As no progress was made on this question in the midsixties, the Italians could claim a certain justification for dragging their heels in the negotiations with Morocco, Tunisia, Spain, and Israel, thereby prolonging their preferential access to North European markets for their agricultural products.[14] As in many other cases of agricultural politics, the prominence given the issue considerably surpassed its economic importance. By 1970, only 10.3 percent of Italy's gross domestic product came from agriculture, forestry and fishing (but the sector employed 19 percent of the work force). Only some 10 percent of its orange production is exported—and thus affected by the potential competition of other Mediterranean producers in other EEC markets.[15] Nevertheless, Italian opposition to agricultural concessions continues in the early 1970s to be probably the greatest obstacle to the conclusion of economically significant agreements between the EEC and nonmember Mediterranean countries.

The links between some of the other particularities are also instructive. So long as France obstructed an agreement with Israel, other governments, such as the Dutch, blocked accords with countries, such as Spain or Algeria, whose interests France appeared to be defending. The point about the unacceptability of Spain's political system thus became not only a reflection of domestic politics and conviction but also a justification for a position taken partly to defend Israel's interests. When de Gaulle left office, the logjam was broken by a package deal in which France lifted its vetoes on Britain and the other full applicants, Israel and Yugoslavia; Italy stopped retarding Mediterranean agreements in general; and the other members consented to the agreement with Spain. Language was used in the agreements (owing largely to Dutch and German pressure) that attempted to reconcile them with the GATT.

COMMUNITY INSTRUMENTS

If politics has determined whether there would be agreements, and economic factors determined what the issues would be, the content of the resulting agreements depends in large part on the instruments available to the community, on the areas in which it has legal and administrative competence. What matters is not so much the legal form of the agreement—whether it is called an association (Greece, Turkey, Malta, and Cyprus), partial association (Morocco and Tunisia) or preferential agreement (Spain, Israel, Portugal, Egypt, and Lebanon); the Treaty of Rome provides for associations "characterized by reciprocal rights and obligations"

(Article 238), but it does not define the nature of said rights and obligations. In practice, the term "association" has been used for two quite distinct relationships: (1) that of countries eventually expected (at least in theory) to become full members, but whose present stage of development requires an abnormally long preparatory period; and (2) that with former colonies, who now get preferential trade and aid treatment (Convention of Yaoundé; agreements with Morocco and Tunisia). More significant, because of the exclusions it implies, is Article 237, which specifies that only European states may apply for full membership in the community—though even here no definition is made of what constitutes "European-ness."

What matters more is the economic content of the agreements. This reflects the degree of economic integration achieved in the community, i.e., the number of policy sectors that the member states have agreed to handle in common. It is striking that of the half-dozen or so sectors where a unified community policy could have a substantial impact on its Mediterranean neighbors, the community has well-established competence in only one—trade. The others are still predominantly subject to national policy and control. It may be useful to review the situation in the other areas.

Energy

The critical role of petroleum in EEC-Mediterranean relations emerged earlier in this essay. The dispositions that exist within the community for energy in general or petroleum in particular do not merit the title "common policy"; some restrictions still exist, for example, on trade *within* the EEC in petroleum products. But external tariffs and tariff-free quotas do fall under the community authority, and decisions about these matters have thus been required. The course followed so far has been to set a nil duty on crude, while discouraging the development of refining capacities outside the EEC by setting the tariff-free quotas on refined products at uneconomically low levels; e.g., 100,000 tons per year is the limit specified in several of the agreements with Mediterranean countries.[16] Two sources of pressure may lead to changes in this policy in the future: (1) in the oil sellers' market of the 1970s the community could bargain away the low quotas on refined products in exchange for commitments regarding the rate, amount, and price of supplies of petroleum products; (2) Algeria is likely to refuse any agreement with the community that does not specify realistic quotas that could accommodate the refining capacity in which it has invested for export purposes—and it has some high cards with which to play, including its own petroleum supplies. Moreover, environmental considerations may lead member countries to countenance the transfer of some petroleum-refining activity to areas beyond their borders.

Migrant Workers

Although the Treaty of Rome provides for free circulation of workers inside the community—and therefore provides a theoretical guarantee to Italian workers of nondiscriminatory treatment in other community countries—the workers coming to the community from nonmember countries generally do so under the terms of bilateral agreements negotiated between the governments of the sending and receiving countries. The community is merely notified of them. Recruitment, to the extent that it is done officially, is also primarily on a national basis.

There are some exceptions to this. The Greek and Turkish associations have free-labor-movement provisions. The Turkish association, which calls for the removal of restrictions on labor movements between 1976 and 1986, could be quite significant, in view of the potential numbers involved (according to the Danieli estimate, half of the increase in the migrant-labor force over the next decade could come from Turkey, and a third could come from Yugoslavia); but some doubt exists about whether it will in fact be fulfilled. And the situation may be changing, in part because of dissatisfaction with the problems associated with present migratory patterns—particularly the tendency of foreign workers to serve as a regulating reservoir for the labor market, as a function of the business cycle. Since 1970 the community has had a standing commitee on employment to consider these questions.[17] Pressure to deal with this subject in the framework of the Mediterranean agreements has already been exerted by Algeria, Turkey, and Yugoslavia.

Public Aid and Private Investment

Of the various Mediterranean agreements in force, only the Greek and Turkish associations provide for EEC aid, and from 1967–74 this provision was not applied to Greece. Out of the total of approximately $1 billion in financial resources transferred each year from the community countries to the Mediterranean partners, only the $40 million or so granted to Turkey passes through community channels. In addition, the community has provided about 0.5 million tons of grain since 1967 to Mediterranean countries, out of a total of about 1.4 million tons given to all countries; and it has given other food aid to UNRWA (Palestine) and to the FAO's World Food Program. The EEC's aid fund, the European Development Fund (EDF), is used exclusively for aid to the Yaoundé Convention partners of sub-Saharan Africa. There is no EEC scheme for guaranteeing or encouraging private investment in the Mediterranean or elsewhere, although this idea has on occasion been proposed, notably by President Pompidou.

Environment

If its own powers and program in this field had been defined the EEC would be a logical agent to take the lead in cooperating with the other littoral countries for purposes of environmental protection in and around the Mediterranean Sea. Since about 1970 the subject has been receiving much attention, and the EEC commission has made proposals, but as of this writing the community remains largely powerless in this activity.[18]

Tourism

While tourism within the EEC is affected positively by the dismantling of customs barriers, extra-EEC tourism is not directly touched by the community. Such embryonic rules and pressures as have been agreed, for the purpose of discouraging economic and administrative impediments to tourism—such as restrictions on the currency tourists may take out of the country—have rather been developed in the OECD.

This litany of impotence could go on. Arguably, the community variable that most affects the Mediterranean countries economically is its rate of growth. Macroeconomic policy is still determined nationally. To the extent that it is becoming a community concern, in the framework of the program to achieve economic and monetary union, it will be of great moment for the community's associate members and principal Mediterranean trade partners; but there is so far little sign of their having a voice in its formulation, though Spain's monetary authorities have been consulted on occasion. Similarly, if European countries such as Greece, Turkey, and Spain are envisaged as full-fledged members of the community, their economic problems might best be regarded as special cases of the general problem of regional imbalance within it.[19] A community regional policy would thus be an appropriate instrument to use; at the moment of enlargement, such a policy scarcely exists, but British and Italian pressure may lead to significant regional actions in the future. It has been agreed to establish a regional-development fund, but what its resources and scope of action will be are still unknown.

Given this paucity of instruments, the community has relied heavily in its agreements on manipulations of the Common External Tariff, over which, as a customs union, it has undisputed authority. The complicated network of agreements that have been concluded, based upon a kind of "fine tuning" in the degree of preference that they accord various countries, represents an attempt by the community to make its single instrument—which commission spokesmen are quick to recognize as inadequate —serve a variety of situations that vary considerably, economically and politically, from one Mediterranean country to another. What has made that attempt at least somewhat viable is that the one area of internal policy that the community has fully elaborated, agriculture, happens to be the one that is required to complete its foreign trade authority—for Mediterranean countries are highly dependent upon agricultural exports. However, while the community has the legal authority to negotiate changes in its Common Agricultural Policy (CAP) for the purposes of its foreign economic relations, important changes have seldom been politically possible.

In fact, the nature of the CAP has posed a series of problems for the Mediterranean countries. Those countries, notably Greece and Turkey, that signed agreements in the early 1960s were told that many of the agricultural concessions they wanted could not be granted because the CAP had not yet been formulated. Even after its main guidelines were specified in early 1962, it was only slowly extended to the types of commodities that were of major interest to Mediterranean producers: fruits and vegetables in 1967, wine and tobacco in 1970. When the rules were formulated, they turned out to be sufficiently protectionist to constitute bad news for Mediterranean suppliers. The high support levels that characterize the CAP encourage much relatively inefficient production of goods that could be imported more cheaply. The cultivation of fruit and vegetables in ever more northerly parts of Europe by greenhouse techniques is a vivid example. The method of protection used for many commodities, that of the variable levy, also seems tailor-made to cause maximum difficulties to the would-be supplier of EEC markets. It puts him entirely at the mercy of supply conditions within the community: if the supply is adequate, the levy rises to prohibitive levels and his sales may suddenly fall to zero. The problem that this unpredictability causes for investment plans—particularly for such long lead-time products as cattle, or vineyards—is evident. To remove from itself the onus of appearing protectionist, the EEC has sometimes made concessions on agricultural products from Mediterranean countries on condition that the suppliers respect specified "reference prices." The result is that the supplier, rather than the EEC customs agent, pockets the difference between the low asking price and the price at which it is acceptable to sell the commodity in the EEC; but by respecting the reference price, he loses much or all of his competitive advantage and thus becomes an agent in enforcement of the EEC's protectionism. Finally, the intra-EEC political balance on which the CAP depends is so intricate and precarious that there is little inclination to complicate the bargaining further by considering the interests of parties outside the community.[20] The implication is that when economic change requires someone to pay the social cost, better it should be paid outside than inside the EEC.

CONTENT OF THE EXISTING AGREEMENTS
WITH SOUTHERN EUROPEAN COUNTRIES

The first of the community's Mediterranean agreements was its association
with Greece, which took effect on November 1, 1962, following an application made by the Greek government in June, 1959.[21] The atmosphere
was that of welcoming a fellow NATO ally into another part of the
Western club, and of proving an "outward-looking-ness" of the community at a time when the failure of the talks on a Europe-wide trade area
called that into question. It was the first time that meaning had to be given
to Article 238 (providing for association) of the Treaty of Rome, and
this accounts in part for the length of time needed to reach agreement. It
also explains why the Turkish request, which was presented only a month
after that of Greece, was left on the back burner during this period of
definition of the meaning of "association." It was taken up immediately
after Greece, and went into effect on December 1, 1964.

Nearly six years then elapsed before the next European agreement, that
with Spain, which took effect at the same time as that with Israel on
October 1, 1970. This was the outcome of over eight years of negotiations
and political maneuvers since Spain had first presented its request in 1962;
although the original application was for association, the resulting agreement was not so labelled. The agreement with Malta—which *is* called an
association, but which is similar to the Spanish agreement in content—
took effect on April 1, 1971. An agreement with Portugal was negotiated
in 1971/72 in the context of the arrangements made for those members
of the European Free Trade Association (EFTA) that did not join the
community; it took effect on January 1, 1973, at the same time as the
accession of the new members. Finally, the association with Cyprus was
signed on December 19, 1972.

Certain issues or contents are common to all the agreements discussed
here. All provide for some liberalization of both industrial and agricultural
trade. All except that with Yugoslavia aim at least formally at virtual free
trade; they propose to get to that point via a multistage process, but the
nature and length of the stages and the automaticity of the transition vary
from one case to another. All must be defended in terms of Article 24 of
the GATT, which authorized departures from most-favored-nation trade
arrangements only for groupings that are free-trade areas or customs
unions in the making. Some of the requirements for reconciling agreements with the GATT—such as fixed calendars for the liberalization of
trade and the establishment of inverse preferences, i.e., preferences given
to community goods by the trade partner—tend to conflict with the political requirements for concluding the agreements.

Partly because of the preferential aspect of the agreements, there is a certain inherent momentum: each accord that is reached tends to produce new claims, as countries that would otherwise be disadvantaged now claim the right to the same preferential status. The most dramatic example of this is Iran's request to be included by the community in the area covered by a "global Mediterranean policy" (see below). In order to cope with this interrelated trade pattern, the community has been obliged to consider the general trade equilibrium in the region when making its agreements. The best example was the unilateral community decision, taken in 1969 but later rescinded after attacks in the GATT, to grant a 40 percent preference for oranges, tangerines, mandarines, and lemons coming from Turkey, Spain, and Israel in order to counterbalance the 80 percent preference which had just been negotiated for Morocco and Tunisia (and, by extension, for Algeria). Finally, with the possible exception of Yugoslavia (whose socialist and neutral status may be incompatible with membership in a group that so far includes—Ireland excepted—only nonneutral and nonsocialist countries), all of the European partners are potential candidates for ultimate membership. Only the accords with Greece and Turkey mention this possibility explicitly, in both cases in the preamble and in identical form: the parties, "recognizing that the support given by the EEC to the efforts of the Greek [Turkish] people to improve its standard of living will facilitate subsequently the adhesion of Greece [Turkey] to the community . . . have decided to conclude an agreement. . . ." Later articles in both agreements commit both sides merely to examine the possibility of adhesion when "the functioning of the agreement permits Greece [Turkey] to envisage the total acceptance of the obligations stemming from" the Treaty of Rome.

Greece

The basic commitment of the Greek agreement is the establishment of a customs union for industrial products over a period of twelve years for most products and twenty-two years for more sensitive products. There is a certain assymmetry in the obligations and the practice of the two parties in removing their restrictions; the community immediately granted intracommunity treatment to Greece, with the result that Greek goods obtained duty-free entry in 1968, and are also subject to intracommunity arrangements on quotas. Full reciprocity is not called for before 1974 or 1984, depending on the products, and Greece is also not obliged to align on the community's Common External Tariff until those dates. Timetables are established for reaching these targets, but, again, certain departures are authorized for Greece in view of its stage of development.

For agriculture, the extensive provisions of the agreement and its various protocols combine certain specific concessions with a more general and vague commitment by the community to take Greek interests and views into account in forming its Common Agricultural Policy, which had yet to be established at the time the agreement was concluded. The concessions took the form of a list of products that would be subject to the normal twelve-year liberalization timetable—citrus fruits, figs, grapes, peaches, nuts, and dried fruits, among others. This was, however, subject to a safeguard clause, insisted upon by Italy. Wine exports were subjected to different treatment by the different member states, until—and even after—the establishment of a common market organization in 1970. And tobacco, which accounted for 35 percent of Greece's exports to the EEC, was granted a 50 percent tariff reduction with a promise of complete liberalization at a later date; it was given as of January 1, 1968. The tobacco market was also organized within the community only in 1970. As agriculture accounted for over 70 percent of Greece's total exports, and as roughly half of that went to the Six, these arrangements were clearly important ones.

The third important section of the agreement was the financial protocol, which provided for concessionary loans to be made to Greece by the European Investment Bank (EIB) in the amount of $125 million over a five-year period.[22] Only some $70 million of this had been committed when that period expired. Other parts of the treaty deal with free movement of labor and services, rules of competition, general economic policy, and liberalization of capital movements.

Following the colonels' coup of April, 1967, the EEC Commission, spurred on by the European Parliament, took the initiative in freezing the association, i.e., of limiting the application of the agreement to "current management." No more loans were granted and the financial protocol was not renewed. The decision was convenient in that it diminished the community's obligation to harmonize the CAP with Greek interests, an undertaking that was proving more and more difficult in pace with the growing problems of the CAP itself. Even before that decision, the Greeks had complained that the agreement had not lived up to expectations: their trade gap with the community had widened, the application of the financial arrangements was slow, and they were not enjoying the agricultural benefits they hoped for (such as access to the community's agricultural fund).

Nevertheless, the accomplishments of the EEC-Greece association are far from negligible. By mid-1968, Greece had benefitted from completely free entry for its industrial products and substantial preferences for its major agricultural exports: zero tariff for tobacco and dried raisins, 80–100 percent tariff reduction for fresh fruits and vegetables, and 75–85 percent reduction for canned fruits and vegetables. Greece has also continued its liberalization program, so that by November 1, 1974, those community products subject to the twelve-year regime will have duty-free access. These arrangements appeared to have had some effect. As the following table shows, by 1970 the community was taking a substantially higher share of Greece's exports than a decade earlier (though less than in 1956). From 1961 to 1966 Greek exports to the community increased by 111 percent, compared to 69 percent toward the rest of the world, and agricultural exports increased by 117 percent, as against 64 percent to the rest of the world.

PERCENTAGE SHARE OF EXPORTS TO EEC (6)

	(1956)	1961	1962	1968	1969	(1970)
Greece	50	30.5	35.7	47.6	45.1	40.4
Turkey		36.9	40.4	33.1	40.0	
Portugal		21.9	23.2	16.8	17.9	
Spain		37.7	38.0	28.6	31.5	
Yugoslavia		(1960) 25.5		28.1		
Cyprus		(1960) 40.4		(1967) 23.8		

Source: SOEC, Basic Statistics and a study by the GATT secretariat, reproduced in Conflitti e Sviluppo nel Mediterraneo (Rome: Istituto Affari Internazionale, 1970).

Turkey

The Ankara accord was a much less detailed document than that of Athens, and it has had a happier life as a result. In view of Turkey's stage of development, it provided for a preparatory period of at least five years, during which the EEC was to help Turkey strengthen its economy without any reciprocal concessions. During that period, financial aid worth $175 million was to be provided by the EIB, and in addition the community granted intracommunity tariff treatment up to specified limits for certain agricultural products of interest to Turkey: raw tobacco, dried raisins and figs, and fruits and nuts. The termination of the preparatory period depended on a judgment to be made after at least four years by all parties, who would then define the modalities of the following "transitional" phase, which was to last twelve years. Following that there will be a "final" phase in which the customs union will be completed.

It took in fact just over six years for agreement to be reached, on November 23, 1970, on the content of the "additional protocol" that defined the conditions, methods, and pace of adjustment during the "transitional" period. That protocol took effect January 1, 1973. Notable among its terms is free entry (already in effect since 1971) for Turkish industrial products into the community; this is qualified only by a tariff-free quota of 200,000 tons for refined-petroleum products, and certain restrictions on cotton textiles. Community preferences are granted to over

90 percent of Turkey's agricultural exports. These are somewhat more generous than those accorded during the preparatory period, and include tariff exemption on tobacco and raisins without quantitative limitation. Free movement of workers will gradually be achieved between 1976 and 1986, according to procedures still to be defined. A new financial protocol provides for concessionary loans amounting to 195 million units of account (equal to pre-1971 dollars) over a five-and-half year period. Other provisions cover the right of establishment, services, transport, and the alignment of economic policies. In return, Turkey will dismantle its customs duties on EEC imports over a period covering twelve or twenty-two years, according to product.

Yugoslavia

The nonpreferential trade agreement signed by the EEC and Yugoslavia on March 19, 1970, was the first trade agreement concluded by the community in a year when the right to do so officially passed from the member governments to the community. As such, it was an important constitutional development. Its economic importance, however, is relatively limited. The principal community concession consists in reducing the import levy applied to Yugoslav "baby beef," a product in which the Yugoslavs had invested specifically to cater to the Italian market but one that had encountered unexpectedly and at times prohibitively high import levies (65 percent in 1968, for example). The agreement had been blocked up to 1973 by France, partly out of an ambition (never to be fulfilled, as it turned out) to become a beef exporter. It was also believed that the veto was imposed in order to grant a Soviet request. Apart from that source of contention, Yugoslav exports to the community appear to have suffered little from the CAP.

YUGOSLAV EXPORTS
(In Millions of United States Dollars)

	Total		To EEC	
	All Products	Agriculture	All Products	Agriculture
1960	566	203	145	78
1963	790	256	268	130
1967	1252	349	371	186

Source: OECD, Agricultural Development in Southern Europe.

Spain

The form of the agreement with Spain represents an attempt to square two political realities. To get the agreement accepted in the GATT it was necessary to stress that the ultimate objective was a free-trade area consistent with Article 24. To win the approval of the Dutch—and, at times, of other fiercely democratic spokesmen from within the community—it was necessary to withhold association, or the economic equivalent thereof, until the political system in Spain had become more democratic. The compromise is an agreement the aim of which "is the gradual elimination in two stages—with due respect for the provisions of GATT—of the obstacles to the main body of mutual trade. Only the provisions governing the first stage, lasting at least six years, were negotiated. The opening of negotiations on what is to happen in the second stage and on the transition from one stage to the next will be subject to the agreement of the two parties."[23]

The EEC concessions include tariff reductions of 60 percent on industrial products by January 1, 1973; some products are totally excepted, however, and others are limited to a 40 percent concession over six years. In agriculture, there are tariff reductions for citrus fruits and olive oil equivalent to those offered other nonassociated Mediterranean suppliers, and a 50 percent reduction for certain preserves, fruits and vegetables, and wines. Spain will liberalize some 95 percent of industrial imports of community origin over six years, the other, sensitive products being variously handled according to special lists.

The experience against which the agreement was concluded was one in which the share of Spain's total exports taken by the community was declining (see table, p. 225) but the share of agricultural exports was remarkably constant: 43.6 percent of Spain's agricultural exports went to the EEC in 1961 and, after some slight variation in intervening years, 43.2 percent was still exported to that destination in 1966.[24]

Malta

The association agreement with Malta calls for the establishment of a customs union in two stages, in principle of five years each. The agreement contains the terms of the first stage, and negotiations on the second stage are to begin eighteen months before expiration of the first. The community grants a 70 percent reduction of duties for Maltese industrial products, while Malta is gradually reducing its duties on all imports from the community by up to 35 percent or to the most-favored-nation level, whichever is lower. At the first session of the association council, which was held April 24, 1972, in Luxembourg, the volatile Mr. Dom Mintoff demanded that the agreement as it stands be complemented by various additional features, including technical assistance, access for Maltese students to European universities, and preferential access to the community for Maltese agricultural exports. The community has agreed to examine whether and how the accord could be extended to new areas to take account of Maltese demands.[25]

Portugal

As a member of EFTA, Portugal benefitted from the EEC's decision to make free trade in industrial products the central provision of its offer to noncandidate EFTA countries. Since the countries in question presented a number of individual problems, six individual, bilateral agreements were concluded, each of which qualified that principle in ways appropriate to the specific country. In the case of Portugal, the modifications recognized its low degree of industrialization by providing (1) an extended timetable for tariff dismantlement by Portugal on imports from the EEC, and (2) limited concessions for certain agricultural and marine commodities (canned fish, tomato concentrate, and some wines). The timetable allows Portugal until 1980 to abolish its trade restrictions on most community goods, and until 1985 for certain sensitive products amounting to some 10 percent of the EEC's total exports to Portugal. The concessions on canned fish and tomato concentrates are intended to take account of the fact that around 25 percent of Portugal's exports to the enlarged EEC fall into the community's definition of agricultural products, whereas to a considerable extent the same commodities were treated as industrial products under EFTA rules and thus enjoyed liberalized access to British and Danish markets that, in the absence of corrective action, they now would have risked losing. The correction amounts to about a one-third reduction in the basic duties for both commodities; this means that the United Kingdom and Denmark will raise their duties from zero to two-thirds of those of the EEC tariff. Many textile products are excluded from the agreement. In spite of these limitations, the agreement seems to leave Portugal slightly better off than before.[26]

Cyprus

Like the Maltese agreement, the Cyprus association provides for the establishment of a customs union through two stages. The terms of the first stage, which is to end on June 30, 1977, are specified in the present agreement; the second stage, which in principle will last five years, will be negotiated in detail later. The community gives an immediate reduction of 70 percent of its tariff on imports of industrial products from Cyprus. By the beginning of the fifth year, Cyprus will reduce its tariffs on imports from the EEC by 35 percent or to MFN level, whichever is lower. On agricultural products, the EEC grants Cyprus a 40 percent tariff reduction on citrus fruits, and access to British and Irish markets on the same terms as before accession. The negotiation of the agreement, and its entry into force, have gotten into the tangle of Greek-Turkish communal relations in Cyprus, since the Turkish community has no representation in the delegation with which the EEC treated. Voices were raised in the EEC to question the desirability or even the legality of concluding an agreement under those conditions.

Others

Gibraltar, at its own request and to the chagrin of the Spanish government, is in the legally complicated position of being subject to the Treaty of Rome (under Article 227, which refers to European territories for whose external relations a member country is responsible) but is not within the EEC's customs area; it can thus retain its free-port status. The treaty does not apply to the United Kingdom's "sovereign base areas" in Cyprus. Albania does not enjoy and has never requested special status with the EEC.

ENLARGEMENT AND THE "GLOBAL MEDITERRANEAN POLICY"

The implications of the entry of Denmark, Ireland, and the United Kingdom for the EEC's Mediterranean relations were multiple. First, for legal and mechanical reasons it became necessary to modify the existing agreements with Mediterranean countries in order, e.g., to enlarge quotas, to specify the way(s) in which the new members' trade with them would have to be adapted, etc. In this situation, the communiuty was the *demandeur*, since the inconvenience of an ambiguous legal situation—with possible consequences such as deviations of trade, lawsuits brought before the European Court by exporters, etc.—would have fallen mainly on it.

Second, for some of the agreements—notably those with Israel and Spain—enlargement raised serious problems. Those countries export considerable quantities of agricultural commodities to the new member countries, especially the United Kingdom, where they enter on terms much more favorable than those of the Community's import regime, even as modified in their preferential agreements. Spain's agricultural exports to the United Kingdom in 1969 amounted to $185 million. Only 24 percent of those commodities would be covered under the existing agreement, while—as a result of past market specialization—63 percent of Spain's agricultural exports to the Six are covered. For Israel, the situation was similar.[27] These two countries in a major way, and others such as Malta and Turkey in a minor way, used the leverage given them by the first point (their signatures being required on the "additional protocols" sought by the community) in order to bargain for concessions by the community —in the form of major revisions of the agreements—on the second point.

The timetable was tight, for the protocols were needed by enlargement day. It would have been physically and politically difficult to negotiate the new trade concessions called for within the time available, with French national elections impending.

Third, owing to the "accident" of Portugal's membership of EFTA, an anomalous situation had resulted, one that it seemed desirable to correct, whereby the latecoming Iberian partner obtained a more favorable agreement than Spain did, though its political regime was no more palatable than Spain's.

Add to these considerations the coincidental facts that (1) the dates for renegotiating several of the Mediterranean agreements were drawing near, and (2) the prospect of a future petroleum shortage was beginning to be perceived, and one has identified the major stimuli that led the community in 1972 to embrace the idea of a "global Mediterranean policy." The initiative was first taken by the Dutch and French delegations, which may have seen in this concept the possibility of buying off the Mediterranean countries with concessions in aid (much of which would presumably come from Germany) and in trade in industrial products and of thereby avoiding politically and socially painful concessions in agriculture. The idea was quickly endorsed by the commission, which saw in it both the prospect of enlarging its array of policy instruments and a means of dealing with the immediate problems of Spain and Israel. It made some concrete suggestions about what the global policy might involve, toward the end of September, 1972,[28] and so the idea was conveniently available when the community summit met in Paris the following month—an attractively concrete and specific item on an agenda that was otherwise somewhat lacking in these qualities. The summit endorsed the principle of "an overall and balanced approach" to the Mediterranean agreements. Armed with that holy writ, the community's council of ministers defined a number of principles of the global policy that would serve as "working hypotheses" during the process of precise definition of the policy's contents. These principles are as follows:

(1) Geographical area: the policy will apply to those coastal Mediterranean countries (including Portugal), plus Jordan, that apply for it.

(2) Throughout that area, a free-trade area in industrial products, qualified by exceptions for sensitive products, should be gradually established.

(3) Some "reciprocity" should exist between the EEC and the partner countries, but this need not necessarily take the form of reverse preferences.

(4) A "considerable" (but numerically undefined) percentage of agricultural goods should be covered, these concessions to be periodically reviewed. Safeguard clauses would apply. The concessions would not be

uniform, but would take account of variations from country to country.

(5) All agreements would include a "cooperation" section, but financial aid would be excluded for Spain, Portugal, Israel, and Yugoslavia.

(6) The "global" agreements should enter into force if possible at the beginning of 1974.[29]

These principles are consistent with, but considerably less precise than, the Commission's general document, which also speaks of provisions for Mediterranean workers and for environmental protection.[30] They succeeded in inducing Spain and Israel to sign the "additional protocols," which specify that until the end of 1973 the new member countries would apply to imports from those countries the same import regime as they had before joining the community. At the time of writing (April, 1973), it is difficult to foresee what content the global policy will have. Upon the enlargement of the community, responsibility for the Mediterranean was bureaucratically split in the EEC Commission, as it had not been before—the northern littoral is grouped with other nonmember European countries, the eastern and southern littorals with the developing countries. The discriminatory character of the agreements is being opposed with extreme vigor by the United States. There is some evidence that the British Conservative government feels reverse preferences are not worth the political cost of defending them in the face of such opposition, while for the Pompidou government they may well be a *conditio sine qua non* of having a Mediterranean policy. The French presumably fear that eliminating reverse preferences for the Mediterranean would lead to their also being eliminated with the associated African countries, with whom the French are keen on preserving their export advantages. In the background, and recently given official expression for the first time, lies the possibility of American-EEC rivalry for the Mediterranean and Mideast oil and the EEC potential for using its trade agreements as a weapon in such a war.[31]

CONCLUSIONS

The full range of economic and political relations between the member countries of the EEC and the nonmember countries of the Mediterranean littoral is rich and diverse. Compared to that richness, the formal agreements that embody the EEC's existing Mediterranean "policy" express and shape those relations only in the palest and most limited way. They embody mainly tariff reductions on industrial products, defined in a relatively narrow way and largely excluding some of the most significant items, such as textiles and refined-petroleum products.

While they may prove to be important in the long run as stimuli to export-oriented investment, such measures have not had very dramatic effects so far. Much fuss has been made by both sides (the community, especially France; and the United States) about reverse preferences, but it is far from clear that they have had significant trade effects.

A serious policy would appear to involve, at a minimum, (1) major concessions on agricultural trade, and this would entail considerable social change within the community countries; (2) the organized transfer of substantial resources, whether through an "internal" instrument such as a regional-development fund or an aid program conceived of as aiding outsiders; and (3) a regularization of the flow of migrant labor, specifying the rights and obligations that exist on a community scale. It may well prove impossible to have a coherent community policy for the Mediterranean area so long as its members follow independent policies on oil, since this is by far the most important commodity in Mediterranean politics. It will require impressive measures of dynamism and generosity for the community to take such steps on a scale worthy of the title "global Mediterranean policy."

POSTSCRIPT: DECEMBER, 1974

Much has happened since mid-1973: spectacular political changes in Portugal and Greece, war in Cyprus, further muffled political evolution in Spain and Turkey, and the energy/economic crisis. Except in the case of Greece, where the governmental change has led to the "unfreezing" of the association agreement with the European Economic Community, and consequently to the resumption of economic aid, no change in these countries' formal status with the community is involved. (Portugal's former colonies will also become eligible for association with the EEC on terms similar with other countries of sub-Saharan Africa.) But in the new circumstances the timing, probability, and desirability of accession of various countries to full membership must be seen in a new light. The indications given by the Constantine Caramanlis government that Greece seeks early admission to the EEC, indications that must be interpreted in the light of Cyprus diplomacy rather than accepted at face value, and the apparent soul-searching in Madrid about how to relate to the EEC during this fluid period of Iberian politics, provide two illustrations of the new state of affairs.

Economically, the interdependence of Mediterranean and trans-Alpine Europe, which was consolidated during the years of prosperity, is being demonstrated to be just as real in conditions of adversity. New restrictions on migrant labor have been introduced in the past year or so by France, Germany, Belgium, and the Netherlands. While the return flow of migrants so far has turned out, mercifully, to be neither so early nor massive as seemed probable a year ago, the trend is clear. The fall-off in remittances, as well as the diminished outlet for employment, will hurt all the more as it coincides with a downturn in tourism and an oil-induced worsening of the trade balances of the Mediterranean countries of Europe. There have been some gratuitous additions to this list of misfortunes for specific countries. Yugoslavia, for example, suffers particularly from the EEC's recent ban on beef imports.

The first negotiations under the "global policy"—with Spain, Israel, Algeria, Morocco, Tunisia, and Malta—have got underway in recent months. The disparity between the limited agenda for these talks, on the one hand, and the vital issues still being handled bilaterally (or, in the case of migration, unilaterally) is even more striking today than before the oil crisis. An alternative negotiating forum—the Nine's multilateral talks with the members of the Arab League— comes somewhat closer to the EEC's real Mediterranean-related concerns: how to assure the community against interruptions in future oil supplies from the Middle East, and how to finance oil imports at the new prices. Compared to the EEC's vital need for delicate diplomatic footwork to avoid having to choose between the United States and the Arabs, the "global Mediterranean policy" has become a less urgent concern.

APPENDIX I

TRADE BETWEEN THE MEDITERRANEAN COUNTRIES
AND THE ENLARGED COMMUNITY (10)
(In Millions of 1968 United States Dollars)

	Exports of Mediterranean Countries			Imports of Mediterranean Countries		
	World	EC (10)	EC (10) as Share of Total Percentage	World	EC (10)	EC (10) as Share of World Percentage
I. Agreements Concluded						
Greece	467.8	244.8	52.3	1,391.7	769.2	55.3
Turkey	496.4	207.2	41.7	770.5	392.8	51.0
Morocco	442.3	304.3	68.8	542.8	299.9	55.3
Tunisia	157.5	79.7	50.6	218.0	126.2	57.9
Spain	1,589.2	653.5	41.1	3,505.2	1,527.7	43.6
Israel	640.2	253.6	39.6	1,081.0	563.3	52.1
Malta	33.9	19.0	56.0	123.4	90.7	73.5
Total I:	3,827.3	1,762.1	46.0	7,632.6	3,769.8	49.4
II. Agreements in Negotiation						
Algeria	830.2	687.9	82.9	815.0	599.2	73.5
Arab Republic of Egypt[a]	622.0	83.9	13.5	665.7	192.5	28.9
Lebanon[a]	195.0	76.8	39.4	599.0	314.5	52.5
Cyprus[a]	88.2	63.4	71.9	170.0	110.0	64.6
Portugal[a]	734.0	300.2	40.1	1,043.0	530.5	50.9
Total II:	2,469.4	1,212.2	49.1	3,292.9	1,746.7	53.0
III. Others						
Albania	—	—	—	—	—	—
Gibraltar	—	—	—	—	—	—
Libya	1,867.4	1,599.9	85.7	644.0	364.8	56.6
Syria	168.1	27.8	16.5	311.9	92.6	29.7
Total III:	2,035.5	1,627.7	80.0	955.9	457.4	47.9
IV. Yugoslavia	1,259.5	423.2	33.6	1,796.5	800.1	44.5
Total Medit. (I-IV)	9,591.7	5,025.2	52.4	13,677.9	6,774.0	49.5

[a]Negotiation subsequently completed

Source: SOEC/OECD (taken from Loeff, op. cit.).

APPENDIX II

(Tables on Migration in Europe Taken from McLin, *op. cit.*)
(Tables 1, 2, 3, 4)

TABLE 1[a]
DISTRIBUTION OF FOREIGNERS IN THE COUNTRIES OF IMMIGRATION ACCORDING TO THEIR ORIGIN

(In Thousands)

Country of Immigration / Country of Emigration	FRG	France	Austria	Switzerland	Sweden	Belgium	Netherlands	U.K.	Total
Yugoslavia	265.0	43.0	45.5	21.0	14.0	3.5	3.0	2.5	397.5
Percent	17.7	1.4	74.6	2.2	10.1	0.8	4.6	0.1	
Italy	350.0	632.0	1.5	532.0	5.5	176.0	9.5	21.0	1727.5
Percent	23.3	21.1	2.5	54.7	4.0	38.6	14.4	1.1	
Spain	143.0	668.0	0.5	98.0	3.0	48.0	11.5	21.5	993.5
Percent	9.5	22.1	0.8	10.1	2.1	10.5	17.4	1.1	
Portugal	30.0	367.0	—	2.0	0.5	4.5	2.0	4.5	410.5
Percent	2.0	12.2	—	0.2	0.4	1.0	3.0	0.2	
Greece	191.0	11.0	0.5	9.0	6.0	14.0	1.5	4.0	237.0
Percent	12.7	0.3	0.8	0.9	4.3	3.1	2.3	0.2	
Turkey	244.0	7.0	6.5	10.0	2.0	11.5	15.0	3.0	298.0
Percent	16.3	0.2	10.6	1.0	1.4	2.5	22.7	0.2	
Others	278.0	1281.0	6.0	300.0	108.0	198.5	23.5	1856.5	4051.5
Percent	18.5	42.6	9.8	30.9	77.7	43.5	35.6	97.1	
TOTAL	1501.0	3009.0	60.5	972.0	139.0	456.0	66.0	1913.0	8116.5
	100.0	100.0	100.0	100.0	100.0	100.0	100.0	100.0	100.0

[a]This chart was compiled by Professor M. Livi-Bacci for the Second European Population Conference, held in Strasbourg Aug. 31–Sept. 7, 1971. It may be found on page 7 of Council of Europe Document CDE (71) T. IV, *Report on the Demographic and Social Pattern of Migrants in Europe, Especially with regard to International Migrations*. The figures should be regarded as only approximate. They have been estimated by a variety of means and refer to different periods. By now the data are all somewhat out of date. For example, at the end of 1972 there were some 2.3 million foreign workers (over 3 million including family) in the Federal Republic. Also, the total number of Yugoslav migrants is now about 900,000, or more than double that indicated in the chart.

NOTE: The figures for the FRG, Austria, Switzerlnad, and the Netherlands represent foreign workers only; for the other countries, they represent the total foreign population.

TABLE 2[a]
INTRA-EUROPEAN EMIGRATION FROM MEDITERRANEAN COUNTRIES
(In Thousands)

Year	Portugal	Spain	Italy	Yugoslavia	Greece	Turkey	Total
1960	3.8	30.5	309.9	5.7	27.0	—	376.9
1961	6.0	43.0	329.6	13.0	41.5	1.2	434.3
1962	9.2	64.8	315.8	33.2	62.1	11.2	496.3
1963	17.1	83.7	235.1	27.7	75.6	36.1	475.3
1964	38.4	102.0	216.5	27.7	80.2	75.8	540.7
1965	71.5	74.5	232.4	48.9	88.1	67.6	583.0
1966	87.0	56.8	219.4	78.9	53.8	45.9	541.8
1967	63.9	25.9	164.0	32.5	16.4	18.4	321.1
1968	53.4	66.7	158.4	109.9	25.0	65.1	478.5
1969	41.6	80.0[b]	176.3	243.5	63.1	160.0[b]	764.5[b]

[a]Livi-Bacci
[b]Provisional estimates

NOTE: Portugal, Italy, and Greece: total emigration; other countries: workers only. Seasonal workers from Spain (who number some 100,000–130,000) and temporary workers from Greece (the 50,000–70,000 who emigrate for less than one year, mainly seamen) are not included.

TABLE 3[a]
VARIOUS NATIONALITIES IN TOTAL IMMIGRATION INTO THE EUROPEAN COMMUNITY
(In Percentages)

1968		1969		1970	
Italians	27	Yugoslavs	24	Yugoslavs	25
Yugoslavs	16	Italians	17	Turks	16
Turks	13	Turks	15	Italians[b]	13
Spaniards	11	Portuguese	11	Portuguese	13
Portuguese	7	Spaniards	9	Spaniards	8
Greeks	7	Greeks	8	Greeks	7
		N. Africans[c]	4	N. Africans[c]	5

[a]Commission des Communautés européenes, *La libre circulation de la main d'oeuvre et les marchés du travail dans la C.E.É. 1971*, projet de rapport.
[b]Estimates
[c]Algerian workers in France not included (a significant omission)

TABLE 4[a]

LABOR SURPLUSES AND SHORTAGES IN EUROPE IN 1980

	Variants for Labor Demand	Scarcities (—) or Redundancies (+) (In Millions)
Group I		
(industrialized market countries)	Low	— 4.7
	Central	—11.2
	High	—12.8
Group II		
(countries of emigration)	High	+ 7.6
	Low	+10.5
Group III		
(centrally-planned countries),		
inc. Soviet Union	High	+15.9
	Low	+24.5
Group III		
excl. Soviet Union	High	+ 4.1
	Low	+ 6.8

[a]Luisa Danieli, "Labour Scarcities and Labour Redundancies in Europe by 1980: An Experimental Study," in *The Demographic and Social Pattern of Emigration from the Southern European Countries*, Florence: Dipartimento Statistico Matematico, 1971.

APPENDIX III

NET RECEIPTS OF INDIVIDUAL DEVELOPING COUNTRIES AND TERRITORIES
Net Official Receipts from DAC Countries and Multilateral Agencies
(1968–69 Annual Averages in Millions of United States Dollars)

	Bilateral	Multilateral	Total	Per Capita
Europe, Total	336.40	118.90	445.30	4.74
Cyprus			4.56	7.33
Gibraltar			1.68	67.20
Greece			92.53	10.51
Malta			16.85	52.82
Spain			85.92	2.63
Turkey			230.87	6.88
Yugoslavia			15.74	—.78
Other			7.16	—
North Africa, Total			110.91	8.57

TOTAL DAC[a] DIRECT INVESTMENT IN EUROPEAN DEVELOPING COUNTRIES,
1965–70
(Average Annual Flows by Sector in Millions of United States Dollars)

	Petroleum	Mining	Manufacturing	Other	Total
1965–66	44	10	124	90	268
1967–68	19	3	130	55	207
1969–70	60	5	224	59	348

[a]DAC = Development Assistance Committee
Source: OECD Development Assistance: 1971 Review (Paris, 1971).

APPENDIX IV

SHARE OF MEDITERRANEAN COUNTRIES
OF WORLD PRODUCTION AND WORLD EXPORTS
OF SOME AGRICULTURAL PRODUCTS IN 1965–67

(In Percentages)

	Mediterranean Countries		Italy	
	Production	Exports	Production	Exports
Olive Oil	61.9	83.4	34.4	7.2
Raw Tobacco	8.1	19.4	1.6	0.6
Wine	21.8	62.0	24.6	9.1
Oranges and				
Mandarines	23.2	70.7	5.6	5.0
Grapefruit	31.4	45.0	—	0.2
Lemons	18.8	28.6	21.4	51.6
Raisins	54.7	50.5	0.1	—
Tomatoes (fresh)	20.8	—	1.41	—

Source: GATT Secretariat, "Gli Scambi della regione: problemi e prospettive," in *Conflitti e sviluppo nel Mediterraneo* (Rome: Istituto Affari Internazionali, 1970).

NOTES

Unless otherwise noted, statistics used are based on compilations by the Statistical Office of the European Communities (SOEC).

1. The countries in question are Yugoslavia, Albania, Greece, Turkey, Cyprus, Syria, Lebanon, Israel, Jordan, Egypt, Libya, Algeria, Tunisia, Morocco, Malta, Spain and Portugal. The six original EEC members are Belgium, France, Italy, Luxemburg, the Federal Republic of Germany, and the Netherlands.

2. J. Loeff, "La Communauté élargie et l'éspace méditerraneen," address delivered at the College of Europe for Bruges Week, in March, 1972. Adjusting these figures for the absence of Norway would change them very little. Loeff was at the time the commission official responsible for relations with Mediterranean countries.

3. *BP Statistical Review of the World Oil Industry, 1970.* These figures have subsequently changed, as a function of supply/demand factors and of Franco-Algerian relations, which worsened in 1971.

4. Figures compiled by Loeff. See appendix I.

5. Ibid.

6. Ibid.

7. See appendix II.

8. Jon McLin, *International Migrations and the European Community,* (JM–1–72), Fieldstaff Reports, West Europe Series, vol. 7, no. 1.

9. See appendix II, table IV.

10. M. Livi-Bacci, *Report on the Demographic and Social Pattern of Mi-*

grants in Europe, Especially with Regard to International Migrations, Second European Population Conference (Strasbourg), Council of Europe Document CDE (71), T.IV.

11. Loeff, op. cit., for these figures plus that in preceding paragraph.

12. See appendix III.

13. A good, if brief, discussion of these factors may be found in John Lambert, "The Cheshire Cat and the Pond: EEC and the Mediterranean Area," *Journal of Common Market Studies*, vol. 10, no. 1 (September, 1971).

14. See appendix IV.

15. Altiero Spinelli, "L'Italie: vocation méditerranéene ou communautaire," in *La Communauté et les pays mediterranéens* (Brussels: Université Libre de Bruxelles, 1970).

16. Guy de Carmoy, *Le Dossier de l'Energie*.

17. McLin, op. cit.

18. Jon McLin, *European Organizations and the Environment*, (JM-2-72), Fieldstaff Reports, West Europe Series, vol. 7, no. 2.

19. Wolfgang Hager, "A Meriterranean Policy for the Enlarged Community," in *A Nation Writ Large* (London: Macmillan, 1973).

20. Jon McLin, *Rethinking the Common Agricultural Policy*, (JM-5-69), Fieldstaff Reports, West Europe Series, vol. 4, no. 5.

21. On the specific agreements, and the Community's foreign economic relations in general, see the following works: Werner Feld, *The European Common Market and the World* (Englewood Cliffs: Prentice-Hall, 1967); Stanley Henig, *External Relations of the European Community*, no. 19 in European Series of Chatham House/PEP (October, 1971); and Gordon Weil, *A Foreign Policy for Europe?* (Bruges: College of Europe, 1970).

22. Joseph Licari, "The European Investment Bank," *Journal of Common Market Studies*, vol. 8, no. 3 (March, 1970).

23. Commission of the European Communities, *Fourth General Report on the Activities of the Communities, 1970*, (Brussels, 1971).

24. OECD, *Agricultural Development in Southern Europe* (Paris, 1969).

25. *Telex Méditerranée*, no. 5 (2 May, 1972). This biweekly newsletter is a source of prime importance for those wishing to stay current on the community's Mediterranean relations. It is published at Rue Hobbema 13, 1040 Brussels, Belgium.

26. Pedro Alvares, "Portugal and the Common Market," *EFTA Bulletin* (January/February, 1973).

27. Commission of the European Communities, *Rapport de la Commission au Conseil sur les Contacts avec les pays co-contractants dans le bassin mediterranéen au sujet des problèmes posés par l'élargissement*, Document No. SEC (71) 2963 (Sept. 14, 1971).

28. Commission of the European Communities, Spokesman's Group, Information Note No. P-48, *The Relations between the Community and the Mediterranean Countries* (October, 1972).

29. *Agence Europe* (Nov. 7, 1972).

30. Basing itself on the Portuguese case, the commission argues that at least 80 percent of all the agricultural exports of each partner country to the enlarged Community should be affected by concessions: "In the case of Portugal

91 percent are covered in all (100 percent of exports of manufactured goods and 64 percent of exports of agricultural products to the Ten). In order to reach an equally high rate of coverage for the countries concerned, approximately 80 percent of agricultural exports would have to be included, since these account for between 50 and 60 percent of these countries' total exports to the Ten, as against 26 percent in the case of Portugal." From the source cited in note 28.

31. Speech by Henri Simonet, the commissioner responsible for energy questions, Mar. 28, 1973.

Afterword

WILTON S. DILLON*

MUSEUMS LIKE the Smithsonian Institution, the British Museum, or the great repositories of Paris, Rome, Warsaw, or Madrid are shelters of artifacts, including great art, which can tell us a lot about what humans of earlier times exchanged with each other in that cradle of Western civilization, those European and African lands around the Mediterranean Sea. Ornaments, arms, minerals and edibles moved back and forth between capital and province, between the microclimates of highlands and lowlands, islands and continental shores, and country and city. How fascinating, therefore, to speculate on what value this book may have in the future when scholars try to unravel the invisible, or less tangible, social structures set up late in the twentieth century to try to pull the heterogeneous societies of Mediterranean Europe into a larger web of give and take. Curators might have a plastic detergent bottle or a fragment of an automobile chassis to exhibit, but few records of the organizational techniques used to get the goods and services moving from place to place. In another part of the world, far from Western economists' preoccupation with the market, the museum keepers of Sydney, Suva, and Honolulu depend on Malinowski's *Argonauts of the Western Pacific* for accounts of the organization of the Trobriand islanders' *kula* ring institution to "explain" the cowry shells, beads, or bowls that travelled in clockwise and counterclockwise traffic patterns in the South Pacific. Such "markets" are uncommon. But they, too, make up part of the mosaic of human experience in organizing a system of distributing the things produced by technology.

Edward Shils' essays on macrosociology, *The Center and the Periphery* (Chicago: The University of Chicago Press, 1974), provide another appealing framework for further analysis of fact and insight to be found in this novel and useful collection of studies on Mediterranean Europe and its ties to the European Economic Community. For one must go through the ever widening rings or concentric circles—from the worlds of Greek

---

*Director, Symposia and Seminars, Smithsonian Institution.

cultivators of olives to Maltese shipbuilders, and from Fiat and Olivetti assemblymen to Turkish poppy growers—to appreciate more fully the intricate linkages that make Southern Europe economically, strategically, culturally, and politically a vital part of an evolving "world system." The energy crisis dramatizes the point that nothing acts in isolation. Washington can manipulate the economies of Israel and Chile, and Moscow can intervene with the outer fringe of its spheres, the subsystems of Cairo, Havana, and, if one believes Joseph Alsop, the new regime in Lisbon and ultimately Lorenzo Marques. (Cuban cigars reach American tobacco buffs in Washington through the generosity of Russian or Polish diplomats.) Trade channels are not rational. Ghana must use intermediaries to buy gold-mining technology from South Africa. Formal and informal structures, Common Market and Sicilian-style interpersonal networks help create the bonds that slowly bring Europe together. But how are these organizational inventions to compare in effectiveness to Arab oil prices and the lag in discovering new substitutes for fossil fuels as factors in creating trading communities? Geography isn't everything. Europe organizes itself as protection against the American or Japanese challenge, and rolls over pliantly like Romulus and Remus to suckle oil from sheiks and shahs who are backed by very old traditions of bargaining in bazaars. The capitals and the provinces are constantly shifting or changing roles. This book captures some important points in time.

Eric Baklanoff is to be commended for his initiatives in bringing these original essays under the covers of one book. In addition to tables and charts vital to understanding the political economy of recent times, the book has symbolic value for encouraging future attention by universities in the American South to do further work in the field of "Southern studies" on a worldwide basis. Traditional civic and residential architecture of *our* South already shows our predisposition to study the Greeks and the Romans and the provinces of their old empires. Yet our liking for the columns and cornices of Greek revival style is merely an aesthetic indicator of our growing awareness that we have some profound affinities with developing countries wherever they are. Every country, region, or civilization I know has its *Midi*, its south, with special characteristics of food and family, politics, religion, and economic behavior. How better to understand, in the wake of our new awareness of limits of economic growth, the dynamics and structure of being "poor but proud"? And how, once our fortunes change and we patronize and protect those on whom we once depended, can we move to the larger community of interdependence that we have to invent lest we die? Much of such human economic and social history can be learned from comparative studies of the Mediterranean and the American South. Here is a splendid start.

Index